W9-BYF-505

PRESENTED TO:

_____

FROM:

_____

His Miracles

Produced with the assistance of The Livingstone Corporation (www.LivingstoneCorp.com). Introductions written by Neil Wilson. Project staff includes David Veerman, Linda Taylor, Christiana Freking, Ashley Taylor, Kirk Luttrell, Tom Taylor, Carol Fielding, Sharon Wright.

Cover & Interior Design: Brand Navigation, LLC—DeAnna Pierce, Terra Peterson, Bill Chiaravalle, www.brandnavigation.com

Cover & Interior Images: Steve Gardner, PixelworksStudio.net

ISBN 1-59145-271-6

Printed and bound in China.

04 05 06 07 08   Regal   7 6 5 4 3 2 1

DEVOTIONS *for* EVERY DAY *of the* YEAR

His

MIRACLES

The MOST MOVING WORDS EVER WRITTEN
ABOUT *the* MIRACLES *of* JESUS

INTEGRITY®
PUBLISHERS

TABLE OF CONTENTS

(The miracles are chronological within topics.)

INTRODUCTION

Welcome to this collection of thoughts on the signs, wonders, and miracles of Jesus. Across the ages, Christians have marveled over the matter-of-factness with which the accounts of Jesus' life record His miracles. The miraculous certainly lies close to the heart of Christianity. The Gospels begin and end with miracles. Almost every page includes examples of the exercise of God's power through Jesus. Yet John admitted at the close of his biography of the Lord, "Jesus provided far more God-revealing signs than are written down in this book. These are written down so you will believe that Jesus is the Messiah, the Son of God, and in the act of believing, have real and eternal life in the way he personally revealed it" (John 20:30–31 MSG).

We will meditate on the miracles of Jesus not only because they help us to believe but also because they brilliantly illustrate how God moved through His creation, altering lives wherever He went. He remains the miracle-working God.

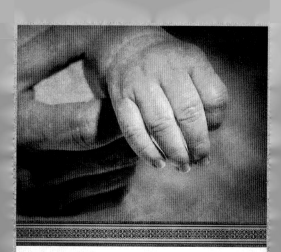

JESUS'
MIRACULOUS
BIRTH

"Behold, the virgin shall be with child,
and bear a Son, and they shall call
His name Immanuel," which is
translated, "God with us."

MATTHEW 1:23 NKJV

Pile enough coincidences on each other and soon you will be tempted to talk about "God-incidences." The miracles surrounding the birth of Jesus combine the telltale fingerprints of God and all the awkward actions that mortals bring to any situation. Angels announced, and humans questioned, doubted, cowered, and reacted. Stars moved across the sky, and people wondered and wandered. Perhaps the greatest miracle is simply that God accomplished so much with such reluctant participants. But here and there God found men and women who stepped out in faith and discovered that God does what He promises.

The Incarnation may now be a matter of public record, but the event itself had all the marks of a sneak attack. Creation was primed for God's visit, yet the mode and method of His coming caught everyone by surprise. The powers of evil were primed for a battle; they never expected God to slip into their stronghold as a baby. These meditations will explore the unexpected lessons and insights surrounding Jesus' birth.

GOD CAME

ISAIAH 7:14 NRSV

Therefore the Lord himself will give you a sign.
Look, the young woman is with child and shall
bear a son, and shall name him Immanuel.

This is the way God entered into humanity to bring a second Adam. God the Son enfleshed Himself—the Holy Spirit bringing about conception . . . the virgin beginning—without the intervention of the normal reproductive cycle of man. That is why Jesus is called the Son of God. He was not the son of Joseph, and He was not the son of a Roman soldier. He was not the son of any human father. He was conceived by the Holy Spirit. God brought about virtually a second creation, a second man, without the original sin of the male line from Adam. Linking Jesus into the family tree of Mary, how-ever, made Him a descendant of David and Abraham, which fulfilled the various promises that God had made to them. Further, it was from His mother, Mary, that the Lord received His human nature. So Jesus Christ was unique, conceived by the Holy Spirit, but of "the house and lineage of David" (Luke 2:4 NKJV).

PAT ROBERTSON

DAY 2

A LIFE *of* MIRACLES

ISAIAH 33:13 NIV
You who are far away, hear what I have done;
you who are near, acknowledge my power!

You simply cannot disentangle Jesus from miracles.
Scholars in the last century tried very hard to discover a nonmiraculous Jesus. They utterly failed. Every
single strand of material in the Gospels shows Jesus as
Someone who was different in His powers from other
people. Through Him God acted in a way impossible to
understand if we think of Him simply as a good Man.
The miracles begin at His birth, without human father.
They continue in His ministry: miracles of healing and of
exorcism, nature miracles (such as His feeding of the multitude or His walking on the sea in a storm), and
supremely His raising from the dead Lazarus, the widow
of Nain's son, and Jairus's daughter. Last of all comes the
greatest of miracles . . . His own resurrection from the
grave—not just to a further *span* of life but to a new quality of life over which death has no power. That is the only
Jesus for whom there is any shred of evidence—a remarkable Being exercising unheard-of powers. . . . He exhibited miraculous powers, and not once or twice but
continually.

MICHAEL GREEN

4   HIS MIRACLES

HUMBLE BEAUTY

ISAIAH 7:14 NKJV
Therefore the Lord Himself will give you a sign:
Behold, the virgin shall conceive and bear a Son,
and shall call His name Immanuel.

Let us notice at the very first glance *His miraculous conception.* It was a thing unheard of before, and unparalleled since, that a virgin should conceive and bear a son. The first promise concerned *the seed of the woman,* not the offspring of the man. Since a venturesome woman led the way in the sin that resulted in paradise lost, she, and she alone, ushers in the Regainer of Paradise. . . . His mother has been described simply as "the virgin," not a princess or prophetess, nor a woman of influence. True, the blood of kings ran in her veins; and her mind was not weak or untaught, for she could sweetly sing a song of praise. Yet how humble her position, how poor the man to whom she was engaged, and how miserable the accommodation provided for the newborn King!

Immanuel—God with us in our nature, in our sorrow, in our daily work, in our punishment, in our death, and now with us, or rather we with Him, in resurrection, ascension, triumph, and Second Advent splendor.

CHARLES HADDON SPURGEON

A VIRGIN SHALL CONCEIVE

ISAIAH 11:10 KJV

And in that day there shall be a root of Jesse, which shall stand for an ensign of the people; to it shall the Gentiles seek: and his rest shall be glorious.

A Virgin shall conceive, a Virgin bear a Son!
From Jesse's root behold a Branch arise,
Whose sacred Flow'r with Fragrance fills the Skies.
Th'Aethereal Spirit o'er its Leaves shall move,
And on its Top descends the Mystic Dove.
Ye Heav'ns! from high the dewy Nectar pour,
And in soft Silence shed the kindly Show'r!
The Sick and Weak the healing Plant shall aid;
From Storms a Shelter, and from Head a Shade.
All Crimes shall cease, and ancient Fraud shall fail;
Returning Justice lift aloft her Scale;
Peace o'er the World her Olive-Wand extend,
And white-rob'd Innocence from Heav'n descend.
Swift fly the Years, and rise th'expected Morn!
Oh spring to Light, Auspicious Babe, be born!

ALEXANDER POPE

NAME *above* ALL NAMES

LUKE 1:31 NIV
"You will be with child and give birth to a son,
and you are to give him the name Jesus."

When the mighty angel entered that humble home in Nazareth unannounced and called Mary by name, the teenage girl must have looked like she'd seen a ghost. Gabriel recognized Mary's fear and told her not to be afraid. Then he told her something that would have seemingly frightened her more. Even though she wasn't married and was still sexually innocent, she was about to have a baby. Not just any baby, however. This child "will be great and will be called the Son of the Most High" (Luke 1:32 NIV). This child would be the promised Messiah. The angel instructed Mary to give her child an Aramaic name: Jesus. Like the Hebrew equivalent, Joshua, the name means "the Lord saves." . . .

Only the sinless Son of Mary has ever offered living—and dying—proof that the Lord has saved us from our sins. He did it on the cross. The reason there is something about the name Jesus is because there is something unique about the One who was given that name. He is Master, Savior, and eternal King. He is Jesus, who saves us from our sins.

GREG ASIMAKOUPOULOS

A MIRACLE *of* DIVINE POWER

LUKE 1:34 MSG
Mary said to the angel,
"But how? I've never slept with a man."

Your religious life is every day to be a proof that God works impossibilities; your religious life is to be a series of impossibilities made possible and actual by God's almighty power. That is what the Christian needs. He has an almighty God that he worships, and he must learn to understand that he does not need a little of God's power, but he needs—with reverence be it said—the whole of God's omnipotence to keep him right, and to live like a Christian.

The whole of Christianity is a work of God's omnipotence. Look at the birth of Christ Jesus. That was a miracle of divine power, and it was said to Mary: "With God nothing shall be impossible." It was the omnipotence of God. Look at Christ's resurrection. We are taught that it was according to the exceeding greatness of His mighty power that God raised Christ from the dead.

ANDREW MURRAY

HOLY OFFSPRING

LUKE 1:34-35 NASB

*Mary said to the angel, "How can this be, since
I am a virgin?" The angel answered and said to her,
"The Holy Spirit will come upon you, and the power of
the Most High will overshadow you; and for that reason
the holy Child shall be called the Son of God."*

The virgin birth is an underlying assumption in *every-thing* the Bible says about Jesus. To throw out the virgin birth is to reject Christ's deity, the accuracy and authority of Scripture, and a host of other related doctrines that are the heart of the Christian faith. No issue is *more* important than the virgin birth to our understanding of who Jesus is. If we deny that Jesus is God, we have denied the very essence of Christianity. Everything else the Bible teaches about Christ hinges on the truth we celebrate at Christmas—that Jesus is God in human flesh. If the story of His birth is merely a fabricated or trumped-up legend, then so is the rest of what Scripture tells us about Him. The virgin birth is as crucial as the resurrection in substantiating His deity. It is not an optional truth. Anyone who rejects Christ's deity rejects Christ absolutely—even if he pretends otherwise.

JOHN MACARTHUR

HE ENTERS HIS WORLD

———

LUKE 1:35 NRSV

The angel said to her, "The Holy Spirit will come upon you, and the power of the Most High will overshadow you; therefore the child to be born will be holy; he will be called Son of God."

Why is it that this miracle is so difficult for many of us to believe? That the Lord God who formed mankind from the dust of the earth and breathed into his nostrils the breath of life could impregnate one of his creation to form a human person in which His Spirit would reside does not seem at all unreasonable to me. What would be far more difficult to believe would be that any ordinary man, conceived and born as we all are in sin, could possibly be divine in any sense. A virgin birth seems a most appropriate and creative way for God to enter His world.

PAUL SMITH

GOD *with* US

MATTHEW 1:23 NKJV
*"Behold, the virgin shall be with child, and bear
a Son, and they shall call His name Immanuel,"
which is translated, "God with us."*

One of the most debilitating emotions is loneliness. . . . That is why one of the most comforting names given to our Savior is Immanuel—God with us. Because of the indwelling Christ, believers are never separated from His permanent presence. We are in Christ and He is in us. What an encouragement! What a comfort! What an assurance! We always have a shoulder to lean on—the broad shoulders of Immanuel. We always have Someone to listen to our heartache—our constant Companion and Friend, Jesus. . . .

Don't let the adversary and accuser rob you of the peace and joy that come from experiencing and enjoying the sweet presence of our God. No sin, no deed, no trial can ever diminish the full presence and acceptance of Christ once you have become His child through faith.

God is with you. God is for you. God loves you. Allow His presence to fill any void.

CHARLES STANLEY

INTO OUR HEARTS

———

MATTHEW 1:23 KJV
*Behold, a virgin shall be with child, and shall bring
forth a son, and they shall call his name Emmanuel,
which being interpreted is, God with us.*

How fitting that the name "Emmanuel" means "God
with us." Jesus embodied what God's plan had been
all along: to be with us. From the beginning of time, this
has been God's desire. Genesis 3:8 tells of God walking
with Adam and Eve in the Garden of Eden. Then sin separated this first man and woman from Him. . . .

So He sent His Son, Jesus, as the ultimate sacrifice for
sin; then He sent His Holy Spirit, "the Spirit of truth" to
live with us and be in us (John 14:17 KJV). . . .

God wants to share our lives and be invited into our
hearts. He wants to laugh at our jokes and hang out in our
homes. He enjoys our kids and understands our weaknesses. When others leave or reject us, He will stay. When
we're angry with Him, He won't turn away. We go
through nothing alone.

God is with us in our doubts, in our confusion, and
even in our darkness. This has always been His plan. How
do you respond to this message of love?

DEBBIE CARSTEN

HEAVEN *to* EARTH

MATTHEW 1:23 NIV
*"The virgin will be with child and will give birth
to a son, and they will call him Immanuel"—
which means, "God with us."*

This thought of God fixing His tent of flesh and living among us is a stupendous one. It is almost inconceivable. It staggers the imagination. Yet that is precisely what happened with the Incarnation.

The miracle and the marvel of Immanuel—God with us—defies description. The hands of God that had tumbled solar systems into space became the small chubby hands of an Infant. The feet of God that had roamed through fiery planets became the infant feet of a Baby. Jesus was the heart of God wrapped in human flesh. He was God in the garb of humanity. He was God walking the earth in sandals.

From that feeding trough in the cattle shed of lowly Bethlehem, the cry from that Infant's throat broke through the silence of centuries. For the first time on Planet Earth, there was heard the voice of God from human vocal [cords]. Immanuel speaks to us of the mighty miracle and marvel of God becoming Man and dwelling with us.

HENRY GARIEPY

MADE MAN

LUKE 1:46–47 KJV

And Mary said, My soul doth magnify the Lord,
and my spirit hath rejoiced in God my Saviour.

It ought not to be a matter of wonder that a miracle was wrought by God; the wonder would be if man had wrought it. Rather ought we to rejoice than wonder that our Lord and Saviour Jesus Christ was made man, than that He performed divine works among men. It is of greater importance to our salvation what He was made for men, than what He did among men: it is more important that He healed the faults of souls, than that He healed the weaknesses of mortal bodies. But as the soul knew not Him by whom it was to be healed, and had eyes in the flesh whereby to see corporeal deeds, but had not yet sound eyes in the heart with which to recognize Him as God concealed in the flesh, He wrought what the soul was able to see, in order to heal that by which it was not able to see.

AUGUSTINE

NUMBERED *among* MEN

LUKE 2:1, 4 KJV

*And it came to pass in those days, that there went out
a decree from Caesar Augustus, that all the world should
be taxed. . . . And Joseph also went up from Galilee, out
of the city of Nazareth, into Judaea, unto the city
of David, which is called Bethlehem; (because he
was of the house and lineage of David).*

To Bethlehem they went to be enrolled;
And there, in Caesar's census book of old,
His name was written 'mong the sons of men
As Caesar's subject: "Jesus"—followed then
By "Son of Mary, born in David's Town,
Of David's line"—the record thus set down.
In a world's book of life, a place they gave
To "Jesus" who was born a world to save.
They numbered Him with sinful men and poor,
Though He was Son of God, divine and pure.

KAY MCCULLOUGH

ANGELS CAME

LUKE 2:13 NRSV
*And suddenly there was with the angel a
multitude of the heavenly host. . . .*

How glorious is the world as men of the Bible knew it!

Jacob saw a ladder set up on the earth with God standing above it and the angels ascending and descending upon it. Abraham and Balaam and Manoah and how many others met the angels of God. . . .

Angels were present to tell of Jesus' coming birth and to celebrate that birth when it took place in Bethlehem; angels comforted our Lord when He prayed in Gethsemane; angels are mentioned in some of the inspired epistles, and the Book of the Revelation is bright with the presence of strange and beautiful creatures intent upon the affairs of earth and heaven.

Yes, the true world is a populated world. The blind eyes of modern Christians cannot see the invisible but that does not destroy the reality of the spiritual creation. Unbelief has taken from us the comfort of a personal world. We have accepted the empty and meaningless world of science as the true one, forgetting that science is valid only when dealing with material things and can know nothing about God and the spiritual world.

A. W. TOZER

THE MIRACLE MAN

LUKE 2:52 NRSV
*And Jesus increased in wisdom and in years,
and in divine and human favor.*

This man Jesus was much more of a human being than I had previously thought. I suppose that somewhere in the recesses of my mind I had stored a mixed-up impression of a being of supernatural perfection and certain supernatural powers. I believed, and indeed still do believe, that Jesus was both God and man. But the conclusion grew upon me that the Jesus of the Gospels really *was* man, not a demi-god and certainly not God playing, however convincingly, the part of man. I have written of the mental and spiritual toughness which co-existed in Jesus with extraordinary sympathy and compassion. So that when I came to the "miracles" of the Gospels I did not find in them anything incompatible with his character or his declared mission. They did not give me the impression of being celestial conjuring-tricks designed to produce faith. Indeed the records insist that Jesus did not want publicity for his acts of physical or mental healing. I think it is difficult for us today to appreciate the spiritual power of a man uniquely integrated and dedicated, and who spent many hours in solitary communion with God.

J. B. PHILLIPS

5/28/09 THURS.

GOD MADE FLESH

JOHN 1:1 NRSV
*In the beginning was the Word, and the Word
was with God, and the Word was God.*

He [Jesus] went far beyond any prophetic ministry to be found in the Old Testament. It was chiefly in his words that a prophet made known the truth of God. No doubt qualities of godliness in them provided illustration of the truth they proclaimed, although this was not always the case. Balaam and Hosea represent two extremes here. In the case of Jesus, however, lip and life were completely in harmony, so much so that John can speak of him as the Word of God made flesh (John 1:1-18). Here the revelation of God comes in the total event of Christ, not simply in his verbal utterances. This is what the writer to the Hebrews means when he says that God has now spoken in a Son (Hebrews 1:1f.). Hebrews 1 contains no reference to the teaching given by Jesus but concentrates on his person and his activities in creation and redemption. It is in the full fact of Christ that God is heard and seen.

GEOFFREY W. GROGAN

6/5/09 Friday

LIFE *in* HIM

JOHN 1:4 NLT
*Life itself was in him,
and this life gives light to everyone.*

I think we finally have to say that Jesus' enduring relevance is based on his historically proven ability to speak
to, to heal and empower the individual human condition.
He matters because of what he brought and what he still
brings to ordinary human beings, living their ordinary
lives and coping daily with their surroundings. He promises wholeness for their lives. In sharing our weakness he
gives us strength and imparts through his companionship
a life that has the quality of eternity.

He comes where we are, and he brings us the life we
hunger for. An early report reads, "Life was in him, life
that made sense of human existence" (John 1:4). To be
the light of life, and to deliver God's life to women and
men where they are and as they are, is the secret of the
enduring relevance of Jesus. Suddenly they are flying
right-side up, in a world that makes sense.

DALLAS WILLARD

✓ 6/9/09

LIGHT *of the* WORLD

JOHN 1:10 NASB
He was in the world, and the world was made through Him, and the world did not know Him.

When God reports that Christ was in the world and the world neither recognized nor knew Him, He was not referring to the created clouds and hills and rocks and rivers. He was referring to human society, the world of mankind, and it was this organized world of man that knew Him not.

John testified that God's Word, His only begotten Son, became flesh and dwelt among us. What was He doing in our kind of world, in our kind of fallen society?

Before the incarnation, He was the all-permeating Word of God moving creatively in His universe. When Jesus Christ became man, God incarnate in a human body, He did not cease to be the all-permeating Word of God. To this very day, the all-permeating Word still fills the universe and moves among us.

How few men there are who realize His presence, who realize that they have Him to deal with. He is still the Light of the world. It is He that lighteth every man that cometh into the world. After His ascension from Olivet's mountain, He still remains as the all-permeating, vitalizing, life-giving Word operative in the universe.

A. W. TOZER

FULL *of* GRACE

JOHN 1:14 NLT

*So the Word became human and lived here
on earth among us. He was full of unfailing
love and faithfulness. And we have seen his glory,
the glory of the only Son of the Father.*

Through the stunning mystery of the Incarnation, this same Jesus is present to those caught in a midlife crisis, to those suffering debilitating illness or addiction, to those in the dark woods of depression, despair, and overwhelming fear. With a compassion that knows no boundary or breaking point, he startles those caught up in the love of pleasure, trapped by fierce pride, or consumed by ravenous greed with a flash of insight, suddenly revealing that their lives are a senseless, chaotic blur of misdirected energies and flawed thoughts.

The Savior, who sets us free from fear of the Father and dislike of ourselves, stirs the defeated through the painful discovery that our efforts to extricate ourselves from the shambles of our lives are self-contradictory, because the source of the shambles is our imperious ego. Huffing and puffing, scrambling for brownie points, and thrashing about trying to fix ourselves is an exercise in futility. Jesus waits and then sends a disciple to the weary soul in order to reveal the staggering meaning of grace.

BRENNAN MANNING

FAR *upon the* EASTERN ROAD

MATTHEW 2:1-2 KJV

There came wise men from the east to Jerusalem, saying,
Where is he that is born King of the Jews? for we have
seen his star in the east, and are come to worship him.

This is the month, and this the happy morn,
   Wherein the Son of heaven's eternal King,
Of wedded maid and virgin mother born,
Our great redemption from above did bring;
For so the holy sages once did sing,
   That he our deadly forfeit should release,
And with his Father work us a perpetual peace. . . .

See how from far upon the eastern road
The star-led wizards haste with odours sweet!
O run, prevent them with thy humble ode,
And lay it lowly at his blessed feet;
Have thou the honour first thy Lord to greet,
   And join thy voice unto the angel quire,
From out his secret altar touched with hallowed fire.

JOHN MILTON

THE MEDIATOR

JOHN 10:30 KJV
I and my Father are one.

Jesus Christ is the only proof of the living God. We only know God through Jesus Christ. Without his mediation there is no communication with God. But through Jesus Christ we know God. All who have claimed to know God and to prove his existence without Jesus Christ have done so ineffectively. But to prove Christ we have the prophecies which are reliable and palpable proofs, and which, being fulfilled and shown to be true by events, show that these truths are certain. Therefore they prove the divinity of Jesus Christ. In him and through him, we know God. Apart from him, and without Scripture, without original sin, without the necessary Mediator who was promised and who came, it is impossible to prove absolutely that God exists, or to teach sound doctrine and sound morality. But through and in Jesus Christ we can prove God's existence, and teach both doctrine and morality. Jesus Christ therefore is the true God of men.

BLAISE PASCAL

THE MESSAGE *of* CHRISTMAS

ROMANS 6:23 NASB
*For the wages of sin is death, but the free gift of
God is eternal life in Christ Jesus our Lord.*

And so Christmas is first of all a celebration of God's love toward man. The babe in a manger is more than just a tender child. He is the image of God, the *prototokos*. He took on a body of human flesh so that He might bear in that body the sins of the world. He made possible the gift of God—eternal life (Romans 6:23). That is the sum of the Christmas message.

Don't get lost in the scope of it all. The incarnation of God in Jesus Christ is nothing if it is not personal. God loves you, individually. He knows you better than you know yourself, yet He loves you. He entered this world, took on human flesh, and died on a cross to bear your sin, to pay the penalty for your iniquity, to remove your guilt. He did it so that you might enter into His presence.

You must respond.

JOHN MACARTHUR

HUMAN, YET DIVINE

———

PHILIPPIANS 2:7 KJV
*[He] made himself of no reputation, and took
upon him the form of a servant, and was
made in the likeness of men.*

Why then did He not appear by means of other and nobler parts of creation, and use some nobler instrument, as the sun, or moon, or stars, or fire, or air, instead of man merely? . . . the Lord came not to make a display, but to heal and teach those who were suffering. . . . Now nothing in God's creation had gone astray with regard to their notions of God save man only. . . .

With reason, then, since it were unworthy of the Divine Goodness to overlook so grave a matter, while yet men were not able to recognize Him as ordering and guiding the whole, He takes to Himself as an instrument a part of the whole, the human body, and unites Himself with that, in order that since men could not recognize Him in the whole, they should not fail to know Him in the part; and since they could not look up to His invisible power, might be able at any rate, from what resembled themselves, to reason to Him and to contemplate Him.

ATHANASIUS

ALL FULLNESS

COLOSSIANS 1:19 NKJV
*For it pleased the Father that in
Him all the fullness should dwell.*

C hrist Himself is the greatest miracle of history. The incarnation, as the central miracle, helps us interpret the miracles done by the "I Am;" Yahweh with us. . . .

The question is, Do miracles still happen? Yes! The miracle of life, our salvation, the transformation of personality, and specific interventions of healing and blessing. A study of the miracles leads us to an "all things are possible" kind of faith for daily living and our needs. Physical, emotional, and spiritual healings are still being done daily by the Great Physician through the Holy Spirit.

Focus on the needs of people in the context of the miraculous power available to us. Fyodor Dostoevsky was right: "Faith does not, in the realist, spring from miracles, but miracles from faith!" We believe that faith comes from the Holy Spirit focusing us on the love and forgiveness of the cross; that faith then dares to believe that as God's miracles we can expect and take special delight in the miracles He will do all around us.

LLOYD JOHN OGILVIE

CONSTANT SURPRISES

COLOSSIANS 2:9 NKJV
*For in Him dwells all the fullness
of the Godhead bodily.*

The second greatest miracle, next to Christ, is what happens to a person who comes to know Christ personally. When we commit our lives to Him and invite Him to live in us, our days are filled with a constant succession of surprises. He is Lord of all life, has unlimited power, and can arrange events and circumstances to bless us. Our only task is to surrender our needs to Him, and then leave the results to Him.

Christ did not use the word "miracle." He talked about the "works of God." Wherever He went, He did "works" which defied both the expected and the anticipated. The reason was that He was the power of God, the "fullness of the Godhead bodily" (Colossians 2:9 NKJV). . . .

Where do you need a miracle—what to you seems impossible? Persist! Don't give up. At all costs make your way to the Master. Tell Him your need, and then leave it with Him. Even greater than the miracle you seek will be the miracle you become by seeking Him, touching Him, and experiencing His matchless love.

LLOYD JOHN OGILVIE

THOU KNOWEST

HEBREWS 2:17 NKJV
Therefore, in all things
He had to be made like His brethren.

May our prayer, O Christ, awaken all Thy human reminiscences, that we may feel in our hearts the sympathizing Jesus.

Thou hast walked this earthly vale and hast not forgotten what it is to be tired, what it is to know aching muscles, as Thou didst work long hours at the carpenter's bench.

Thou hast not forgotten what it is to feel the sharp stabs of pain, or hunger, or thirst.

Thou knowest what it is to be forgotten, to be lonely.

Thou dost remember the feel of hot and scalding tears running down Thy cheeks.

O we thank Thee that Thou wert willing to come to earth and share with us the weaknesses of the flesh, for now we know that Thou dost understand all that we are ever called upon to bear.

We know that Thou, our God, art still able to do more than we ask or expect. So bless us, each one, not according to our deserving, but according to the riches in glory of Christ Jesus, our Lord. Amen.

PETER MARSHALL

JESUS' MIRACLES
OVER NATURE

———

Many believed in His name when
they saw the signs which He did.
JOHN 2:23 NKJV

JESUS' MIRACLES OVER NATURE

Nature may groan and suffer as a result of the fall of humanity (Romans 8:22), but it remains obedient to the Master's voice. Creation may be marred by sin, but it is not deaf to the Creator. Nature's awesome power instantly yielded to Jesus' instructions. People gave mixed reactions to Jesus' words; but winds and waves obeyed. People clung to old wineskins while water gleefully became wine. Dried fish and crusty loaves multiplied in a small cascade of food enough to fill a multitude. Fish found their way to the other side of a boat and waiting nets.

Jesus' power over nature carried a quiet, sure demeanor. His actions were deft. It wasn't His command or His prayer that got people's attention; it was what happened after He spoke. As you read these reflections on Jesus' ongoing role as ruling Creator, visualize the effects of His authority in your life. Listen for His voice.

THE ROLE *of* JESUS' MIRACLES

LUKE 4:18 NRSV

"The Spirit of the Lord is upon me, because he has anointed me to bring good news to the poor. He has sent me to proclaim release to the captives and recovery of sight to the blind, to let the oppressed go free . . ."

Those miracles confirmed what Jesus had taught earlier in the synagogue in Nazareth, when He claimed to fulfill the prophecy of the One who, as the Lord's anointed, would bring "good news to the poor," would bring God's salvation, would bring the answer to the judgment that was facing those who had rebelled against God. The evidence of this would be the mighty miracles they would see performed. So the miracles were not only intended to accomplish wonderful things, although they did that; they were also intended to establish Jesus' identity and ultimately to give credibility to the good news He had come to proclaim.

You understand, then, the role of Jesus' miracles. They were a proof of the existence of this Person or Force beyond nature who could act within it. That's good news! They revealed Him as the Power who could reverse the very forces of death and destruction that plague our world. That is certainly good news!

PAUL SMITH

LIBERTY *to the* CAPTIVES

LUKE 4:18 NKJV

". . . to proclaim liberty to the captives . . ."

The enemy which Jesus confronted and challenged in his ministry was not the Roman oppressor but the spiritual power of darkness, the dominion of Satan. "If I by the finger of God cast out demons," he said, "then the kingdom of God has come upon you" (Luke 11:20). The proclamation of the advent of the divine kingdom stirred up specially hostile activity in the realm of evil, which felt its dominion threatened. The superior power of the kingdom of God was seen in the release of those whose minds and bodies were held in spiritual bondage: Jesus not only proclaimed but effected "liberty to the captives and release to the enchained" (Isa. 61:1). In doing so he knew himself to be the agent of the Father who desired the well-being, not the suffering, of his children.

F. F. BRUCE

DIVERTED WRATH

———

LUKE 4:19 NIV
" . . . to proclaim the year of the Lord's favor."

The air in the synagogue was hot and tight. The attendant handed Jesus the scroll of Isaiah. He quietly unrolled it, found the verse He was looking for, and began to speak with the voice of uncommon authority. . . .

He stopped in the middle of the verse. Just like that, Jesus left it unfinished and sat down. The eyes of everyone were fastened on Him. Little wonder, they had never heard Isaiah 61 read in such a way, like the words were His own. Finally Jesus broke the silence, "Today this Scripture is fulfilled in your hearing." . . .

Jesus made it clear that His agenda was not to execute the wrath of God, but to bear in His own body that same wrath. I'm heartbroken by that statement: Jesus, precious Savior, did not come to execute the wrath of God, but to bear in His own body God's fury. All of the Father's white-hot anger against my sin was poured out on the cross. Because of Jesus, the Father has no anger left for you and me.

JONI EARECKSON TADA

TOTAL DEPENDENCE

JOHN 5:30 NIV
*"By myself I can do nothing; I judge only as
I hear, and my judgment is just, for I seek not
to please myself but him who sent me."*

Have you ever noticed how humble, unassuming and unmiraculous the miracles of Jesus are? The first one, turning water into wine, was recognized only by a few slaves at the wedding feast in Cana. "Go fill up those water jars," he said. Then, "Now take it to the master of ceremonies." Did you miss it? The miracle happened.

We could say the same about the feeding of the five thousand. There was no shouting, no waving of arms in the air, no hocus-pocus. Jesus simply prayed and passed the food out.

There was something indescribable about the way Jesus performed his miracles that always miraculously directed the attention away from himself and toward the Father. Jesus heals someone who is sick, and those who witness the healing inevitably "praise God." Jesus wins praise for the Father, not himself. "I can do nothing without the Father," Jesus said, thereby winning praise for God. Indeed, Jesus was not ashamed to confess his total dependence on God.

MICHAEL CARD

UNVEILING HIS GLORY

JOHN 5:36 NIV

*"I have testimony weightier than that of John.
For the very work that the Father has given
me to finish, and which I am doing,
testifies that the Father has sent me."*

We must, however, observe that His miracles were, as Erasmus remarked, acted parables. Jesus sought to bring all His miracles into the realm of the spiritual. In this sense they become eloquent sermons, preaching Christ's readiness to come to the remedy of all in need. Unlike the prophets of the Old Testament the miracles of Jesus were not an alien and occasional addition to His person and vocation. They were profoundly "natural" to Jesus. . . . His miracles were, so to speak, the forth-flashings of His total being. . . . The miracles of Jesus were a service of love and grace; yet for all those who had hearts to understand they were of such a nature as to bear witness to Him as sent by the Father (John 5.36). The miracles of Jesus are part of the fact of Jesus. They demonstrate the reality of blessings from the throne of God upon men and they proclaim the saving deeds of the gospel. They are of a pattern with the Person self-disclosed in the record. In a very definite manner they unveil His glory (John 2.11; 11.4).

H. D. McDONALD

OVER, ABOVE, *and* OUTSIDE

MARK 3:7-8 NLT

*Jesus and his disciples went out to the lake, followed
by a huge crowd from all over Galilee, Judea, Jerusalem,
Idumea, from east of the Jordan River, and even from
as far away as Tyre and Sidon. The news about his
miracles had spread far and wide, and vast numbers
of people came to see him for themselves.*

A Christian believes in natural law—i.e., that things
behave in a certain cause-and-effect way almost all
the time. But in maintaining this, he does not restrict
God's right and power to intervene when and how He
chooses. God is over, above, and outside natural law, and
is not bound by it. . . .

Many miracles were done in public. They were . . . performed over a period of time and involved a great variety
of powers. He had power over nature, as when He turned
the water to wine; He had power over disease, as when
He healed the lepers and the blind; He had power over
demons, as was shown by His casting them out; He had
supernatural powers of knowledge, as in His knowing that
Nathaniel was under a fig tree; He demonstrated His
power of creation when He fed 5,000 people from a few
loaves and fish; and He exhibited power over death itself
in the raising of Lazarus and others.

PAUL LITTLE

BELIEVABILITY *of* MIRACLES

JOHN 21:24 NRSV

This is the disciple who is testifying to these things and has written them, and we know that his testimony is true.

An imbecile habit has arisen in modern controversy of saying that such and such a creed can be held in one age but cannot be held in another. Some dogma, we are told, was credible in the twelfth century, but is not credible in the twentieth. You might as well say that a certain philosopher can be believed on Mondays but cannot be believed on Tuesdays. You might as well say of a view of the cosmos that it was suitable to half-past three, but not suitable to half-past four. What a man can believe depends upon his philosophy, not upon the clock of the century . . . the point is not whether it was given in our time, but whether it was given in answer to our question.

G. K. CHESTERTON

THE CREDIBILITY *of* MIRACLES

JOHN 21:24 NASB
*This is the disciple who is testifying
to these things and wrote these things,
and we know that his testimony is true.*

Sometimes the credibility of the miracles is in an inverse ratio to the credibility of the religion. Thus miracles are (in late documents, I believe) recorded of the Buddha. But what could be more absurd than that he who came to teach us that Nature is an illusion from which we must escape should occupy himself in producing effects on the Natural level—that he who comes to wake us from a nightmare should *add* to the nightmare? The more we respect his teaching the less we could accept his miracles. But in Christianity, the more we understand what God it is who is said to be present and the purpose for which He is said to have appeared, the more credible the miracles become. That is why we seldom find the Christian miracles denied except by those who have abandoned some part of the Christian doctrine. The mind which asks for a non-miraculous Christianity is a mind in process of relapsing from Christianity into mere "religion."

C. S. LEWIS

VERIFYING *the* TRUTH

ACTS 2:22 NASB

"Men of Israel, listen to these words: Jesus the Nazarene, a man attested to you by God with miracles and wonders and signs which God performed through Him in your midst, just as you yourselves know."

The early Christians did not need to prove that Jesus had performed miracles. They simply appealed to the knowledge of their listeners. Less than two months after Jesus' crucifixion, on the day of Pentecost, Simon Peter . . . appeals to the knowledge of hostile witnesses, that they themselves were aware of the miracles of Jesus. That He wasn't immediately shouted down demonstrates that the wonders Jesus performed were well known. It is significant that this kind of first-hand testimony to the miraculous does not occur either in other religions or in Greek or Roman mythology. . . .

The miracles of Jesus are in keeping with reality. They do not appear as the fantasies of imagination. Rather, they are presented as serious historical events which we might expect to occur if a supernatural God were attempting to verify a truth by breaking into the natural order.

JOSH MCDOWELL

UNDER *the* FIG TREE

JOHN 1:48 NLT

*"How do you know about me?" Nathanael asked.
And Jesus replied, "I could see you under the
fig tree before Philip found you."*

From Nathanael's perspective, no thinking man would just accept that Jesus was the Messiah. So he went to Jesus, not with faith but with a head and heart full of doubt. Then Jesus rocked Nathanael's world. Before they had ever met, Jesus knew all about him. He knew what Nathanael was doing. He knew what he was thinking. He knew where he had been. When Nathanael realized that Jesus knew everything about him, he was stunned.

"How do you know about me?" he asked. . . .

It wasn't really a question as much as a declaration of wonder. Nathanael instantly realized that Jesus knew everything about him because he had been an eyewitness to his entire life.

The realization that Jesus knows and sees everything is either frightening or enlightening. If you are frightened, you will attempt to hide from him. But if you are enlightened, you will declare like Nathanael, "You are the Son of God" (v. 49) and follow him every day for the rest of your life.

STEPHEN ARTERBURN

YOU ARE *the* SON *of* GOD!

JOHN 1:48–49 NRSV
Nathanael asked him, "Where did
you get to know me?" Jesus answered, "I saw
you under the fig tree before Philip called you."
Nathanael replied, "Rabbi, you are the Son
of God! You are the King of Israel!"

Well, that was quick. Nathanael's skepticism is blown away by one slight show of divine ESP. There was no sleeping on it. No consultation with theologians in Jerusalem. No FBI check on the man from Nazareth. No struggle. Instant conversion, from skeptic to believer in ten seconds. One sniff of a miracle, and Nathanael has his reason for believing.

Nathanael's faith is real enough for Jesus. Faith is faith, after all. Even if you do not have the most convincing reason for believing, you can still believe; and your faith can be a power for the rebirth of your life. Jesus does not question Nathanael's faith at all. He knows that Nathanael has a reason for believing, which he still was to discover. He has grabbed hold of the first reason that came along, and this is real enough for the time being. He has an explanation that makes sense to him now. But one day he would actually experience the real reason.

LEWIS B. SMEDES

THE PARTY

JOHN 2:1–2 NCV

Two days later there was a wedding in the town of Cana in Galilee. Jesus' mother was there, and Jesus and his followers were also invited to the wedding.

May I state an opinion that may raise an eyebrow? May I tell you why I think Jesus went to the wedding? . . . I think Jesus went to the wedding to have fun.

Think about it. It's been a tough season. Forty days in the desert. No food or water. A standoff with the devil. A week breaking in some greenhorn Galileans. A job change. He's left home. It hasn't been easy. A break would be welcome. Good meal with some good wine and some good friends . . . well, it sounds pretty nice. So off they go.

His purpose wasn't to turn the water to wine. That was a favor for his friends. His purpose wasn't to show his power. The wedding host didn't even know what Jesus did. His purpose wasn't to preach. There is no record of a sermon.

Really leaves only one reason. Fun. Jesus went to the wedding because he liked the people, he liked the food, and heaven forbid, he may have even wanted to swirl the bride around the dance floor a time or two. (After all, he's planning a big wedding himself. Maybe he wanted the practice?)

MAX LUCADO

To Have Faith Is *to* Trust

———

JOHN 2:3, 5 NRSV

*When the wine gave out, the mother of Jesus said
to him, "They have no wine."* . . . *His mother
said to the servants, "Do whatever he tells you."*

Even when Mary did not understand what Jesus was
going to do, even when it seemed that he had refused
her request, Mary still believed in him so much that she
turned to the serving folk and told them to do whatever
Jesus told them to do. Mary had the faith which could
trust even when it did not understand. She did not know
what Jesus was going to do, but she was quite sure that he
would do the right thing. In every life come periods of
darkness when we do not see the way. In every life come
things which are such that we do not see why they came
or any meaning in them. Happy is the man who in such
a case still trusts even when he cannot understand.

WILLIAM BARCLAY

The Creator *of* All

John 2:7 NLT
Jesus told the servants, "Fill the jars with water."

An incredible history of response has followed these stories, ranging from the reverential to the ridiculous, from the artistic to the philosophical. Capturing the beauty of the conversion of the water into wine, the poet Alexander Pope said, "The conscious water saw its Master and blushed." That sublime description could be reworked to explain each one of these miracles. Was it any different in principle for a broken body to mend at the command of its Maker? Was it far-fetched for the Creator of the universe, who fashioned matter out of nothing, to multiply bread for the crowd? Was it not within the power of the One who called all the molecules into existence to interlock them that they might bear His footsteps? Why were they not making that connection?

But is this not the very impertinence that grasps the gift and ignores the giver? Naturalism by its purpose engineers the displacement of the miracle and puts in its place explanations that defy reason. Those who smirk at His walking on water have forgotten the miracle He has already performed in the very composition of water.

Ravi Zacharias

OVERFLOWING GRACE

JOHN 2:7-8 NKJV

Jesus said to them, "Fill the waterpots with water."
And they filled them up to the brim. And He
said to them, "Draw some out now, and take it
to the master of the feast." And they took it.

He does not give to men just enough for their necessity, but he gives up to the higher degree which we call enjoyment. Here he turns good wholesome water into a sweeter, richer, more nourishing beverage; perhaps we little know how truly good and sustaining that God-made drink was to those who were privileged to taste it. Our dear Master will give to all those who are his followers a joy unspeakable and full of glory. They shall not only have enough grace to live by so as barely to hope and serve; but they shall drink of "wines on the lees well refined," and shall have grace to sing with, grace to rejoice with, grace to fill them with assurance, and cause them to overflow with delight. Our Beloved has not only brought us to the house of bread, but to the banquet of wine. We have heaven here below. Jesus does not measure out grace by the drop, as chemists do their medicines; but he gives liberally, his vessels are filled to the brim.

CHARLES HADDON SPURGEON

SAVING *the* BEST *for* LAST

———

JOHN 2:10 KJV
And saith unto him, Every man at the beginning
doth set forth good wine; and when men have
well drunk, then that which is worse: but thou
hast kept the good wine until now.

The Lord Jesus . . . is always giving something better.
As the taste is being constantly refined, it is provided
with more delicate and ravishing delights. That which
you know of Him today is certainly better than that you
tasted when first you sat down at his board. And so it will
ever be. The angels, as his servants, have orders to bring
in and set before the heirs of glory things which eye hath
not seen, and man's heart has not conceived, but which
are all prepared. The best of earth will be below the sim-
plest fare of heaven. But what will heaven's best be! If
wine in the peasant's house is so luscious, what will be the
new wine in the Father's kingdom! What may we not
expect from the vintages of the celestial hills! What will it
be to sit at the marriage supper of the Lamb, not as guests,
but as the Bride! Oh, hasten on, ye slow-moving days; be
quick to depart, that we may taste that ravishment of bliss!
But for ever and ever, as fresh revelations break on our
glad souls, we shall look up to the Master of the feast and
cry, *"Thou has kept the best until now."*

F. B. MEYER

REVEALING *the* DIVINE

JOHN 2:11 NIV

This, the first of his miraculous signs, Jesus performed at Cana in Galilee. He thus revealed his glory, and his disciples put their faith in him.

Jesus' life was a blaze of miracles. His miracles are important not only because of the benefits people received from them, but also because of what they indicate about Jesus Himself.

Before we examine the first of Jesus' recorded miracles, we must first look at the role they play in general. Some argue that the purpose of miracles is to demonstrate the existence of God. But this reverses the role miracles play in the Bible. Before a miracle can be perceived as a miracle, the existence of God must be established first. It is the existence of God that makes miracles possible in the first place. . . .

To believe in the miracles is to believe in what the miracles signify. It is to embrace what the signs make manifest. John declares that the sign of Cana manifested the glory of Christ. It was this significance that the disciples realized and then believed in Him. The sign revealed glory and the manifestation of Christ's glory provoked the disciples to faith. The disciples heard the nonverbal testimony of the works of Jesus and they put their trust in Him.

R. C. SPROUL

HIS OWN ARCHITECT

JOHN 2:11 KJV

*This beginning of miracles did Jesus in Cana
of Galilee, and manifested forth his glory;
and his disciples believed on him.*

Christ's miracles are object lessons. They are living pictures. They talk to us. They have hands which take hold of us. Many valuable lessons do these miracles teach us. In their diversity, they refresh us. They show us the matchless power of Jesus Christ, and at the same time discover to us His marvelous compassion for suffering humanity. These miracles disclose to us His ability to endlessly diversify His operations. God's method in working with man is not the same in all cases. He does not administer His grace in rigid ruts. There is endless variety in His movements. There is marvelous diversity in His operations. He does not fashion His creations in the same mould. Just so our Lord is not circumscribed in His working nor trammeled by models. He works independently. He is His own architect. He furnishes His own patterns which have unlimited variety.

E. M. BOUNDS

PROOFS *of* OUR FAITH

JOHN 2:23 NKJV
*Now when He was in Jerusalem at the Passover,
during the feast, many believed in His name
when they saw the signs which He did.*

The prophecies of Scripture, even the miracles and proofs of our faith, are not the kind[s] of evidence that are absolutely convincing. At the same time it is not unreasonable to believe in them. There is thus evidence and obscurity, to enlighten some and confuse others. But the evidence is such as to exceed, or at least balance, the contrary evidence, so that it is not reason that decides us against following the faith. Therefore the only things that keep us from accepting the evidence must be lust and the wickedness of heart. There is therefore enough evidence to condemn and yet not enough to convince, so that it is obvious that those who follow it are prompted to do so by grace and not by reason. Those who evade its message are induced to do so by lust and not by reason.

BLAISE PASCAL

TRUTH ITSELF

JOHN 4:48 NRSV

*Then Jesus said to him, "Unless you see signs
and wonders you will not believe."*

A craving for miracles was a symptom of the sickly condition of men's minds in our Lord's day; they refused solid nourishment and longed for mere wonders. The Gospel that they so greatly needed they would not have; the miracles that Jesus did not always choose to give they eagerly demanded. Even today there are many who must see signs and wonders or they will not believe. . . . Do you think that He will submit to this? My Master has a generous spirit, but He also has a royal heart. He rejects all orders and maintains His sovereignty of action. Why, dear reader, if this is your case, do you crave signs and wonders? Isn't the Gospel its own sign and wonder? Isn't this the miracle of miracles, that "God so loved the world, that he gave his only Son, that whoever believes in him should not perish"? Surely that precious word, "Let the one who desires take the water of life—without price" and that solemn promise, "Whoever comes to me I will never cast out" are better than signs and wonders! A truthful Savior ought to be believed. He is truth itself. Why will you ask the One who cannot lie for proof?

CHARLES HADDON SPURGEON

HE WENT *on* HIS WAY

LUKE 4:24, 28-30 NIV

"I tell you the truth," he continued, "no prophet is accepted in his hometown." . . . All the people in the synagogue were furious when they heard this. They got up . . . in order to throw him down the cliff. But he walked right through the crowd and went on his way.

On another occasion there is a hint that something miraculous took place when the crowd tried to lay hands on him. The mob wanted to lynch him and mysteriously Jesus "walked right through the crowd and went on his way" (Lk 4:30).

If Jesus was resolute in facing death on some occasions, he was equally quick to avoid it on others. Why? Was he stronger on some days than others?

The New Testament never suggests that sacrifice and suffering are in themselves good. Jesus faced the cross . . . not because it was virtuous to do so but because suffering and death were the price he had to pay to achieve his purpose. . . .

He saw no virtue in suffering for suffering's sake, and he avoided it where possible. Moreover, his outlook on suffering was not morbid, neurotic or masochistic. He saw beyond the pain to glory and victory.

JOHN WHITE

POWERLESS, APART *from* CHRIST

LUKE 5:4 NRSV

*When he had finished speaking, he said
to Simon, "Put out into the deep water and
let down your nets for a catch."*

When God works without instruments, He is glorified; but He has selected this plan of human involvement as being that by which He is most magnified in the earth. *The means themselves can accomplish nothing.* "Master, we toiled all night and took nothing!" What was the reason for this? Were they not experienced fishermen going about their business? They were not novices; they understood the work. Was the problem that they lacked skill? No. Were they lazy? No; they had worked. Did they lack perseverance? No; they had *worked all night*. Was there a lack of fish in the sea? Certainly not, for as soon as the Master came, they swam to the net in large numbers. What then is the reason? It is because there is no power in the means themselves apart from the presence of Jesus. Without Him we can do nothing. But with Christ we can do all things. . . . Let us work until the night comes, and we will not labor in vain, for He who tells us to let down the net will fill it with fish.

CHARLES HADDON SPURGEON

DEEP WATERS

LUKE 5:5-6 NRSV

Simon answered, "Master, we have worked all night long but have caught nothing. Yet if you say so, I will let down the nets." When they had done this, they caught so many fish that their nets were beginning to break.

Picture the scene: Simon and other experienced, career fishermen have been trying all night to catch fish. They know the lake, and they know their trade, yet they have caught nothing. Jesus, a carpenter, tells them to move out into the deeper water and try again. Simon and the others must have felt like telling Jesus he should stick to building furniture and leave the fishing to the experts . . . but they didn't. Instead, they obeyed him. Have you ever been in a situation where you felt that Jesus couldn't possibly understand your needs? Many acts of service and enterprises for God require moving out into deeper water. Learn a lesson from a bunch of fishermen: Listen to Jesus and obey his commands, however difficult they may be to do.

LIFE APPLICATION BIBLE COMMENTARY—LUKE

MASTER *of* FISH—AND MEN

LUKE 5:9 NIV
*For he and all his companions were astonished
at the catch of fish they had taken.*

Peter, obviously feeling Jesus should stick to preaching and leave him to figure out his trade, reluctantly complied. "Because you say so, I will let down the nets," he muttered (v. 5). Peter probably respected the Lord too much to tell Him that fish generally feed in the dark and not in the light, and seeing they had toiled all night and caught nothing it was highly improbable that they would come up with anything in broad daylight. . . .

How like us this is! We think Jesus needs to live in the religious section of our lives. He can look after that part, we say, but He can't really understand the secular part of us. "What can He know about my job?" we question. . . .

We need to grow to understand that if we are fishermen, He, the Maker of fish and men, is the expert and can make us far better fishermen than others ever could. . . .

Peter, overwhelmed with the miracle of the fishes, finally began to grasp this fact. Here was no mere religious guru, but more—perhaps even God?

JILL BRISCOE

WHY ARE YE FEARFUL?

MATTHEW 8:23-24 KJV

And when he was entered into a ship, his disciples
followed him. And, behold, there arose a great
tempest in the sea, insomuch that the ship was
covered with the waves: but he was asleep.

Christ sleeps. If He had been awake when the storm came on, either the disciples wouldn't have been afraid and wouldn't have sought His help, or else they wouldn't have thought He could do anything about it. Therefore, He sleeps. He makes them nervous and gives them a clearer perception of what was happening. People don't look at what happens to others in the same way as what happens to themselves. So when the disciples saw others benefiting and not themselves, they became apathetic. Because they couldn't see or enjoy their own blessings from Him, Christ allowed the storm. Then, by their deliverance from it, they could gain a better perception of their benefits. Christ doesn't do this in the presence of the crowd—they might be condemned as having little faith. Instead, He takes them aside, corrects them in front of stormy waters, and ends the storms raging in their souls. Christ rebukes His disciples, and says, "Why are ye fearful, O ye of little faith?" He teaches them that fear isn't caused by approaching trials, but by weakness of the mind.

CHRYSOSTOM

LITTLE SHIPS

MARK 4:36 KJV
And when they had sent away the multitude,
they took him even as he was in the ship.
And there were also with him other little ships.

It is well to sail with Jesus, even though it be in a little ship. When we sail in Christ's company, we may not make sure of fair weather, for great storms may toss the vessel which carries the Lord Himself, and we must not expect to find the sea less boisterous around our little boat. If we go with Jesus we must be content to fare as He fares; and when the waves are rough to Him, they will be rough to us. It is by tempest and tossing that we shall come to land, as He did before us. When the storm swept over Galilee's dark lake all faces gathered blackness, and all hearts dreaded shipwreck.

When all creature help was useless, the slumbering Saviour arose, and with a word, transformed the riot of the tempest into the deep quiet of a calm; then were the little vessels at rest as well as that which carried the Lord. . . . Winds and waves will not spare us, but they all obey Him; and, therefore, whatever squalls may occur without, faith shall feel a blessed calm within. He is ever in the centre of the weather-beaten company: let us rejoice in Him. His vessel has reached the haven, and so shall ours.

CHARLES HADDON SPURGEON

TRANQUILITY RESTORED

MARK 4:37 KJV

And there arose a great storm of wind, and the
waves beat into the ship, so that it was now full.

Thou hast heard an insult, it is the wind; thou art
angry, it is a wave. When therefore the wind blows,
and the wave swells, the ship is endangered, the heart is in
jeopardy, the heart is tossed to and fro. When thou hast
heard an insult, thou longest to be avenged; and, lo,
avenged thou hast been, and so rejoicing in another's
harm thou hast suffered shipwreck. And why is this?
Because Christ is asleep in thee. What does this mean,
Christ is asleep in thee? . . . Awake Him up then, call Him
to remembrance. The remembrance of Him is His word;
the remembrance of Him is His command. And then
wilt thou say if Christ, awake in thee, What manner of
man am I, who wish to be avenged! Who am I, who deal
out threatenings against another man? . . . Therefore will
I refrain myself from my wrath, and return to the repose
of my heart. Christ hath commanded the sea, tranquility
is restored.

AUGUSTINE

DON'T YOU CARE?

MARK 4:38 NIV
Jesus was in the stern, sleeping on a cushion.
The disciples woke him and said to him,
"Teacher, don't you care if we drown?"

God, don't you care?" . . .

It's the timeless question. The question asked by literally every person that has stalked this globe. There has never been a president, a worker, or a businessman who hasn't asked it. There has never been a soul who hasn't wrestled with this aching question. Does my God care? Or is my pain God's great goof?

As the winds howled and the sea raged, the impatient and frightened disciples screamed their fear at the sleeping Jesus. "Teacher, don't you care that we are about to die?" He could have kept on sleeping. He could have told them to shut up. He could have impatiently jumped up and angrily dismissed the storm. He could have pointed out their immaturity. . . . But he didn't.

With all the patience that only one who cares can have, he answered the question. He hushed the storm so the shivering disciples wouldn't miss his response. Jesus answered once and for all the aching dilemma of man—"Where is God when I hurt?"

Listening and healing. That's where he is. He cares.

MAX LUCADO

CAPTAIN *of* SALVATION

MARK 4:38 KJV

*And he was in the hinder part of the ship,
asleep on a pillow: and they awake him, and say
unto him, Master, carest thou not that we perish?*

Learn from the experience of the disciples. In their alarm they aroused Him with the aspersion, "Carest thou not that we perish?" *He* care? Who could care more than the Merciful One, the Compassionate Christ? Has He ever forsaken His own, failed them in their extremity, forgotten them? Never! Where He leads He loves, where He points He protects, where He plans He provides, where He sends He saves. Winds and waves will obey the word of Him, who makes the storm a calm. When sailing under the order of the great Captain of our salvation, only be sure that the blast of the enemy means blessings ahead, and not breakers. Riot often precedes revival, as panic does promotion. The devil will do his utmost to drive you back from the center of God's will and the outstretching of His power through you, or will try to drown you in the depths of despair and defeat. Sail on, despite Satan's sneers, snares, or storms.

V. RAYMOND EDMAN

TRUE REST

LUKE 8:24 NLT
*The disciples woke him up, shouting,
"Master, Master, we're going to drown!"*

To be fair to the disciples, we must remember that up to this point almost everything their Leader had done had been done for others in distress, not for them personally. This was the first time they themselves were in a real jam, and His presence and power had extricated them from sure disaster. For the first time it was they themselves who had to be delivered. For the first time it was they who were not the onlookers but the leading characters in the life-and-death drama enacted before their own eyes. For the first time—if they were to be saved in this hopeless situation—they had to exercise viable faith of their own in Christ. For the first time they had to pocket their pride as a group, come implicitly to the Master, expecting help and finding Him faithful to provide it.

He was there in the storm with them. They knew it. Happily, they were humble enough, sensible enough, and sincere enough to seek salvation from the One who could deliver them. And He did. God, in Christ, by His Spirit, is in all the storms of His followers' lives. It is when we give up battling them in our own ability and turn to Him that we find relief and rest.

W. PHILLIP KELLER

CONFIDENCE AMIDST CRISIS

MATTHEW 8:26 NKJV
*But He said to them, "Why are you fearful,
O you of little faith?"*

When we are afraid, the least we can do is pray to God. . . . Yet our trust is only in God up to a certain point, then we turn back to the elementary panic-stricken prayers of those people who do not even know God. We come to our wits' end, showing that we don't have even the slightest amount of confidence in Him or in His sovereign control of the world. To us He seems to be asleep, and we can see nothing but giant, breaking waves on the sea ahead of us.

"O you of little faith!" What a stinging pain must have shot through the disciples as they surely thought to themselves, "We missed the mark again!" And what a sharp pain will go through us when we suddenly realize that we could have produced complete and utter joy in the heart of Jesus by remaining absolutely confident in Him, in spite of what we were facing. . . .

It is when a crisis arises that we instantly reveal upon whom we rely. If we have been learning to worship God and to place our trust in Him, the crisis will reveal that we can go to the point of breaking, yet without breaking our confidence in Him.

OSWALD CHAMBERS

LORD *of* EARTH, *and* AIR, *and* SEA

LUKE 8:24 KJV

And they came to him, and awoke him,
saying, Master, master, we perish. Then he arose,
and rebuked the wind and the raging of the water:
and they ceased, and there was a calm.

Lord of earth, and air, and sea,
  Supreme in power and grace,
Under thy protection, we
Our souls and bodies place.
Bold an unknown land to try,
We launch into the foaming deep;
Rocks, and storms, and deaths defy,
With Jesus in the ship.

Who the calm can understand
In a believer's breast?
In the hollow of his hand
Our souls securely rest:
Winds may rise, and seas may roar,
We on his love our spirits stay;
Him with quiet joy adore,
Whom winds and seas obey.

CHARLES WESLEY

DIVINE DEMOCRACY

MATTHEW 8:27 NRSV

They were amazed, saying, "What sort of man is this,
that even the winds and the sea obey him?"

The chief difference between Christianity and the thousand transcendental schools of today is substantially the same as the difference nearly two thousand years ago between Christianity and the thousand sacred rites and secret societies of the Pagan Empire. The deepest difference is this: that all the heathen mysteries are so far aristocratic that they are understood by some, and not understood by others. The Christian mysteries are so far democratic that nobody understands them at all.

G.K. CHESTERTON

TRULY AWED

MARK 4:41 NLT
And they were filled with awe and said
among themselves, "Who is this man, that
even the wind and waves obey him?"

When was the last time you felt truly awed? . . .
The disciples of Jesus certainly had plenty of
"awe-full" moments. In the passage cited above, they
were caught with Jesus in a sudden storm on the Sea of
Galilee. It must have been a severe squall—at least four of
these men were experienced fishermen, but they were
absolutely panicked.

Awakened from a peaceful sleep, Jesus calmly rebuked
the tempest. And immediately the sea became like glass.

But the storm wasn't over. Not by a long shot. Banished from the sea, it kicked up in the racing hearts and
spinning minds of the Twelve. Dripping wet, the men
were left to quietly ponder what they had just experienced. . . .

One thing is true. When God, in his glory, is manifest
in our midst, we experience awe. Everything is both
"awe-full" and awesome.

Allow God to invade your day. Look for his glory, his
manifestation, in the most mundane of tasks you have
before you today. Worship him in those moments.

iWORSHIP DAILY DEVOTIONAL BIBLE

EVEN THIS

LUKE 8:25 NIV
*"Who is this? He commands even the winds
and the water, and they obey him."*

E*ven.*
Is there something you are facing—whether in your outer circumstances or in your inner character—that seems impossible to command? Something that has baffled you and outwitted you a thousand times, and appears that it will win over you in the end? Something as deaf to your command as the wind, or wild waters?

Don't despair. Don't shrug and give up.

Our Lord—your Lord and mine—can command even the most difficult, unruly thing that seems as if it will never be commanded.

Let His word "even" be a comfort to you. He who commands even the winds and water (and they must obey Him)—He can say to that "even" of yours, "Peace, be still . . ."

And there will come for you "a great calm" (Mark 4:39 KJV).

AMY CARMICHAEL

WHERE IS YOUR FAITH?

LUKE 8:25 KJV

And he said unto them, Where is your faith? And they being afraid wondered, saying one to another, What manner of man is this! for he commandeth even the winds and water, and they obey him.

A temptation has sprung up; it is the wind; thou art disturbed; it is a wave. Awake up Christ then, let Him speak with thee. "Who is this, since the winds and the sea obey Him?" Who is this, whom the sea obeyeth? "The sea is His, and He made it." "All things were made by Him." Imitate the winds then, and the sea rather; obey the Creator. At Christ's command the sea giveth ear; and art thou deaf? The sea heareth, and the wind ceaseth: and dost thou still blow on? What! I say, I do, I devise; what is all this, but to be blowing on, and to be unwilling to stop in obedience to the word of Christ? Let not the wave master you in this troubled state of your heart. Yet since we are but men, if the wind should drive us on, and stir up the affections of our souls, let us not despair; let us awake Christ, that we may sail on a tranquil sea, and so come to our country.

AUGUSTINE

HE HAD COMPASSION *on* THEM

MATTHEW 14:14 NLT

*A vast crowd was there as he stepped from the boat,
and he had compassion on them and healed their sick.*

When Matthew writes that Jesus had compassion on the people, he is not saying that Jesus felt casual pity for them. No, the term is far more graphic. Matthew is saying that Jesus felt their hurt in his gut . . .

And once he felt their hurts, he couldn't help but heal their hurts. He was moved in the stomach by their needs. He was so touched by their needs that he forgot his own needs. He was so moved by the people's hurts that he put his hurts on the back burner. When Jesus arrived at Bethsaida, he was sorrowful, tired, and anxious to be alone with the disciples. No one would have blamed him had he dismissed the crowds a second time. No one would have criticized him had he waved away the people. But he didn't. Later he would. Later he would demand their departure and seek solitude.

But not before he "healed their sick" (Matthew 14:14) and taught them "many things" (Mark 6:34 NLT). Self was forgotten and others were served by the compassionate Savior.

MAX LUCADO

DEMONSTRATING *the* KINGDOM *of* GOD

LUKE 9:11 NIV

The crowds learned about it and followed him. He welcomed them and spoke to them about the kingdom of God, and healed those who needed healing.

All that I have said about worldviews points toward one conclusion: Christians' worldviews affect their theology. If Christians have a worldview that is affected by Western materialism, they will probably deny that signs and wonders are for today. Though they may use a theological rationale, the real issue is that it upsets their worldview. In contrast to this, a second group of Christians have a worldview that is affected by Western rationalism; they might acknowledge signs and wonders, but consign them to the irrational. These people seek signs and wonders for the thrill of the experience, as an end in itself. They do not understand the purpose of signs and wonders: to *demonstrate* the kingdom of God.

If we believe in a theology that does not include the possibility of contemporary Christians doing the works of Jesus—including signs and wonders—we will not have a practice of signs and wonders.

JOHN WIMBER

THOU HAST A PLAN!

JOHN 6:5-6 KJV

When Jesus then lifted up his eyes, and saw a great company come unto him, he saith unto Philip, Whence shall we buy bread, that these may eat? And this he said to prove him: for he himself knew what he would do.

At this very hour you may have to come face to face with a most tremendous need, and Christ stands beside you looking at it and questioning you about it. He says, in effect, "How are you going to meet it?" He is scrutinizing you . . . watching you with a gentle tender sympathy. How many of us have failed in the test! We have taken out our pencil and our paper and commenced to figure out the two hundred pennyworth of bread; or we have run off hither and thither to strong and wealthy friends to extricate us; or we have sat down in utter despondency; or we have murmured against Him for bringing us into such a position. Should we not have turned a sunny face to Christ saying: *Thou hast a plan! Thine is the responsibility, and Thou must tell me what to do. I have come so far in the path of obedience to Thy Guiding Spirit: and now, what art Thou going to do?*

C. G. MOORE

A CHANCE *to* BLESS

MATTHEW 14:17-18 KJV
*And they say unto him, We have here but five loaves,
and two fishes. He said, Bring them hither to me.*

Are you encompassed with needs at this very moment, and almost overwhelmed with difficulties, trials, and emergencies? These are all divinely provided vessels for the Holy Spirit to fill, and if you but rightly understood their meaning, they would become opportunities for receiving new blessings and deliverances which you can get in no other way.

Bring these vessels to God. Hold them steadily before Him in faith and prayer. Keep still, and stop your own restless working until He begins to work. Do nothing that He does not Himself command you to do. Give Him a chance to work, and He will surely do so; and the very trials that threatened to overcome you with discouragement and disaster, will become God's opportunity for the revelation of His grace and glory in your life, as you have never known Him before.

A. B. SIMPSON

BREAK THOU *the* BREAD *of* LIFE

LUKE 9:16 NKJV

Then He took the five loaves and the two fish, and looking up to heaven, He blessed and broke them, and gave them to the disciples to set before the multitude.

Break Thou the bread of life, dear Lord, to me,
As Thou didst break the loaves beside the sea;
Beyond the sacred page I seek Thee, Lord;
My spirit pants for Thee, O living Word!

Bless Thou the truth, dear Lord, to me, to me,
As Thou didst bless the bread by Galilee;
Then shall all bondage cease, all fetters fall;
And I shall find my peace, my all in all.

Thou art the bread of life, O Lord, to me,
Thy holy Word the truth that saveth me;
Give me to eat and live with Thee above;
Teach me to love Thy truth, for Thou art love.

O send Thy Spirit, Lord, now unto me,
That He may touch my eyes, and make me see:
Show me the truth concealed within Thy Word,
And in Thy Book revealed I see the Lord.

MARY A. LATHBURY

DAY 68

MUCH *with* LITTLE

JOHN 6:11 NLT
Then Jesus took the loaves, gave thanks to God, and passed them out to the people. Afterward he did the same with the fish. And they all ate until they were full.

The disciples should have known that the power of God was present with them. To prove the point, Jesus determined to show them that *nothing* was too big or too small for Him to do. As the disciples stuttered and made excuses, Jesus asked for the five loaves and the two fish. Taking them in hand, He looked up to heaven, blessed and broke them, and gave them to His men to hand out to the multitude.

This isn't the only way Jesus could have performed the miracle, of course. He could have materialized the food out of nothing. He could have done "special orders"— surf for her, turf for him. Or He could have caused manna to fall on the ground, as it did for ancient Israel. Instead, He asked His disciples for what they had, regardless of how little it seemed.

We see an important spiritual principle here: God wants but does not need our participation in His work . . . God can do much with little.

GREG LAURIE

HIS MIRACLES

FED *and* FILLED

JOHN 6:12 NIV
*When they had all had enough to eat,
he said to his disciples, "Gather the pieces
that are left over. Let nothing be wasted."*

W hen did the reality of what had happened finally
get through to the disciples? Was Andrew holding a full basket in his hands when he offered the bread
and fish to someone who said, with a mouth already full,
"No thanks! I couldn't eat one more bite!"? Did he try
passing it to someone else, who also refused it, saying, "I
don't know when I've had so much to eat!"? Did Andrew
then straighten up, look out over the orderly yet festive
crowd that seemed to stretch almost to the horizon, and
suddenly realize that *everyone had been fed?* Did he grip the
basket with trembling hands, staring hard at the contents,
until his thoughts focused? *It's a miracle! It's a miracle! We fed
thousands of people with only five loaves and two fish!*

It was such a quiet, unobtrusive miracle. Nothing flashy
or showy or manipulative or spectacular. No one would
have even known a miracle had taken place, except that
Jesus had lifted up five loaves and two fish in front of
everyone when He asked His Father's blessing. There had
been no adequate resources to feed so many people at
once, yet everyone was not only fed but also filled!

ANNE GRAHAM LOTZ

He Only Needed a Word

John 6:15 NIV

Jesus, knowing that they intended to come and make him king by force, withdrew again to a mountain by himself.

At the literally mundane level, Jesus knew how to transform the molecular structure of water to make it wine. That knowledge also allowed him to take a few pieces of bread and some little fish and feed thousands of people. He could create matter from the energy he knew how to access from "the heavens," right where he was.

It cannot be surprising that the feeding of the thousands led the crowds to try to force him to be their king. Surely one who could play on the energy/matter equation like that could do anything. Turn gravel into gold and pay off the national debt! Do you think he could get elected president or prime minister today?

He knew how to transform the tissues of the human body from sickness to health and from death to life. He knew how to suspend gravity, interrupt weather patterns, and eliminate unfruitful trees without saw or ax. He only needed a word. Surely he must be amused at what Nobel prizes are awarded for today.

Dallas Willard

REAL BELIEVERS

JOHN 6:26 ESV

*Jesus answered them, "Truly, truly, I say to you,
you are seeking me, not because you saw signs,
but because you ate your fill of the loaves."*

After the feeding of the five thousand, the people
wanted to take Jesus by force and make him king.
When Jesus realized this, he immediately "withdrew
again to the mountain by himself" (John 6:15 ESV). When
the people caught up with him, they asked him, "Rabbi,
when did you come here?" (6:25). "Jesus answered them,
'Truly, truly, I say to you, you are seeking me, not because
you saw signs, but because you ate your fill of the loaves.
Do not labor for the food that perishes, but for the food
that endures to eternal life, which the Son of Man will
give to you. For on him God the Father has set his seal'"
(6:26-27). Jesus was pushing to turn their focus away from
free food to the truth of the gospel. In this narrative Jesus'
difficult teaching on the bread of life came next (6:28-
59). "When many of his disciples heard it, they said, 'This
is a hard saying; who can listen to it?'" (6:60). The result
was that "After this many of his disciples turned back and
no longer walked with him" (6:66). Jesus would rather
have a few real believers than many followers who came
along for the wrong reason.

AJITH FERNANDO

TO BEAR THY CROSS

JOHN 6:26 KJV

Jesus answered them and said, Verily, verily, I say unto you, Ye seek me, not because ye saw the miracles, but because ye did eat of the loaves, and were filled.

Jesus hath now many lovers of the heavenly kingdom, but few bearers of His Cross. He hath many desirous of consolation, but few of tribulation. He findeth many companions of His table, but few of His abstinence. . . . Many reverence His miracles, few follow the ignominy of His Cross. Many love Jesus so long as no adversities befall them, many praise and bless Him so long as they receive any consolations from Him; but if Jesus hide Himself and leave them but a little while, they fall either into complaining or into too much dejection of mind. . . .

If thou bear the Cross cheerfully, it will bear thee, and lead thee to the desired end, namely, where there shall be an end of suffering, though here there shall not be. If thou bear it unwillingly, thou makest for thyself a burden and increasest thy load, and yet notwithstanding thou must bear it. If thou cast away one cross, without doubt thou shalt find another, and that perhaps a more heavy one.

THOMAS À KEMPIS

IN *the* PATH *of the* STORM

MATTHEW 14:22 NIV
*Immediately Jesus made the disciples get into
the boat and go on ahead of him to the other side,
while he dismissed the crowd.*

Obedience, yes, I said *obedience,* often puts us in the path of a storm. Jesus sent them into danger so that they might be delivered from a greater danger, namely, the temptation to be swept away with the crowd. Let us never forget that it was Jesus who asked them to go to the other side. It was the Master of the winds who planned that they would row directly into a storm. . . .

Sometimes we have the mistaken notion that a storm is proof that we are "out of the will of God." Yet, it is in the center of God's will, in obedience to Him, that we might encounter the fiercest opposition. Let's not fall into the error of thinking that we have made a wrong decision just because we are sailing into high winds. Sometimes our greatest trial comes when we are walking in obedience to the Lord's command.

ERWIN LUTZER

BATTERED *by the* WAVES

MARK 6:47-48 NASB
*When it was evening, the boat was in the middle
of the sea, and He was alone on the land.
Seeing them straining at the oars . . .
He came to them, walking on the sea.*

There were the disciples being battered by the waves
and wind. The harder they rowed in one direction,
the harder the wind pushed in the other direction. Mark
pictures them "straining at the oars" (Mark 6:48). These
boys were sweating. And they didn't even want to be out
there.

Are you in a storm today? Can you feel the wind pushing against you? You say, "Tony, I'm not only in a storm,
but I'm being pushed backwards."

I hear you. I've been in those kinds of trials too. The
first thing I want to tell you about trials is that for a Christian, there is no such thing as random, pointless trials. If
Jesus sent you into the storm, His authority is reigning
over it even though it may be raining on you.

If you are in a trial, God has a point to it. God can even
hit the target with a crooked arrow. He can take a trial
caused by our sin and failure and still make something out
of it. The power and authority of Christ are not threatened by trials.

TONY EVANS

THE RIGHT TIME

MARK 6:48 NCV

*He saw his followers struggling hard to row the
boat, because the wind was blowing against them.
Between three and six o'clock in the morning,
Jesus came to them, walking on the water.*

Mark tells us that during the storm Jesus "saw his
followers struggling" (Mark 6:48). Through the
night he saw them. Through the storm he saw them. And
like a loving father he waited. He waited until the right
time, until the right moment. He waited until he knew it
was time to come, and then he came.

What made it the right time? I don't know. Why was
the ninth hour better than the fourth or fifth? I can't
answer that. Why does God wait until the money is gone?
Why does he wait until the sickness has lingered? Why
does he choose to wait until the other side of the grave to
answer the prayers for healing?

I don't know. I only know his timing is always right. I
can only say he will do what is best. . . . Though you hear
nothing, he is speaking. Though you see nothing, he is
acting. With God there are no accidents. Every incident
is intended to bring us closer to him.

MAX LUCADO

DO NOT BE AFRAID

*They were terrified, but he called out to them,
"I am here! Don't be afraid."*

Everyone has to deal with some fear in his or her life. It comes in many different forms: fear of dying, of going to the dentist, of heights, of spiders, of small spaces, of speaking in public. . . .

It is interesting that in the Bible, whenever God makes an appearance to a human being—directly or in the form of the angel of the Lord—usually the first thing he says to the person is, "Fear not." Something about the presence of God causes us to fear; but something in his nature also will not allow fear to stay. . . .

In his book *Lifesigns*, the late Henri Nouwen wrote: "Why is there no reason to fear any longer? Jesus himself answers this question succinctly when he approaches his frightened disciples walking on the lake: 'I am here. Do not be afraid.'"

We can face our fears with confidence, knowing that God is with us even in the storms. Take your fears to the One who alone can deal with and overcome them.

As you spend time with God right now, tell him your biggest fears. Then repeat Jesus' words, "I am here. Don't be afraid."

IWORSHIP DAILY DEVOTIONAL BIBLE

LORD, WHOM WINDS *and* SEAS OBEY

JOHN 6:20 NKJV
But He said to them, "It is I; do not be afraid."

Lord, whom winds and seas obey,
Guide us through the watery way;
In the hollow of thy hand
Hide, and bring us safe to land.

Jesus, let our faithful mind
Rest, on thee alone reclined;
Every anxious thought repress,
Keep our souls in perfect peace.

Keep the souls whom now we leave,
Bid them to each other cleave;
Bid them walk on life's rough sea;
Bid them come by faith to thee.

Save, till all these tempests end,
All who on thy love depend;
Waft our happy spirits o'er;
Land us on the heavenly shore.

CHARLES WESLEY

LIFE'S BAD WEATHER

MARK 6:50 NIV

Immediately he spoke to them and said,
"Take courage! It is I. Don't be afraid."

You can't avoid all the bad weather in life. You can try to anticipate some of it, but much is unavoidable and must be faced. On occasion there is no alternative but to sail right through the eye of the storm. Peter was about to learn this very salutary lesson. . . .

Looking back at the incident, Peter must have smiled to himself. With the advantage of hindsight he would have understood many things obscured by the terror of the moment. . . .

Peter would face many fierce storms before he arrived in glory. . . . Storms of doubts, despair, and ill discipline would plague him—storms of suffering and deprivation. As leader of the church, he would be caught up in hurricanes of hostility from inside the church fellowship and face headwinds from the world that would leave him just as battered and bruised as his Galilean experience. When the squalls blew up across the lake of his life, Peter must have often drawn strength from the Lord's great cry of presence and help: "Take courage! It is I. Don't be afraid."

JILL BRISCOE

KEEP *on* WALKING

MATTHEW 14:28-29 AMP.
And Peter answered Him, Lord if it is You,
command me to come to You on the water. He said,
Come! So Peter got out of the boat and walked
on the water, and he came toward Jesus.

Peter stepped out at the command of Jesus to do something he had never done before. As a matter of fact, no one had ever done it except Jesus.

It required faith!

Then Peter made the mistake of spending too much time looking at the storm. He became frightened. Doubt and unbelief pressed in on him, and he began to sink. He cried out to Jesus to save him, and He did. . . . You and I can be aware of our circumstances and yet, purposely, keep our mind on something that will build us up and edify our faith.

The devil brings storms into your life to intimidate you. We glorify God when we continue to do what we know is right even in adverse circumstances.

When the storms come in your life, dig in both heels, set your face like flint, and be determined in the Holy Spirit to stay out of the boat!

JOYCE MEYER

SERIOUS INVOLVEMENT

MATTHEW 14:28-29 NKJV

*And Peter answered Him and said, "Lord, if it is You,
command me to come to You on the water." So He said,
"Come." And when Peter had come down out of the
boat, he walked on the water to go to Jesus.*

Jesus came to the disciples one night out in the middle
of the Sea of Galilee, walking on the water in the midst
of a violent storm. Who out of all the disciples jumped
out of the boat? Peter. *There's the Lord,* he must have
thought. *I'm here; I've got to go where the action is. . . .* Before
anyone knew it, Peter was out of the boat, walking on the
water. The rest of the disciples were still clinging to their
seats, trying to make sure they didn't fall overboard in the
storm. But Peter was out of the boat without giving it a
second thought. That is involvement—serious involvement. Only after he left the boat and walked some distance did Peter think about the danger and start to sink.

People often look at that incident and criticize Peter's
lack of faith. But let's give him credit for having faith to
leave that boat in the first place.

JOHN MACARTHUR

RECOGNIZING JESUS

MATTHEW 14:30 NKJV
*But when he saw that the wind was
boisterous, he was afraid; and beginning to sink
he cried out, saying, "Lord, save me!"*

The wind really was boisterous and the waves really were high, but Peter didn't see them at first. He didn't consider them at all; he simply recognized his Lord, stepped out in recognition of Him, and "walked on the water." Then he began to take those things around him into account, and instantly, down he went. Why couldn't our Lord have enabled him to walk at the bottom of the waves, as well as on top of them? He could have, yet neither could be done without Peter's continuing recognition of the Lord Jesus.

We step right out with recognition of God in some things, then self-consideration enters our lives and down we go. If you are truly recognizing your Lord, you have no business being concerned about how and where He engineers your circumstances. The things surrounding you are real, but when you look at them you are immediately overwhelmed, and even unable to recognize Jesus. Then comes His rebuke, " . . . why did you doubt?" (14:31). Let your actual circumstances be what they may, but keep recognizing Jesus, maintaining complete reliance upon Him.

OSWALD CHAMBERS

ANCHORS *of* FAITH

MATTHEW 14:30-31 NIV

But when he saw the wind, he was afraid and,
beginning to sink, cried out, "Lord, save me!"
Immediately Jesus reached out his hand and caught him.
"You of little faith," he said, "why did you doubt?"

This is the God Who walks with us and helps us carry our heavy loads. He knows our frames, our makeup, and our limitations. He remembers that we are frail, and He has promised not to give us more than we can take. This is the quiet knowing that we have as we carry our individual burdens through life.

When Peter's mother-in-law was sick, Jesus took her by the hand and "lifted her up" (Mark 1:31 KJV). . . .

When Peter's faith failed and he began to sink, the Lord took him by the hand and lifted him into the boat (see Matt. 14:30-31).

When we are burdened and feel overwhelmed . . . about to sink beneath the load, we must focus our faith on Him and not on our circumstances. . . . It is the difficulties, the weights of life, that cause us to depend on Him. They are often the very things that keep us anchored to Him.

GIGI GRAHAM TCHIVIDJIAN

BRINGING GOD *into* FOCUS

MARK 6:51 NRSV

*Then he got into the boat with them and the
wind ceased. And they were utterly astounded.*

The miracles constitute a claim by Jesus as to who He
really is. The nature miracles are a good example of
this. The Old Testament is clear that it is *God* who mul-
tiplies food and feeds the hungry, but on two occasions
Jesus Himself does this for thousands of people. Do you
see the implicit claim? Think of Jesus walking on the
water of the turbulent Sea of Galilee. Was that to show
off? Not at all. It was to teach the terrified disciples a crucial lesson: that Jesus does what God does. In the Psalms
we read that it is God who stills the raging of the sea;
when the waves rise, He stills them. But what God does
in the Old Testament Jesus does in the Gospels! The conclusion is evident. Jesus embodies God, brings Him into
focus, as nobody else has ever done. The miracles are
acted claims. They point to who Jesus really is.

MICHAEL GREEN

ANOTHER GROUP, ANOTHER MIRACLE

MATTHEW 15:30, 32–33 NRSV

Great crowds came to him. . . . Then Jesus called his disciples to him and said, "I have compassion for the crowd, because they have been with me now for three days and have nothing to eat; and I do not want to send them away hungry. . . ." The disciples said to him, "Where are we to get enough bread in the desert to feed so great a crowd?"

Although the disciples had seen Jesus feed five thousand people, they had no idea what he would do in this situation. Perhaps they didn't expect Jesus to perform the same miracle when the crowd was Gentile and not Jewish (thus revealing their spiritual blindness). This miracle again revealed Jesus' divine power. The crowd was in a *remote place,* and the disciples asked the obvious question: "Where could we get enough bread . . . to feed such a crowd?" Jesus had already found the resources in a previous remote place for an even larger crowd, yet the disciples were completely perplexed as to how they should be expected to feed this crowd. People often give up when faced with difficult situations. Like the disciples, we often forget God's provision for us in the past. When facing a difficult situation, remember what God has done for you and trust him to take care of you again.

LIFE APPLICATION BIBLE COMMENTARY—MATTHEW

GIVE *and* TAKE

MATTHEW 15:32 KJV

Then Jesus called his disciples unto him, and said, I have compassion on the multitude, because they continue with me now three days, and have nothing to eat: and I will not send them away fasting, lest they faint in the way.

Our Lord's mission of grace and truth was at its height. His help was sought with the utmost eagerness. Large numbers of sick were cast at his feet in hot haste. The crumb was given to the woman of Canaan, but whole loaves were distributed to the crowds of Jews, because it was befitting that they should have a full chance to appreciate and accept Christ. For a brief moment they glorified the God of Israel, but the spasm of gratitude was transient. "His own" rejected Jesus. They would have his miracles, but would not own his claims. Take care that you do not become content with getting his help; love him for himself.

Do not suppose that these miracles were confined to his earthly life. He is still the great storehouse of divine and healing energy. He is still moved with compassion, and longs to help each weary and sin-sick soul. His thought still is "lest they faint in the way." The wilderness can place no bar on "the saving strength of his right hand."

F. B. MEYER

BOUNTY *of* CHRIST

MATTHEW 15:36 KJV
And he took the seven loaves and the fishes,
and gave thanks, and brake them, and gave to his
disciples, and the disciples to the multitude.

The bounty of Christ is inexhaustible, and, to evidence that, Christ repeated this miracle, to show that he is still the same for the succour and supply of his people that attend upon him. His favours are renewed, as our wants and necessities are. In the former miracle, Christ used all the bread he had, which was five loaves, and fed all the guests he had, which were five thousand, and so he did now; though he might have said, "If five loaves would feed five thousand, four may feed four thousand;" he took all the seven loaves, and fed with them the four thousand; for he would teach us to take things as they are, and accommodate ourselves to them; to use what we have, and make the best of that which is. Here it was, as in the dispensing of manna, He that gathered much had nothing over, and he that gathered little had no lack.

MATTHEW HENRY

THE HUNGRY ARE FED

MARK 8:8 NKJV
So they ate and were filled.

Tell out, my soul, the greatness of the Lord!
Unnumbered blessings give my spirit voice;
Tender to me the promise of God's word;
In God my Savior shall my heart rejoice.

Tell out, my soul, the greatness of God's name!
Make known God's might, who wondrous deeds
has done;
God's mercy sure, from age to age the same; God's holy
name, the Lord, the mighty One.

Tell out, my soul, the greatness of God's might!
Powers and dominions lay their glory by;
Proud hearts and stubborn wills are put to flight,
The hungry fed, the humble lifted high.

Tell out, my soul, the glories of God's word!
Firm is the promise and God's mercy sure.
Tell out, my soul, the greatness of the Lord
To children's children and forevermore!

TIMOTHY DUDLEY-SMITH

SHEER ABUNDANCE

MARK 8:8 NIV

Afterward the disciples picked up seven basketfuls of broken pieces that were left over.

In the previous feeding episode, Jesus had asked the disciples to divide the crowd into a specific arrangement; this time, he did not do so. The Greek word for "baskets" carries an interesting twist on this story. In the feeding of the five thousand, there were twelve baskets of leftovers, and the "baskets" were *kophinos,* large baskets. After the feeding of the four thousand, there were seven baskets of leftovers, and the "baskets" were different; these were *spuris,* baskets that were large enough to hold a person. (Paul was let down over the Damascus wall in a *spuris*—Acts 9:25.) The abundance of leftovers in these seven baskets may have been more than the leftovers from the twelve baskets in the previous incident. If the disciples took some of the leftovers as their own food supply for the coming days, then the abundance of the supply for them was a reminder over several days of their lack of faith in what Jesus could accomplish.

LIFE APPLICATION BIBLE COMMENTARY—MARK

MIRACLES HAPPEN

JOHN 6:30 NRSV
*So they said to him, "What sign are you going
to give us then, so that we may see it and believe you?
What work are you performing?"*

The most incredible thing about miracles is that they
happen. . . .

The modern mind always mixes up two different ideas:
mystery in the sense of what is marvelous, and mystery in
the sense of what is complicated. That is half its difficulty
about miracles. A miracle is startling; but it is simple. It is
simple because it is a miracle. It is power coming directly
from God (or the devil) instead of indirectly through
nature or human wills. . . .

Nobody can get behind that fundamental difference
about the reason of things; and it is as rational for a theist
to believe in miracles as for an atheist to disbelieve in
them. In other words there is only one intelligent reason
why a man does not believe in miracles and that is that he
does believe in materialism.

G. K. CHESTERTON

ON *the* MOUNTAIN

———

MARK 9:2 NKJV
*Now after six days Jesus took Peter, James, and
John, and led them up on a high mountain apart by
themselves; and He was transfigured before them.*

We have all experienced times of exaltation on the
mountain, when we have seen things from God's
perspective and have wanted to stay there. But God will
never allow us to stay there. The true test of our spiritual
life is in exhibiting the power to descend from the mountain. If we only have the power to go up, something is
wrong. It is a wonderful thing to be on the mountain
with God, but a person only gets there so that he may
later go down and lift up the demon-possessed people in
the valley (see 9:14–18). We are not made for the mountains, for sunrises, or for the other beautiful attractions in
life—those are simply intended to be moments of inspi-
ration. We are made for the valley and the ordinary things
of life, and that is where we have to prove our stamina and
strength. . . .

We are inclined to think that everything that happens
is to be turned into useful teaching. In actual fact, it is to
be turned into something even better than teaching,
namely, character. The mountaintop is not meant to teach
us anything, it is meant to make us something.

OSWALD CHAMBERS

THE LAW *and* PROPHETS

MATTHEW 17:3 NIV
Just then there appeared before them
Moses and Elijah, talking with Jesus.

Why Moses and Elijah? These two are significant not only because of the mysterious character of their respected departures from earth but because of the roles they played in the Old Testament. Moses was the mediator of the Old Covenant as Jesus is the Mediator of the New Covenant. Elijah, whose return was promised in the last prophecy of the Old Testament (see Malachi 4:5), was one of the most important of a long line of Old Testament prophets. Moses and Elijah together represent the Law and the Prophets. The much-used phrase "the Law and the Prophets" served as a summary for the teaching of God in the Old Testament. . . .

On the Mount of Transfiguration the very incarnation and embodiment of the gospel is witnessed in His glory by the Law (Moses) and the Prophets (Elijah).

R. C. SPROUL

COMMON SENSE VS. FAITH

LUKE 9:30-31 NKJV

And behold, two men talked with Him, who were Moses and Elijah, who appeared in glory and spoke of His decease which He was about to accomplish at Jerusalem.

Every time you venture out in your life of faith, you will find something in your circumstances that, from a commonsense standpoint, will flatly contradict your faith. But common sense is not faith, and faith is not common sense. In fact, they are as different as the natural life and the spiritual. Can you trust Jesus Christ where your common sense cannot trust Him? Can you venture out with courage on the words of Jesus Christ, while the realities of your commonsense life continue to shout, "It's all a lie"? When you are on the mountaintop, it's easy to say, "Oh yes, I believe God can do it," but you have to come down from the mountain to the demon-possessed valley and face the realities that scoff at your Mount-of-Transfiguration belief (see Luke 9:28-42). Every time my theology becomes clear to my own mind, I encounter something that contradicts it. As soon as I say, "I believe 'God shall supply all [my] need,'" the testing of my faith begins (Philippians 4:19 NKJV). When my strength runs dry and my vision is blinded, wilt I endure this trial of my faith victoriously or will I turn back in defeat?

OSWALD CHAMBERS

FULFILLED *in* HIM

MARK 9:5-6 NKJV

*Then Peter answered and said to Jesus, "Rabbi,
it is good for us to be here; and let us make three
tabernacles: one for You, one for Moses, and one
for Elijah"—because he did not know what
to say, for they were greatly afraid.*

Our confusion was Peter's confusion which the
Father's voice and the vision of Jesus clarified. On
the Mount of Transfiguration, Moses, representing the
law, and Elijah the prophets, talked with Jesus, the New
Revelation. The Jewish heart of Peter wanted to keep all
three, and put them on the same level—he wanted to
build three tabernacles for them. A voice from the cloud
spoke, "This is My beloved Son. Hear Him"—the law
and the prophets are fulfilled in him; hear him. And when
they lifted up their eyes they saw no man save Jesus only.
He filled their horizon. He must fill ours.

E. STANLEY JONES

STRENGTH *from the* MOUNT

MATTHEW 17:5-6 NRSV

While he was still speaking, suddenly a bright cloud overshadowed them, and from the cloud a voice said, "This is my Son, the Beloved; with him I am well pleased; listen to him!" When the disciples heard this, they fell to the ground and were overcome by fear.

The moment on the mount was absolutely necessary, but it could not be prolonged beyond its own time. . . . Often there come to us moments that we would like to prolong indefinitely. But after the time on the mountain top we must come back to the battle and the routine of life; that time is meant to give us strength for life's everyday.

After the great struggle at Mount Carmel with the prophets of Baal, Elijah, in reaction, ran away. Out into the desert he went and there, as he lay under a juniper tree asleep, an angel twice prepared a meal for him. Then comes the sentence, "[So] he arose and ate and drank, and went in the strength of that food forty days and forty nights" (I Kings 19:8 NASB). To the mountain top of the presence of God we must go, not to remain there but to go in the strength of that time for many days. . . . We cannot live forever in the moment on the mountain but we cannot live at all without it.

WILLIAM BARCLAY

HIS MIRACLES

JESUS ONLY

MATTHEW 17:7-8 KJV

*And Jesus came and touched them, and said,
Arise, and be not afraid. And when they had lifted
up their eyes, they saw no man, save Jesus only.*

Reaching forth His loving hand, our Lord touched each disciple reassuringly, and bade them stand up, fearing nothing. . . . The Lord Jesus alone remained—He who is the same yesterday, today, and forever (Hebrews 13:8).

Jesus is not a mere man who, by dint of spiritual enlightenment and surrender to the Father's will, became more divine than any other man. He is God the Son, one person of the eternal trinity, manifested in the flesh and thus the one mediator between God and man. Peter's confession and the Father's voice after the transfiguration tell the same blessed story. Jesus had to be who He was in order to do what He did. No one less than the Son of God could make propitiation for our sins (1 John 4:10).

The vision passed, but Jesus remained. When the morning came He led His disciples down from that mount of special privilege to face the appalling effects of sin in the valley below, for the time had not yet come for the kingdom to be displayed in universal power and glory.

H. A. IRONSIDE

LITTLE MIRACLES

MATTHEW 17:24, 27 NIV
After Jesus and his disciples arrived in Capernaum,
the collectors of the two-drachma tax came to Peter. . . .
"But so that we may not offend them, go to the lake
and throw out your line. Take the first fish you catch;
open its mouth and you will find a four-drachma coin."

When this same Lord lived in Palestine, he performed smaller-scale miracles: withering a fig tree; finding a coin in the fish's mouth; healing Peter's mother-in-law of a fever; restoring a man's shriveled hand. He performed powerful miracles, but at a different speed and on a smaller scale than when he created the cosmos.

C. S. Lewis said the Lord's earthly miracles are a retelling in small letters of the very same story that is written across the whole universe in letters too large for some to see. How exciting to look up into the heavens and realize that a personal God created in a personal way all that we see. Stars, suns, and galaxies are the very stamp of his power and personality. And this same Lord of creation loves you and me.

JONI EARECKSON TADA

TOUGH WORDS

——

MARK 11:12–14 NIV
The next day as they were leaving Bethany, Jesus was
hungry. Seeing in the distance a fig tree in leaf, he went
to find out if it had any fruit. When he reached it, he
found nothing but leaves. . . . Then he said to the tree,
"May no one ever eat fruit from you again."
And his disciples heard him say it.

Why should anyone trouble to record the incident [of the cursing of the fig tree] as though it had some special significance? Because it did have some special significance. As recorded by Mark, it is an acted parable with the same lesson as the spoken parable of the fruitless fig tree in Luke 13:6–9. In that spoken parable a landowner came three years in succession expecting fruit from a fig tree on his property, and when year by year it proved to be fruitless, he told the man in charge of his vineyard to cut it down because it was using up the ground to no good purpose. The fig tree represents the city of Jerusalem, unresponsive to Jesus as he came to it with the message of God, and thereby incurring destruction. Elsewhere Luke records how Jesus wept over the city's blindness to its true well-being and foretold its ruin "because you did not know the time of your visitation" (Luke 19:41–44 ESV).

F. F. BRUCE

HAVE FAITH

MATTHEW 21:21 NRSV

"Truly I tell you, if you have faith and do not doubt, not only will you do what has been done to the fig tree, but even if you say to this mountain, 'Be lifted up and thrown into the sea,' it will be done."

Jesus had cursed the fig tree; the fig tree had died; the disciples had expressed surprise. Jesus explained that they could ask anything of God and receive an answer. . . . They should not have been surprised that a fig tree could be withered at Jesus' words. Jesus was using a mountain as a figure of speech to show that God could help in any situation: *This mountain* (referring to the Mount of Olives on which they stood) could be *thrown into the sea* (the Dead Sea, that could be seen from the Mount). Jesus' point was that in their petitions to God they must believe without doubting (that is, without wavering in their confidence in God). The kind of prayer Jesus meant was not the arbitrary wish to move a mountain of dirt and stone; instead, he was referring to prayers that the disciples would need to faithfully pray as they faced mountains of opposition to their gospel message in the years to come. Their prayers for the advancement of God's kingdom would always be answered positively—in God's timing.

LIFE APPLICATION BIBLE COMMENTARY—MATTHEW

AN OBJECT LESSON

MARK 11:21 NIV
Peter remembered and said to Jesus, "Rabbi, look!
The fig tree you cursed has withered!"

Jesus withered that fig tree as his disciples watched and wondered. Yet the fig tree was simply doing what its kind does "out of season." What could have been Christ's purpose in that destructive miracle? His lesson for the twelve and for us had to do with faith, or our lack of it.

In Mark's Gospel, the incident brackets the cleansing of the Temple. The authority to disrupt the commercial interests that had taken over this place of prayer was super-human. Jesus' oneness with the Father was its source. "This is my Father's house and you have corrupted it." He cleared the Temple because it fostered prayer-less, faithless living. He cursed the fig tree to make the same point.

Of course, Jesus knew where he was headed: to the cross. He was doing things and saying things now that "sealed his fate." But the teaching is clear: It takes faith to clean out a Temple and faith to dry up a fig tree. Jesus' anger was directed at the corruption he saw in the Temple, and at the continuing shallowness of trust on the part of the twelve. The fig tree simply served as an effective object lesson by its creator.

JAMES WILSON

CREATION SET FREE

ROMANS 8:21 NASB
The creation itself also will be set free
from its slavery to corruption into the freedom
of the glory of the children of God.

One thing we definitely know. God has not deliberately sent tragedy and suffering upon us. Though they are allowed, endured by God, they are not God's *intention* for us. Not once in the gospels does Jesus say that God sends tragedy and pain either to test us or to punish us. Though the blocks that prevent full healing are many and mysterious, the New Testament makes it clear that God is *always* on the side of healing, release, and reconciliation.

We know another thing. We are given the witness in scripture that the day will come when the whole creation will freely accept this love, healing, and reconciliation. There will be no aspect of creation left weeping and alone. There will be no more desire to choose lovelessness. The risk and choice will be there forever, but that risk (that grave gift of God's honor) will be transcended by a creation joyfully and freely united with God in the embrace of lovers.

This is not a bland victory. God has paid a great price for love within freedom.

FLORA SLOSSON WUELLNER

JESUS' MIRACLES
on the SABBATH

Then he turned to his critics and asked,
"Is it legal to do good deeds on the Sabbath,
or is it a day for doing harm? Is this
a day to save life or to destroy it?"

MARK 3:4 NLT

JESUS' MIRACLES *on the* SABBATH

It would be possible to make the case that Jesus was crucified because He broke the accumulated rules about the Sabbath. He challenged a tradition run amuck. At times, we sense that the religious leaders were setting a trap for Him. At other times, He seemed to revel in the opportunity to break their stodgy rules. Jesus dared to say that the religious leaders had missed the point when it came to the Sabbath. The Sabbath was a gift from God to be used as a means for rest and for worship. Many of those who heard Him preferred to leave the Sabbath as an end in itself. They were all about rules; He was all about rest.

Jesus was accused of breaking the Sabbath by those who didn't hesitate to break people made in God's image. They charged Him with not taking the Sabbath seriously when they didn't take it seriously enough. For Jesus, setting people free from diseases and sin were the most relaxing and worship-filled moments of any day, and He wasn't about to forego that pleasure on the one day of the week specially set aside for restful pursuits.

SATAN MUST OBEY

LUKE 4:33, 35 NLT

Once when he was in the synagogue, a man possessed by a demon began shouting at Jesus. . . . Jesus cut him short. "Be silent!" he told the demon. "Come out of the man!"

The Jews believed that the Messiah would crush Satan and destroy his power. That the spirits feared Jesus demonstrated his power over them. In this showdown, Luke established Jesus' credentials by showing that even the evil spirits recognized Jesus as Messiah. Luke emphasized Jesus' conflict with evil powers to show his superiority over them, so he recorded many stories about Jesus driving out evil spirits. Jesus didn't have to conduct an elaborate exorcism ritual. His word was enough to send out the demons. This shows that Jesus was far more than just a teacher. Jesus' power over demons reveals his absolute power over Satan, even in a world that seems to be in Satan's control. Satan is presently under God's authority; when God chooses to command, Satan must obey. Satan's workings are only within God's prescribed limits; he can do no more evil than God allows. In the end, Satan and all his demons will be tormented in the lake of fire forever (Revelation 20:10).

LIFE APPLICATION BIBLE COMMENTARY—LUKE

PRESENT *among* THEM

MARK 1:25-26 NASB
*And Jesus rebuked him, saying, "Be quiet,
and come out of him!" Throwing him into
convulsions, the unclean spirit cried out with
a loud voice, and came out of him.*

At this the wretched man became convulsed and
cried out. It seemed as if his unclean spirits strug-
gled against Jesus' holiness. Finally, in obedience to a
higher power the demons departed, leaving the man sane.

In that devil-haunted world, exorcisms were often
accomplished by incantations and magic, practices forbid-
den in Jewish religion but frequently resorted to by men
and women battling desperately against strange forces that
seemed to threaten them on every side. If some in the
congregation that Sabbath day assumed unthinkingly that
Jesus was merely a clever magician using occult powers,
other people, watching him more closely, observed that
he employed no magic formula and uttered no incanta-
tion, but restored the insane man to sanity simply by the
power of a spoken word. . . .

The cure of the demon-sufferer demonstrated more
conclusively than any sermon that God was present
among them.

ALICE PARMELEE

HOLD THY PEACE

LUKE 4:35 KJV

And Jesus rebuked him, saying, Hold thy peace, and come out of him. And when the devil had thrown him in the midst, he came out of him, and hurt him not.

If there is one aspect of the New Testament Jesus in which he may be said to present himself eminently as a practical person, it is in the aspect of an exorcist. There is nothing meek and mild, there is nothing even in the ordinary sense mystical, about the tone of the voice that says "Hold thy peace and come out of him." It is much more like the tone of a very businesslike lion-tamer or a strong-minded doctor dealing with a homicidal maniac. . . .

Now the first thing to note is that if we take it merely as a human story, it is in some ways a very strange story. I do not refer here to its tremendous and tragic culmination or to any implications involving triumph in that tragedy. I do not refer to what is commonly called the miraculous element; for on that point philosophies vary and modern philosophies very decidedly waver. Indeed the educated Englishman of today may be said to have passed from an old fashion, in which he would not believe in any miracles unless they were ancient, and adopted a new fashion in which he will not believe in any miracles unless they are modern.

G. K. CHESTERTON

HEALED *to* SERVE

LUKE 4:38-39 NIV

*Jesus left the synagogue and went to the home of
Simon. Now Simon's mother-in-law was suffering from
a high fever, and they asked Jesus to help her. So he
bent over her and rebuked the fever, and it left her.
She got up at once and began to wait on them.*

Consider the story of Peter's mother-in-law, found in
Luke 4:38-39. She was struggling with a high fever,
but when Jesus touched her, the fever disappeared. Amazingly, when Peter's mother-in-law was miraculously
healed, she got out of bed and prepared Jesus and the disciples a meal. I call that being healed to serve.

My mother battled with metastatic colon cancer. Naturally, we prayed for her, and I truly believe she experienced healing because she lived longer than anyone with
that type of cancer in this area. She was able to live almost
five years after her original diagnosis, and during that time
she continued to serve in her women's circle, in her
church, and by taking care of her family. When you or
your loved one has experienced healing, God does it for
a reason and He expects you to continue to serve Him.

DAVID HAGER

HEALING PRAYER

MARK 1:30 NASB

Now Simon's mother-in-law was lying sick with a fever; and immediately they spoke to Jesus about her.

Into Simon's house illness had entered; fever in a deadly form had prostrated his mother-in-law; and as soon as Jesus came, they told Him of the sad affliction, and He hurried to the patient's bed. Do you have any illness in the house this morning? You will find Jesus the best physician by far; go to Him at once and tell Him all about the matter. Immediately lay the case before Him. It concerns one of His people, and therefore He will not regard it as trivial. Notice that immediately the Savior restored the ill woman; none can heal as He does. We dare not assume that the Lord will remove all illness from those we love, but we dare not forget that believing prayer for the sick is far more likely to be followed by restoration than anything else in the world; and where this does not happen, we must meekly bow to His will by whom life and death are determined. The tender heart of Jesus waits to hear our griefs; let us pour them into His patient ear.

CHARLES HADDON SPURGEON

NOT *for* SHOW

MATTHEW 8:15 NLT

But when Jesus touched her hand, the fever left her.
Then she got up and prepared a meal for him.

Miracles did not cost Jesus nothing; virtue went out of him with every healing; and beyond a doubt he would be tired. It would be for rest that he came into Peter's house, and yet no sooner was he in it than there came still another demand on him for help and healing.

Here was no publicity; here there was no crowd to look and to admire and to be astonished. Here there was only a simple cottage and a poor woman tossing with a common fever. And yet in those circumstances Jesus put forth all his power.

Jesus was never too tired to help; the demands of human need never came to him as an intolerable nuisance. Jesus was not one of these people who are at their best in public and at their worst in private. No situation was too humble for him to help. He did not need an admiring audience to be at his best. In a crowd or in a cottage his love and his power were at the disposal of anyone who needed him.

WILLIAM BARCLAY

INFINITE POTENTIALITY *of* RELIEF

MATTHEW 8:16 NRSV

That evening they brought to him many who were
possessed with demons; and he cast out the spirits
with a word, and cured all who were sick.

It was evening. The sun was setting, and the Sabbath
past. All that day it had been told from home to home
what had been done in the Synagogue. . . . On that evening no one in Capernaum thought of business, pleasure,
or rest. There must have been many homes of sorrow, care
and sickness there, and in the populous neighbourhood
around. To them, to all, had the door of hope now been
opened. Truly a new Sun had risen on them with healing in His wings. No disease too desperate, when even
the demons owned the authority of His mere rebuke. . . .
No picture of the Christ more dear to us, than this of the
unlimited healing of whatever disease of body or soul. In
its blessed indefiniteness it conveys the infinite potenti-
ality of relief, whatever misery fall on us, or whatever care
or sorrow oppress us. He must be blind, indeed, who sees
not in this Physician the Divine Healer; in this Christ the
Light of the World.

ALFRED EDERSHEIM

JUST A TASTE

—

MATTHEW 8:16–17 NLT

That evening many demon-possessed people were brought to Jesus. All the spirits fled when he commanded them to leave; and he healed all the sick. This fulfilled the word of the Lord through Isaiah, who said, "He took our sicknesses and removed our diseases."

Matthew continues to show Jesus' kingly nature. Through a single touch, Jesus healed (Matthew 8:3, 15); when he spoke a single word, evil spirits fled his presence (Matthew 8:16). Jesus has authority over all evil powers and all earthly disease. He also has power and authority to conquer sin. Sickness and evil are consequences of living in a fallen world. But in the future, when God removes all sin, there will be no more sickness and death. Jesus' healing miracles were a taste of what the whole world will one day experience in God's kingdom.

LIFE APPLICATION BIBLE

DRAWING NEAR

MARK 1:32 NIV
That evening after sunset the people brought
to Jesus all the sick and demon-possessed.

At even, ere the sun was set,
The sick, O Lord, around Thee lay;
O, with how many pains they met!
O, with what joy they went away!

Once more 'tis eventide, and we,
Oppressed with various ills, draw near;
What if Thyself we cannot see?
We know that Thou art ever near.

O Savior Christ, our woes dispel;
For some are sick, and some are sad;
And some have never loved Thee well,
And some have lost the love they had. . . .

Thy touch has still its ancient power.
No word from Thee can fruitless fall;
Hear, in this solemn evening hour,
And in Thy mercy heal us all.

HENRY TWELLS

TOTAL HEALING

LUKE 4:40 NIV
*When the sun was setting, the people brought to
Jesus all who had various kinds of sickness, and laying
his hands on each one, he healed them.*

The electrifying news of such healing miracles spread throughout the land as Luke tells us: "Yet the news about him spread all the more, so that crowds of people came to hear him and to be healed of their sicknesses" (5:15 NIV). Luke, good doctor that he was, perceived the holistic practice of Christ. He records that to those He healed, Jesus said, "Your faith has healed you" (8:48). Only in the forgiveness and cleansing of sin can there be total healing.

It has been estimated that over half the people with illness are suffering from psychosomatic ailments, from the effects of the mind and spirit on the body. Dr. Jung, the famous psychiatrist, says: "About a third of my cases are suffering from no clinically definable neurosis, but from the senselessness and emptiness of their lives."

The healing ministry of Christ to all of us is His healing of our sins. "By his wounds you have been healed" (1 Peter 2:24). He is the Physician who took on Himself our fatal sickness.

HENRY GARIEPY

WE WOULD SEE JESUS

LUKE 4:40 NKJV

*When the sun was setting, all those who had any that
were sick with various diseases brought them to Him;
and He laid His hands on every one of them and
healed them.*

We would see Jesus; lo! his star is shining
Above the stable while the angels sing;
There in a manger on the hay reclining;
Haste, let us lay our gifts before the King.

We would see Jesus, on the mountain teaching,
With all the listening people gathered round;
While birds and flowers and sky above are preaching
The blessedness which simple trust has found.

We would see Jesus, in his working of healing,
At eventide before the sun was set;
Divine and human, in his deep revealing
Of God made flesh, in loving service met.

We would see Jesus, in the early morning,
Still as of old, he calleth, "Follow me!"
Let us arise, all meaner service scorning;
Lord, we are thine, we give ourselves to thee.

J. EDGAR PARK

TOTAL GENEROSITY

MATTHEW 4:24 NKJV
*Then His fame went throughout all Syria;
and they brought to Him all sick people who
were afflicted with various diseases and torments,
and those who were demon-possessed, epileptics,
and paralytics; and He healed them.*

Child of Bethlehem, what contrasts you embrace! No one has ever been so humble; no one has ever wielded such power. We stand in awe of your holiness, and yet we are bathed in your love. . . .

You are the heir to King David's throne, but you renounced all of his royal splendor. Of all his luxurious bedrooms, you chose a stable. Of all his magnificent beds, you chose a feeding-trough. Of all his golden chariots, you chose an ass.

Never was there a king like you! Instead of royal isolation, you made yourself available to everyone who needed you. Instead of high security, you made yourself vulnerable to those who hated you.

It is we who need you, above anything in the world. You give yourself to us with such total generosity, that it might almost seem that you need us. There never was a king like this before!

EPHRAEM OF SYRIA

ONE WAS HEALED

JOHN 5:2-5 NIV

*Now there is in Jerusalem near the Sheep Gate a
pool, which in Aramaic is called Bethesda and which
is surrounded by five covered colonnades. Here a great
number of disabled people used to lie—the blind,
the lame, the paralyzed. One who was there
had been an invalid for thirty-eight years.*

He entered a place where lay a great multitude of sick
folk—of blind, lame, withered; and being the physician of both souls and bodies, and having come to heal
all the souls of them that should believe, of those sick folk
He chose one for healing, thereby to signify unity. If in
doing this we regard Him with a commonplace mind,
with the mere human understanding and wit, as regards
power it was not a great matter that He performed; and
also as regards goodness He performed too little. There
lay so many there, and yet only one was healed, whilst He
could by a word have raised them all up. What, then, must
we understand but that the power and the goodness was
doing what souls might, by His deeds, understand for
their everlasting salvation, than what bodies might gain
for temporal health? For that which is the real health of
bodies, and which is looked for from the Lord, will be at
the end, in the resurrection of the dead.

AUGUSTINE

ARE YOU WILLING?

JOHN 5:5-6 NKJV

Now a certain man was there who had an infirmity thirty-eight years. When Jesus saw him lying there, and knew that he already had been in that condition a long time, He said to him, "Do you want to be made well?"

Why did Jesus ask this man if he wanted to be made well? Wasn't it obvious, given his position near the pool why this crippled man was even present? I think it was an honest question, meaning, "Are you content with your condition? Are you willing to put yourself in my hands? Are you willing to change?"

Surprisingly, social scientists have found that some people really don't want to change. Some people really don't want to be made well.

Not everyone wants to change. That's why Jesus asked the crippled man lying near the pool at Bethesda if he wanted to be made well. The man at the pool was simply hoping Jesus might help him get into the water. But Jesus did even more than that. He healed him on the spot, and the man got up and walked.

GREG LAURIE

A QUESTION *of* HEART

JOHN 5:6 AMP.

When Jesus noticed him lying there [helpless],
knowing that he had already been a long time in
that condition, He said to him, Do you want to become
well? [Are you really in earnest about getting well?]

For many, many years, "Why me, God?" was the cry of my heart, and it filled my thoughts and affected my attitude daily. I lived in the wilderness of self-pity, and it was a problem for me, my family, and the plan of God for my life. . . .

When Jesus addressed His question to the man who had been lying by the pool of Bethesda for thirty-eight years, He knew that self-pity would not deliver this man. "Do you want to become well?" are words of compassion to anyone who is trapped in an emotional prison and who has learned to function with their problem. They are words directed to the heart.

Gaining freedom from hurts and emotional bondages is not easy. I know. It will provoke feelings and emotions that have been "stuffed" rather than faced and dealt with. It may involve very real pain, but to be free and cleansed by the power of forgiveness is the only way to ever be fully well again.

JOYCE MEYER

POWER *of* TRUST

JOHN 5:6 RSV

When Jesus saw him and knew that he
had been lying there a long time, he said to him,
"Do you want to be healed?"

Jesus' authority is demonstrated in both his teaching and his healing miracles that are signs of the power of God to change lives for the better.

The surprising events that occur in Jesus' presence are not done as tricks to astound people. They result from his caring for people and his obedience to the will of God.

Persons in need are confronted by a person who *loves* them and is completely obedient to God's will. This presence of Jesus, and the TRUST or FAITH of those whom he confronts, allow these acts of God's power to occur. This relationship is central. Where these elements are present—Jesus' obedience and love, and the willingness of a person to trust God—evil is overcome and God is glorified.

Do you want to be healed? That's a question Jesus asked the man at Bethesda. Do you want to be healed? is a question he asks today.

Do you want to be healed?

Jesus Christ is still in the business of making *you* well, if you will trust in him.

RICHARD ALLEN WARD

THE NARROW LIMITS *of* OUR FAITH

JOHN 5:7 KJV

The impotent man answered him, Sir, I have no man, when the water is troubled, to put me into the pool: but while I am coming, another steppeth down before me.

This diseased man does what almost all of us are wont to do; for he limits the assistance of God according to his own thought. . . . In this we have a mirror of that forbearance of which every one of us has daily experience: when, on the one hand, we keep our attention fixed on the means which are within our reach, and when, on the other hand, contrary to expectation, he displays his hand from hidden places and thus shows how far his goodness goes beyond the narrow limits of our faith.

Besides, this example ought to teach us patience. Thirty-eight years were a long period, during which God had delayed to render to this poor man that favor which, from the beginning, he had determined to confer upon him. However long, therefore, we may be held in suspense, though we groan under our distresses, let us never be discouraged by the tediousness of the lengthened period. For, when our afflictions are long continued, though we discover no termination of them, still we ought always to believe that God is a wonderful deliverer who, by his power, easily removes every obstacle out of the way.

JOHN CALVIN

ARE WE INDIFFERENT?

MARK 3:1-2 NIV

Another time he went into the synagogue, and a man with a shriveled hand was there. Some of them were looking for a reason to accuse Jesus, so they watched him closely to see if he would heal him on the Sabbath.

Often it's not *what* Jesus did, but *why* He did it. Healing people was, for Jesus, a daily part of His public ministry. But the point behind the above story has to do with *why* Jesus performed the miracle.

The Lord was deeply disturbed by the indifference the congregation showed toward the handicapped person. He was upset that the people were more concerned about the letter of the law and the proper way to do things rather than meeting the need of a hurting person in their midst. It was their cold stubborn apathy that prompted Jesus to act.

There are many reasons for reaching out to meet the needs of people around you. One reason may be to simply lend a helping hand. Another may be to put your gifts and talents to use. But a valid reason could be that you must take action against the nonchalance and indifference others have toward the needs at hand. Many a church has been sorely convicted when a believer steps out and shakes up the status quo!

JONI EARECKSON TADA

RECKLESS FREEDOM

MARK 3:3 NRSV
*And he said to the man who had the
withered hand, "Come forward."*

Now the Pharisees must watch Jesus for other infractions, for every infraction would increase the damage to law and order. They must be ready to challenge this rebel at every opportunity. And virtually every episode provoked such an opportunity, because Jesus with his disciples acted with what must have seemed to be reckless freedom. If a man needed healing, they did not wait until the next day, when it would be entirely legal to heal. They provided the help at once. To postpone the healing would, in their eyes, make the Sabbath an instrument for doing harm, even of killing (3:4). The Messiah came not to observe holy days but to save life. Each act of mercy was a demonstration of the truth that salvation makes all days holy, because every day presents its opportunity to heal and to free. Only the hardness of men's hearts can blind them to this true holiness.

PAUL S. MINEAR

RELIGIOUS SERVICE

MARK 3:4 NLT

*Then he turned to his critics and asked, "Is it
legal to do good deeds on the Sabbath, or is it a day
for doing harm? Is this a day to save life or to
destroy it?" But they wouldn't answer him.*

This passage is fundamental because it shows the clash
of two ideas of religion.

To the Pharisee religion was *ritual;* it meant obeying
certain rules and regulations. Jesus broke these regulations and they were genuinely convinced that he was a
bad man. It is like the man who believes that religion
consists in going to church, reading the Bible, saying
grace at meals, having family worship, and carrying out
all the external acts which are looked on as religious, and
who yet never put himself out to do anything for anyone, who has no sense of sympathy, no desire to sacrifice,
who is serene in his rigid orthodoxy, and deaf to the call
of need and blind to the tears of the world.

To Jesus religion was *service.* It was love of God *and* love
of men. Ritual was irrelevant compared with love in
action. To Jesus the most important thing in the world
was not the correct performance of a ritual, but the spontaneous answer to the cry of human need.

WILLIAM BARCLAY

THE DAY *of* DELIVERANCE

MATTHEW 12:13–14 NRSV

Then he said to the man, "Stretch out your hand."
He stretched it out, and it was restored, as sound
as the other. But the Pharisees went out and
conspired against him, how to destroy him.

Stretch out your hand!" Jesus commanded.
Impressed by the Master's courage in the presence of
his enemies, the man obeyed. He felt blood begin to cir-
culate and muscles flex in his useless hand. His was a test
case indeed, demonstrating God's love and healing power.
Far from destroying the Sabbath, Jesus had fulfilled its
purpose. The holy day was ordained to bring men deliverance from evil and peace of heart, both of which Jesus
had given to the man with the withered hand.

Frustrated in their plan to outwit Jesus, the Pharisees
stormed out of the synagogue. Some day, they knew, they
must destroy Jesus before he ruined their religion by sub-
stituting the welfare of individuals for the immutability of
the Law. Moreover, if the healing they had just witnessed
showed that Jesus shared in God's creative power, the wis-
est of the Pharisees realized that Judaism would eventually
have to be transformed to encompass so amazing a truth.

ALICE PARMELEE

HARDENED HEARTS

MARK 3:6 KJV
*The Pharisees went forth,
and straightway took counsel with the Herodians
against him, how they might destroy him.*

One might have thought that such an exhibition of the grace and power that was in Jesus would have filled every heart with gladness and led to praise and thanksgiving to God for having visited His people so wonderfully. But the miracle had the very opposite effect on these jealous advocates of human traditions as opposed to divine revelation. They exhibited an utter lack of conscience toward God while displaying a punctilious concern for the observance of their traditions and false conceptions of the will of God regarding the observance of the weekly sabbath. The Pharisees, stern champions of orthodoxy that they were, entered into collaboration with the Herodians, the worldly and corrupt politicians of their day. Both groups wanted to lay hold of Jesus and put Him out of the way. Thus did extremes meet then, as often since. Men of entirely opposite views agreed on the rejection of Christ and consulted each other about how He might be destroyed. Such is the inevitable evil of the natural heart in its opposition to God!

H. A. IRONSIDE

HOPE *in* HIM

MATTHEW 12:15 KJV
Great multitudes followed him, and he healed them all.

What a variety of sickness must have been presented to the gaze of Jesus! Yet we do not read that He was disgusted but patiently waited on every case. What a combination of evils must have met at His feet! What sickening ulcers and putrefying sores! Yet He was ready for every new shape of the monster of evil and was victor over it in every form. . . . It is still the case today. Whatever my own condition may be, the beloved Physician can heal me; and whatever may be the state of others whom I may remember at this moment in prayer; I may have hope in Jesus that He will be able to heal them of their sins. My child, my friend, my dearest one—I can have hope for each, for all, when I remember the healing power of my Lord; and on my own account, however severe my struggle with sins and infirmities, I can still rejoice and be confident. He who on earth walked the hospitals still dispenses His grace and works wonders among the sons of men: Let me go to Him immediately and earnestly.

CHARLES HADDON SPURGEON

LOOSED!

Now He was teaching in one of the synagogues on the Sabbath. And behold, there was a woman who had a spirit of infirmity eighteen years, and was bent over and could in no way raise herself up. But when Jesus saw her, He called her to Him and said to her, "Woman, you are loosed from your infirmity."

Causes of disease may be physical, psychological, or spiritual. Regardless of the cause, though, Christians have power over disease. Christians in the first century saw disease as a work of Satan, a weapon of his demons, a way in which evil rules the world. When Jesus healed disease, whether demonically or physically caused, he pushed back the kingdom of Satan. What the devil did, Jesus undid. . . .

In response to attacks from the Pharisees (because Jesus healed her on the Sabbath, a day of rest for the Jews), Jesus said, "You hypocrites! . . . Should not this woman, a daughter of Abraham, *whom Satan has kept bound for eighteen long years,* be set free . . ?" (Luke 13:15-16). His was not a medical explanation. He identified the cause of her problem as Satan's doing. The Pharisees operated with hardness of heart and religious blindness. They hid behind theology, in this case the prohibition of work on the Sabbath.

JOHN WIMBER

TAKE TIME *to* HELP

LUKE 13:14-15 NIV

Indignant because Jesus had healed on the Sabbath, the synagogue ruler said to the people, "There are six days for work. So come and be healed on those days, not on the Sabbath." The Lord answered him, "You hypocrites! Doesn't each of you on the Sabbath untie his ox or donkey from the stall and lead it out to give it water?"

Jesus shamed this synagogue ruler and the other leaders by pointing out their hypocrisy. They would untie their animals and care for them on the Sabbath. Yet these same people refused to see that care for humans is far more important. They were such *hypocrites,* willing to help animals but not willing to help a human being, a *woman, a daughter of Abraham.* What "work" had Jesus done? He had merely reached out and touched her—not even as much work as leading an *ox* or *donkey* to water.

Yet these hypocrites could not see past their laws. They hid behind their own set of laws to avoid love's obligations. People today can use the letter of the law to rationalize away their obligation to care for others (for example, by tithing regularly and then refusing to help a needy neighbor). But people's needs are more important than rules and regulations. Take time to help others.

LIFE APPLICATION BIBLE COMMENTARY—LUKE

WHY WAIT?

LUKE 13:16–17 NIV

*"Then should not this woman, a daughter of
Abraham, whom Satan has kept bound for eighteen
long years, be set free on the Sabbath day from what
bound her?" When he said this, all his opponents
were humiliated, but the people were delighted with
all the wonderful things he was doing.*

Now Satan had bound this woman for eighteen
years. Would it have been right to make her wait
even another hour to be freed? What would we think of
Jesus if He told her to go away and suffer for another day
while He went to the barn to care for His donkey? Anyone who acted like that couldn't be very much like God.
Yet many Christians have been guilty of this very sin.
They have made the people, whom Satan has bound in
the darkness of sin, wait for the Gospel while they take
care of their own pleasures and wants. It is important that
we all pray and do what we can to spread the Gospel message of salvation as quickly as possible. Someone wants to
be saved. Why should they have to wait even one more
day?

RALPH N. WALTER

WHO SINNED?

JOHN 9:1 KJV

*And as Jesus passed by, he saw a man
which was blind from his birth.*

First, while every man is ready to censure others with
extreme bitterness, there are few who apply to themselves, as they ought to do, the same severity. If my brother
meets with adversity, I instantly acknowledge the judgment of God; but if God chastises me with a heavier
stroke, I wink at my sins. . . .

The second error lies in excessive severity; for no
sooner is any man touched by the hand of God, than we
conclude that this shows deadly hatred, and we turn small
offenses into crimes, and almost despair of his salvation.
On the contrary, by extenuating our sins, we scarcely
think that we have committed very small offenses, when
we have committed a very aggravated crime.

Thirdly, we do wrong in this respect, that we pronounce condemnation on all, without exception, whom
God visits with the cross or with tribulation. What we
have lately said is undoubtedly true, that all our distresses
arise from sin; but God afflicts his own people for various
reasons. Sometimes he does not look at their sins, but
only tries their obedience, or trains them to patience.

JOHN CALVIN

"YOU DESERVED IT"

JOHN 9:2 NIV
His disciples asked him, "Rabbi, who sinned,
this man or his parents, that he was born blind?"

There is no death without sin, and there is no suffer-ing without iniquity," taught the Pharisees, who saw the hand of punishment in natural disasters, birth defects, and such long-term conditions as blindness and paralysis. Here is where "the man blind from birth" entered the picture. Steeped in good Jewish tradition, Jesus' disciples debated what could account for such a birth defect. Had the man somehow sinned *in utero?* Or was he suffering the consequences of his parents' sin—a prospect easier to imagine but patently unfair.

Jesus responded by overturning common notions about how God views sick and disabled people. He denied that the man's blindness came from any sin, just as he dismissed the common opinion that tragedies happen to those who deserve them (see Luke 13:1-5). Jesus wanted the sick to know they are especially loved, not cursed, by God. Every one of his miracles of healing, in fact, undercut the rabbinic tradition of "You deserved it."

PHILIP YANCEY

FINDING OUT *the* DETAILS

JOHN 9:2 NLT

*"Teacher," his disciples asked him, "why was
this man born blind? Was it a result of his
own sins or those of his parents?"*

The disciples who first followed Christ were dreadfully out of step with His cause when they pointed out a blind beggar and asked Christ who had sinned—the man's parents, or he in his mother's womb—that he should be born blind (John 9:1-7). No doubt they had seen this beggar many times before and had reacted with the same kind of theological curiosity. What they saw in Christ's response was hardly stand-offish. It clearly demonstrated the distance between Christ and His followers in regard to responding to people's needs. His was a response of compassion, not curiosity and judgment. He marshaled His resources to grant sight to the beggar and claimed that the blindness was actually intended to provide a moment when God could be magnified through Christ's compassionate touch.

Aren't we just like those detached disciples? When we hear of trouble in someone's life we are far more interested in the details and an analysis of what, why, when, and where than we are in finding out what we can do to reach out and help.

JOSEPH STOWELL

CLOSED-BOX THINKING

JOHN 9:2 NRSV

His disciples asked him, "Rabbi, who sinned,
this man or his parents, that he was born blind?"

For the disciples, reality occurred in a box with limited possibilities. Bad things happened to people because it was their own or someone else's fault. Eager to engage Jesus in their thoughtful reflection, they put the choices to him—"Is he blind because of his own sin or his parents' errors?" The Lord immediately corrected their distorted vision with a third alternative; bad things sometimes happen in order to eventually bring glory to God.

Closed-box thinking reveals a severely limited view of God. It actually makes the assumption that there are bad things God cannot handle or change. In that thinking, God becomes subject to the laws of the universe rather than Lord over the universe he created. It generates an attitude in which we say to God, "If we can't figure out how you can bring good out of this situation, then it can't be done." God loves to explode closed-box thinking. Inside the box is darkness, but Jesus is the light. Healing the blind man that day was only a small part of Jesus' light-filling ministry.

NEIL WILSON

FOR A REASON *and* A SEASON

JOHN 9:3 NKJV

Jesus answered, "Neither this man nor his parents sinned, but that the works of God should be revealed in him."

The assurance of Jesus is that because God is with us, we do not have to give in to, sink beneath, or become defeated by troubles. . . .

Jesus taught His followers that all troubles are passing in nature. Sickness and trouble are for a season and for a reason. Storms arose and prevailed—both in the natural on the Sea of Galilee and in the supernatural lives of those possessed and oppressed by the devil for a season and a reason. Jesus' very life was for a season and a reason. Even His death and burial in a tomb were only for a season and a reason!

The passing nature of troubles is something Jesus calls us to recognize. His challenge is to endure, to persevere, to learn, to grow, and to overcome. . . . Why should we be troubled and lose our peace if we remember our Lord's example of living confidently knowing that His Father was watching, directing, caring for, and loving Him and His followers on a daily basis? God will do the same for us.

CHARLES STANLEY

IN CHRISTIAN SUFFERING,
GOD RADIATES

JOHN 9:3 NLT
"He was born blind so the power
of God could be seen in him."

The man's suffering shows what God can do. Affliction, sorrow, pain, disappointment, loss always are opportunities for displaying God's grace. First, it enables the sufferer to show God in action. When trouble and disaster fall upon a man who does not know God, that man may well collapse; but when they fall on a man who walks with God they bring out the strength and the beauty, and the endurance and the nobility, which are within a man's heart when God is there. . . . Any kind of suffering is an opportunity to demonstrate the glory of God in our own lives.

WILLIAM BARCLAY

NOTHING *to* LOSE *but* BLINDNESS

JOHN 9:6 NASB

When He had said this, He spat on the ground, and made clay of the spittle, and applied the clay to his eyes.

For various reasons, this miracle is best enjoyed from the blind man's perspective. Other senses sharpened by the lack of sight, he probably heard every nuance in the familiar discussion that sought to fix blame for his blindness. This time one voice presented a new perspective on his problem, but before he could reflect on Jesus' words, another sound filled his ears—someone spit.

Close by, he heard the soft sounds of dust gradually kneaded into pasty consistency. Then he smelled the fresh mud as Jesus brought his hand up and applied the thick, cold substance on his face, packing it into his eye sockets. The voice instructed him to wash in Siloam's Pool. He had nothing to lose but mud on his face, so he went and came back seeing.

Good repairman that he was, Jesus could have consulted the shop manual on the human prototype (Genesis 2:7), but he already knew what to do. When he made mud to heal the man he was simply using the original manufacturer's replacement parts.

NEIL WILSON

SEEING CHRIST *for* WHO HE IS

JOHN 9:37-38 NASB
*Jesus said to him, "You have both seen Him,
and He is the one who is talking with you." And he
said, "Lord, I believe." And he worshiped Him.*

This poor, blind beggar, who had never seen anything in his life, clearly recognized the Son of God. Meanwhile the religious leaders who thought they knew everything could not even recognize their own Messiah. Spiritual sight is a gift from God that makes one willing and able to believe.

What did this man first see with his newly opened eyes of faith? He saw Christ as sovereign Lord. Verse 38 says, "He worshiped Him." He fell on his knees right there and worshiped. It is a beautiful climax to the story. It was not a question of "making" Christ his Lord; when the scales fell off his spiritual eyes, he saw Him for who He was, and the only possible response was to sink to his knees.

JOHN MACARTHUR

HE CAN MAKE US LIKE HIMSELF

LUKE 14:1-2 NRSV

*On one occasion when Jesus was going to the house
of a leader of the Pharisees to eat a meal on the
sabbath, they were watching him closely. Just then,
in front of him, there was a man who had dropsy.*

It is by no means impossible that the Pharisees "planted"
the man with the dropsy in this house to see what Jesus
would do. They were watching him; and the word used
for *watching* is the word used for "interested and sinister
espionage." Jesus was under scrutiny.

Without hesitation Jesus healed the man. . . .

This passage tells us certain things about Jesus. . . .

It shows us the serenity with which Jesus met life.
There is nothing more trying than to be under constant
and critical scrutiny. When that happens to most people
they lose their nerve and, even more often, lose their temper. They become irritable; and while there may be
greater sins than irritability there is none that causes more
pain and heartbreak. But even in things which would
have broken most men's spirit, Jesus remained serene. If
we live with him, he can make us like himself.

WILLIAM BARCLAY

LORD *of the* SABBATH

LUKE 14:3 NIV
Jesus asked the Pharisees and experts in the law,
"Is it lawful to heal on the Sabbath or not?"

Luke, the physician, identified this man's disease as "dropsy" (also called edema), an abnormal accumulation of fluid in bodily tissues and cavities causing swelling. It may have been related to a heart condition.

Jesus knew what his "watchers" were thinking, so he asked them the question that had caused friction between him and them before: *"Is it lawful to heal on the Sabbath or not?"* That was the crux of the matter. Under any normal circumstances, a person would say that it would be perfectly all right to heal another human being on the Sabbath. Yet because the Pharisees had added so many rules regarding Sabbath observance, and because they allowed the rules to occupy their lives, they would have answered Jesus' question in the negative. Their oral tradition said that it was only lawful to heal on the Sabbath if it was a life-threatening situation. But Jesus would heal on the Sabbath no matter what the Pharisees thought, for he was Lord of the Sabbath.

LIFE APPLICATION BIBLE COMMENTARY—LUKE

REDEFINING ISRAEL

LUKE 14:4-6 NASB

But they kept silent. And He took hold of him, and healed him, and sent him away. And He said to them, "Which one of you will have a son or an ox fall into a well, and will not immediately pull him out on a sabbath day?" And they could make no reply to this.

The two stories in Luke's Gospel about sabbath-breaking emphasize that the sabbath was the most appropriate day for healing to take place. It was the day that signaled release from bondage and captivity. Jesus was indicating that in his view Israel's long-awaited sabbath day was breaking in through his ministry. What was at issue was not "religion" or "ethics" in the abstract. It was a matter of eschatology and agenda. Jesus affirmed Israel's vocation, her belief in her God and her eschatological hope. But this vocation, theology and aspiration were to be redefined around a new set of symbols, appropriate for the new day that was dawning.

N. T. WRIGHT

THE PURSUING LOVE *of* GOD

JOHN 5:19 JB

"I tell you most solemnly, the Son can do nothing by himself; he can do only what he sees the Father doing: and whatever the Father does the Son does too."

Jesus' ministry of service is rooted in his compassion for the lost, lonely, and broken. Why does he love losers, failures, and those on the margin of social respectability? Because the Father does. "I tell you most solemnly, the Son can do nothing by himself; he can do only what he sees the Father doing: and whatever the Father does the Son does too" (John 5:19). In Jesus of Nazareth, the mind of God becomes transparent. There is nothing of self to be seen, only the passionate, pursuing love of God. Jesus lays bare the heart of God through his life of humble service. In fact, when Jesus returns, it will not be with the impact of unbearable glory; he will come as a servant. "Happy those servants whom the master finds awake when he comes. I tell you solemnly, he will put on an apron, sit them down at table and wait on them" (Luke 12:37 JB).

BRENNAN MANNING

JESUS' MIRACLES
OVER SICKNESS

---

*The people were amazed when they saw
the mute speaking, the crippled made well,
the lame walking and the blind seeing.
And they praised the God of Israel.*

MATTHEW 15:31 NIV

JESUS' MIRACLES OVER SICKNESS

Sick people by the hundreds were brought to Jesus. Some of them were sufferers of lifelong handicaps; others were simply ill. Whether blind, deaf, lame, paralyzed, or bleeding, Jesus compassionately healed them all. Whether they stood before Him or were miles away, Jesus' touch changed their lives. Jesus demonstrated an uncanny sense of what really ailed people. And sometimes it wasn't obvious.

Jesus healed them. He used various but not random means. As we will see, Jesus carried out His healing ministry in a way that always indicated His mastery and purposes. Every one of His healing acts conveyed compassion and much more. Unfortunately, many didn't use their eyes to see or ears to hear when they witnessed Jesus' purposeful miracles. In this section we want to relish the marvels of Jesus' power and revel in the message He communicated with His healing touch.

HEARTBROKEN

LUKE 4:18 KJV
"The Spirit of the Lord is upon me, because . . .
he hath sent me to heal the brokenhearted."

When the Prince of Peace came into this dark world He did not come in any private way. He tells us that He came not to see and be seen, but to "seek and to save that which was lost," and also "to heal the brokenhearted." And in the face of this announcement it is a mystery to me why those who have broken hearts will rather carry them year in and year out than just bring them to the great Physician. How many men in Chicago are just going down to their graves with a broken heart? They have carried their hearts weighted with trouble for years and years, and yet when they open the Scriptures they can see the passage telling us that He came here for the purpose of healing the brokenhearted. He left Heaven and all its glory to come to the world—sent by the Father, He tells us, for the purpose of healing the brokenhearted.

D. L. MOODY

HIS MISSION

———

LUKE 6:19 KJV
*And the whole multitude sought to touch him:
for there went virtue out of him, and healed them all.*

During His sojourn on this earth, was He not ever ready to heal diseased bodies? And do you think that He is now unwilling to minister to distressed souls? Perish the thought. He was always at the disposal of the maimed, the blind, the palsied, yes, of the repellent leper too. He was ever prepared, uncomplainingly, to relieve suffering, though it cost Him something—"there went virtue out of him" (Lk 6: 19)—and though much unbelief was expressed by those He befriended. As it was then a part of His mission to heal the sick, so it is now a part of His ministry to bind up the brokenhearted. What a Saviour is ours! The almighty God, the all-tender Man. One who is infinitely above us in His original nature and present glory, yet One who became flesh and blood, lived on the same plane as we do, experienced the same troubles, and suffered as we, though far more acutely. Then how well qualified He is to supply your every need! Cast all your care upon Him, knowing that He cares for you.

ARTHUR W. PINK

LET *the* HEALING STREAMS ABOUND

PSALM 36:9 KJV
*For with thee is the fountain of life:
in thy light shall we see light.*

Thou, O Christ, art all I want,
    More than all in thee I find;
Raise the fallen, cheer the faint,
Heal the sick, and lead the blind.
Just and holy is thy name,
I am all unrighteousness;
False and full of sin I am;
Thou art full of truth and grace.

Plenteous grace with thee is found,
Grace to cover all my sin;
Let the healing streams abound,
Make and keep me pure within.
Thou of life the fountain art,
Freely let me take of thee;
Spring thou up within my heart;
Rise to all eternity.

CHARLES WESLEY

SWALLOW YOUR PRIDE

JOHN 4:46-47 NRSV

*Now there was a royal official whose son lay ill in
Capernaum. When he heard that Jesus had come from
Judea to Galilee, he went and begged him to come down
and heal his son, for he was at the point of death.*

The Greek [for royal official] is *basilikos* which could
even mean that he was a petty king; but it is used for
a royal official and he was a man of high standing at the
court of Herod. Jesus on the other hand had no greater
status than that of the village carpenter of Nazareth. Further, Jesus was in Cana and this man lived in Capernaum,
almost twenty miles away. That is why he took so long to
get back home.

There could be no more improbable scene in the
world than an important court official hastening twenty
miles to beg a favour from a village carpenter. First and
foremost, this courtier swallowed his pride. He was in
need, and neither convention nor custom stopped him
bringing his need to Christ. His action would cause a
sensation but he did not care what people said so long as
he obtained the help he so much wanted. If we want the
help which Christ can give we must be humble enough
to swallow our pride and not care what any man may say.

WILLIAM BARCLAY

BELIEVE *and* OBEY

JOHN 4:50 NLT
*Then Jesus told him, "Go back home.
Your son will live!" And the man believed
Jesus' word and started home.*

This government official not only believed that Jesus could heal, he also obeyed Jesus by returning home, thus truly demonstrating his faith. It isn't enough for us to say we believe that Jesus can take care of our problems. We need to act as if he can. We also need to leave the means, ways, and timing up to him. When we pray about a need or problem, we should live as though we believe Jesus can do what he says.

Notice how the official's faith grew:

He believed enough to ask Jesus to help his son.

He believed to the point of insisting that Jesus come with him to heal his son.

He trusted Jesus' assurance that his son would live, and he acted on it.

He and his whole household believed in Jesus.

Faith grows as we use it.

LIFE APPLICATION BIBLE COMMENTARY—JOHN

THE FAITH *of* OBEDIENCE

JOHN 4:50 PHILLIPS

"You can go home," returned Jesus, "your son is alive."
And the man believed what Jesus had said
to him and went on his way.

What this nobleman did, in going home, was identical to what the servants had done at the wedding in filling the great stone jars with water. They had all done just exactly what they were told to do. This is the faith of obedience. It is the positive response to the command of Christ. This is faith in action. Faith, living faith in God, is having complete confidence in His character. It is an absolute assurance that because of His wholesome (holy) character and impeccable conduct He is totally trustworthy. It is knowing that because He is utterly reliable, one's response to His requests can always be positive. He is ever faithful, ever dependable. So when an individual complies and cooperates quietly with Him in calm assurance, all is well.

W. PHILLIP KELLER

A MIRACLE *of* SPACE

JOHN 4:51–53 NIV

While he was still on the way, his servants met him
with the news that his boy was living. When he inquired
as to the time when his son got better, they said to him,
"The fever left him yesterday at the seventh hour."
Then the father realized that this was the exact time
at which Jesus had said to him, "Your son will live."
So he and all his household believed.

The healing of this man's son was a miracle of *space.* Jesus healed a boy who was twenty miles away. Jesus was not any less in the man's house in Capernaum just because He was actually standing in Cana. The physical presence of Christ does not make Him more present. Indeed, when He promised the Holy Spirit to His disciples, He told them, "It is for your good that I am going away" (John 16:7 NIV) because the Counselor (Comforter, KJV) would come and be with them and in them. Jesus could only be in one place at one time with His earthly body; but by His Spirit He would indwell His people throughout the world.

Two healings took place that day. The father's weak faith was made strong, and the boy's weak body became well. All in the presence of Jesus.

ERWIN LUTZER

TRUE BELIEF

JOHN 4:54 NLT
*This was Jesus' second miraculous sign
in Galilee after coming from Judea.*

The first sign was that of changing the water into wine at a festive and gala wedding party in Cana (John 2:1-11). The second sign performed in Galilee was in a darkened home, under the shadow of death, when a dying child was healed. The point is: True belief in God means belief in his Word. Jesus' miracles, according to the Gospel of John, were signs pointing the people who witnessed them to the one who performed the signs—Jesus, the Messiah, the Son of God. If the miracle produced faith only in a miracle-worker and not in the Son of God, then the purpose of the sign was missed.

PHILIP W. COMFORT AND WENDELL C. HAWLEY

"I WILL"

MARK 1:40–41 RSV

And a leper came to him beseeching him, and kneeling
said to him, "If you will, you can make me clean."
Moved with pity, he stretched out his hand and
touched him, and said to him, "I will; be clean."

I think this indicates something of an awareness on the
leper's part of a divine purpose there may have been in
his affliction. . . . There are times when God wills for his
children to pass through physical affliction. . . . It is not
the teaching of Scripture that everybody must be healed.

This leper is a case in point. Evidently he sensed some
purpose in this, and when he said, "If you will, you can
make me clean," he did not mean by that, "If you're in a
good mood at present . . ." He meant, rather, "If it is not
out of line with the purpose of God, if it is not violating
some cosmic program God is working out, then you can
make me clean." The answer of Jesus is very positive:
"Moved with pity, he stretched out his hand and touched
him, and said to him, 'I will; be clean.'" That "I will" is
like a green light from God. It says the time has come for
the healing to occur. Whatever purpose the leprosy may
have served, it has been accomplished, and the time was
come to set it aside. "I will; be clean."

RAY C. STEDMAN

MIRACULOUS GRACE

MATTHEW 8:2 NIV

A man with leprosy came and knelt before him and said, "Lord, if you are willing, you can make me clean."

When the leper came to Him crying for a remedy He spoke, and we know that His word was enough; but that would not satisfy the graciousness of the Lord Jesus Christ. He would not give the man his cure as He might have given him an alms, or, rather, I should say, as if He had thrown him an alms. The poor man was terribly cut off from his people, looked upon as defiled, and so horrid that nobody would touch him. It is a terrible thing to show disgust at any human being; but these lepers were used to expressions of disgust from their fellow men. There came the graciousness of our Lord Jesus Christ, the grace of Christ, for He must put His hands upon him, saying: "I will, be thou clean." That was not necessary for the leper's sake, but the grace was needful for the poor man's soul and spirit. This is the grace of our Lord Jesus Christ.

GEORGE MACDONALD

GODLY TOUCH

MATTHEW 8:3 NCV
*Jesus reached out his hand and touched the
man and said, "I will. Be healed!" And immediately
the man was healed from his disease.*

Oh, the power of a godly touch. Haven't you known
it? The doctor who treated you, or the teacher
who dried your tears? Was there a hand holding yours at
a funeral? Another on your shoulder during a trial? A
handshake of welcome at a new job? A pastoral prayer for
healing? Haven't we known the power of a godly touch?

Can't we offer the same?

Many of you already do. . . . But others of us tend to
forget. Our hearts are good; it's just that our memories are
bad. We forget how significant one touch can be. We fear
saying the wrong thing or using the wrong tone or acting the wrong way. So rather than do it incorrectly, we do
nothing at all.

Aren't we glad Jesus didn't make the same mistake? If
your fear of doing the wrong thing prevents you from
doing anything, keep in mind the perspective of the lepers of the world. They aren't picky. They aren't finicky.
They're just lonely. They are yearning for a godly touch.

Jesus touched the untouchables of the world. Will you
do the same?

MAX LUCADO

WE LIVE

MARK 1:41–42 KJV

*And Jesus, moved with compassion, put forth his hand,
and touched him, and saith unto him, I will; be thou
clean. And as soon as he had spoken, immediately the
leprosy departed from him, and he was cleansed.*

It is worthy of devout notice that Jesus touched the leper. This unclean person had broken through the regulations of the ceremonial law and pressed into the house, but Jesus so far from chiding him broke through the law Himself in order to meet him. He made an interchange with the leper, for while He cleansed him, He contracted by that touch a Levitical defilement. Even so Jesus Christ was made sin for us, although in Himself He knew no sin, that we might be made the righteousness of God in Him. O that poor sinners would go to Jesus, believing in the power of His blessed substitutionary work, and they would soon learn the power of His gracious touch. That hand which multiplied the loaves, which saved sinking Peter, which upholds afflicted saints, which crowns believers, that same hand will touch every seeking sinner, and in a moment make him clean. The love of Jesus is the source of salvation. He loves, He looks, He touches us, WE LIVE.

CHARLES HADDON SPURGEON

HE IS THERE *for* YOU

LUKE 5:17–18 NASB

One day He was teaching; and there were some
Pharisees and teachers of the law sitting there. . . .
And some men were carrying on a bed a man who
was paralyzed; and they were trying to bring him
in and to set him down in front of Him.

With the special gift of imagination, picture yourself approaching the crowd around Jesus. You
long to get through to him about someone you love.
Now see the crowd part and the open corridor directly
to the Lord made for you. He is there for you. Now stand
before him face to face, heart to heart. He is waiting for
you to ask for what he is ready to give. Tell him about a
person or persons on your heart. Then wait for his
answer. At this very moment you prayed, says Jesus, my
power has been released in the person for whom you
interceded. My will shall be done, in my timing, according to my plan, and for the now and forever blessing of
your loved one. You and I are of one heart now. We both
love and care. Now go your way in faithfulness.

LLOYD JOHN OGILVIE

CREATIVE FAITH

MARK 2:4 NKJV

And when they could not come near Him because of
the crowd, they uncovered the roof where He was.
So when they had broken through, they let down
the bed on which the paralytic was lying.

F aith is full of creativity. The house was full, a crowd
blocked the entry, but faith found a creative way of
getting to the Lord and placing the paralytic before Him.
If we cannot get sinners to Jesus by ordinary methods, we
must use extraordinary ones. It seems, according to Luke
5:19, that roof tiles had to be removed. That would create dust and cause a measure of danger to those below; but
where the case is very urgent, we must be prepared to run
some risks and shock some people. Jesus was there to heal,
and therefore roof or no roof, faith ventured all so that the
poor paralytic might have his sins forgiven. We need more
daring creative faith among us! Dear reader, let us seek it
this morning for ourselves and for our fellow-workers
and try today to perform some gallant act for the love of
souls and the glory of the Lord.

The world is constantly creating and inventing; genius
serves all the purposes of human desire: Can't faith invent
too and by some creative means reach the people who are
strangers to the Gospel?

CHARLES HADDON SPURGEON

TO HEAL *the* SOUL

MARK 2:5 NCV

When Jesus saw the faith of these people, he said to the
paralyzed man, "Young man, your sins are forgiven."

Jesus was moved. So he applauds—if not with his hands,
at least with his heart. And not only does he applaud,
he blesses. And we witness a divine loveburst.

The friends want him to heal their friend. But Jesus
won't settle for a simple healing of the body—he wants
to heal the soul. He leapfrogs the physical and deals with
the spiritual. To heal the body is temporal; to heal the soul
is eternal.

The request of the friends is valid—but timid. The
expectations of the crowd are high—but not high
enough. They expect Jesus to say, "I heal you." Instead he
says, "I forgive you." They expect him to treat the body,
for that is what they see.

He chooses to treat not only the body, but also the spiritual, for that is what he sees.

They want Jesus to give the man a new body so he can
walk. Jesus gives grace so the man can live.

Remarkable. Sometimes God is so touched by what he
sees that he gives us what we need and not simply that for
which we ask.

MAX LUCADO

WHAT MORE PROOF DO WE NEED?

MARK 2:6–7 KJV

But there were certain of the scribes sitting there, and reasoning in their hearts, Why doth this man thus speak blasphemies? who can forgive sins but God only?

What can be more reasonable than to believe a man when he comes and tells us that he is sent from God to heal the diseases of our souls, and in order that we may believe him, he heals all sorts of men, at all times, of all manner of diseases, by a touch or a word. He plainly shows that he can do it when he will, let the disease be what it will. . . . He tells us that he will deliver us from spiritual and eternal death (and also from temporal death), that he will raise us from the dead and give us eternal life, so that we shall live forever and not die. And to prove this he gives us sensible evidence that he has power over men's lives by not only prolonging their lives but even restoring them after they are dead, and besides, he rises from the dead himself. He tells us that he will bestow heavenly glory upon us and will translate us to heaven. And to confirm us in this belief, he tells us that we shall see himself after his death ascend into heaven. What more could we desire from a man, who pretends to come from God and to have power to do these things for us, than to give us such evidences of his power as these?

JONATHAN EDWARDS

HIS MIRACLES

THAT YOU MAY KNOW

MARK 2:9-11 NASB

"Which is easier, to say to the paralytic, 'Your sins
are forgiven'; or to say, 'Get up, and pick up your
pallet and walk'? But so that you may know that
the Son of Man has authority on earth to forgive
sins"—He said to the paralytic—"I say to you,
get up, pick up your pallet and go home."

Jesus claimed to be able to forgive sins. "And Jesus seeing their faith said to the paralytic, 'My son, your sins
are forgiven' " (Mark 2:5; see also Luke 7:48-50). By Jewish law this was something only God could do; Isaiah
43:25 restricts this prerogative to God alone. The scribes
asked, "Why does this man speak that way? He is blas-
pheming; who can forgive sins but God alone?" (Mark
2:7 NASB). Jesus then asked which would be easier, to say,
"Your sins are forgiven"; or to say "Arise and walk"?

According to the Wycliffe Commentary, this is "an
unanswerable question. The statements are equally simple
to pronounce; but to say either, with accompanying performance, requires divine power. An imposter, of course,
in seeking to avoid detection, would find the former
easier. Jesus proceeded to heal the illness that men might
know that he had authority to deal with its cause."

JOSH MCDOWELL

SAY *the* WORD

MATTHEW 8:5-6, 8 RSV

As he entered Capernaum, a centurion came forward to him, beseeching him and saying, "Lord, my servant is lying paralyzed at home, in terrible distress. . . . I am not worthy to have you come under my roof; but only say the word, and my servant will be healed."

Jesus: Then what do you ask, Proclus? Don't you want your servant healed?

Proclus: Yes, indeed I do. But surely you don't need to see him. You've only to say the word, and he'll be cured.

Jesus: What makes you believe that?

Proclus: Sir, I have only to look at you. I know authority when I see it. . . . I know very well that when *you* command, you are obeyed.

Jesus *(vehemently)***:** Do you hear that, all of you? It is amazing. Nowhere have I met faith like this—not in the length and breadth of Israel. . . . Go your way, Centurion, and as you have believed, so it will be.

DOROTHY SAYERS

NO BOUNDARIES

LUKE 7:9-10 NRSV

When Jesus heard this he was amazed at him,
and turning to the crowd that followed him, he said,
"I tell you, not even in Israel have I found such faith."
When those who had been sent returned to the
house, they found the slave in good health.

Love takes us out of ourselves in self-giving to others. The whole life of our Lord was characterized by such an outlook. There are several references in the gospels to his great compassion for the needy crowds of people. . . .

Luke in particular stresses that the love of Christ brought him into contact with those who were despised or under-valued by the society of his day. Lepers were excluded from ordinary society, but he not only cleansed them from their leprosy but even touched them, something no Pharisee would ever have dreamed of doing (Luke 5:12-14). Tax-collectors were regarded as beyond the pale because of their daily contact with Roman officialdom, but he not only ate with them and their despised friends, but actually called one of them to be a member of the inner band of his disciples (Luke 5:27-32). The Roman occupying force was hated, yet he healed the servant of a centurion and remarked upon the greatness of his faith (Luke 7:1-10).

GEOFFREY W. GROGAN

READY *to* HELP

LUKE 7:21 KJV

In that same hour he cured many of their
infirmities and plagues, and of evil spirits;
and unto many that were blind he gave sight.

Here is in this doctrine great encouragement to all persons to look to Christ under all manner of difficulties and afflictions, and that especially from what appeared in Christ when he was here. We have an account in the history of Christ of great numbers under a great variety of afflictions and difficulties, resorting to him for help. And we have no account of his rejecting one person who came to him in a friendly manner for help, under any difficulty whatever. But on the contrary, the history of his life is principally filled up with miracles that he wrought for the relief of such. When they came to him, he presently relieved them, and always did it freely without money or price. We never read of his doing anything for any person as hired to it, by any reward that was offered him. And he helped persons fully, he completely delivered them from those difficulties under which they labored. And by the doctrine of the text we learn that though he is not now upon earth, but in heaven, yet he is the same that he was then. He is as able to help, and he is as ready to help under every kind of difficulty.

JONATHAN EDWARDS

LORD *and* GOD

LUKE 7:21–22 NRSV

Jesus had just then cured many people of diseases, plagues, and evil spirits, and had given sight to many who were blind. And he answered them, "Go and tell John what you have seen and heard . . ."

Jesus showed himself the Prophet *par excellence* by his words and the King *par excellence* by his deeds. His mighty works, as he told the synagogue at Nazareth and the messengers of John, were Messianic signs (Lk. 4:18ff.; Mt. 11:2ff.). The Messiah of contemporary Jewish expectation was one who had a special relationship to God, who would usher in the end of the age and establish the kingdom of God; his deeds would be the deeds of God himself. This was further currently interpreted as meaning the overthrow of the hated Romans and the establishment of a great Jewish empire. Jesus accepted the first part of this equation, and extended it to its utmost limits, but the second part he totally rejected. The Messiah King was both Lord and God, in spite of the fact that he was lowly and rejected, the Suffering Servant. By word and deed he showed himself Lord over wind and wave, over beast and tree, over food and drink, over sickness and death, over demons and Devil.

JOHN W. WENHAM

FREE *of* OFFENSE

LUKE 7:23 NKJV
"And blessed is he who is not offended because of Me."

The response of Jesus is prophetic. He quotes Isaiah, a book very familiar to John. The passages in Isaiah 29:18, 35:4-6 and 61:1 apply to all that John's disciples had observed while they waited to question Jesus. They bore witness of Him as Messiah. But He does not end there. He adds, "And blessed is he who is not offended because of Me."

He was saying, "John, I know you don't understand all that is happening with you and many of My ways, but do not be offended with Me because I do not operate as you expected." He was urging John not to judge by his own understanding of God's ways in the past and in his own life and ministry. John didn't know the whole picture or plan of God, just as we do not know the complete picture today. Jesus was encouraging him, saying, "You've done what was commanded of you. Your reward will be great. Just stay free from offense with Me!"

JOHN BEVERE

TURN YOUR GAZE *upon* HIM

LUKE 8:42 NASB
As He went, the crowds were pressing against Him.

Jesus is passing through the crowd heading for the house of Jairus, so that He might raise the ruler's dead daughter. He is so extravagant in His goodness that He works another miracle on His way there. . . . What delightful encouragement this truth affords us! If our Lord is so ready to heal the sick and bless the needy, then, my soul, do not be slow to put yourself in His path so that He may smile on you. Do not be lazy in asking, since He is so generous in giving. Pay careful attention to His Word now and at all times, so that Jesus may speak through it to your heart. Pitch your tent wherever He is so that you can obtain His blessing. When He is present to heal, may He not heal you? Be certain that He is present even now, for He always comes to hearts that need Him. And do you not need Him? *He* knows the extent of your need; so turn your gaze, look upon your distress, and call upon Him while He is near.

CHARLES HADDON SPURGEON

THE HEM *of* HIS GARMENT

MATTHEW 9:20 KJV

And, behold, a woman, which was diseased
with an issue of blood twelve years, came behind him,
and touched the hem of his garment.

She only touched the hem of His garment
As to His side she stole,
Amid the crowd that gathered around Him,
And straightway she was whole.

Oh, touch the hem of His garment!
And thou, too, shalt be free!
His saving power this very hour
Shall give new life to thee!

She came in fear and trembling before Him,
She knew her Lord had come;
She felt that from Him virtue had healed her,
The mighty deed was done.

He turned with "Daughter, be of good comfort,
Thy faith hath made thee whole!"
And peace that passeth all understanding
With gladness filled her soul.

GEORGE F. ROOT

HIS WILL *to* HEAL

MATTHEW 9:20–21 NKJV

And suddenly, a woman who had a flow of blood for twelve years came from behind and touched the hem of His garment. For she said to herself, "If only I may touch His garment, I shall be made well."

The hymn writer caught the simple pathos of this scene: "She only touched the hem of His garment, as to His side she stole; amid the crowds that gathered around her, and straightway she was whole." Points for our learning include (1) His goodness turns our problems into occasions of hope, v. 20; (2) His greatness makes our needs seem small, v. 21; (3) His graciousness makes our healing sure, v. 22.

In developing a message on physical healing we should be careful to relate healing to the providence and will of God. That He can heal is without question; that it is always His will to heal is another question. We must seek to discern the will of God, that which will be to His glory, as an authentic witness of His presence and purpose. This witness often includes suffering with a spirit of trust in His grace—often as important a witness to the character of the Kingdom as healing. The ministry of healing is the church's privilege more than her program.

MYRON S. AUGSBURGER

THE CAUSE

MARK 5:26 KJV

*And had suffered many things of many physicians,
and had spent all that she had, and was nothing
bettered, but rather grew worse.*

The main subject of these verses is the miraculous healing of a sick woman. Great is our Lord's experience in cases of disease! Great is his sympathy with his sick and ailing members! . . . The Saviour of the Christian is always set before us as gentle, and easy to call on, the healer of the broken-hearted, the refuge of the weak and helpless, the comforter of the distressed, the sick person's best friend. And is not this just the Saviour that human nature needs? The world is full of pain and trouble. The weak on earth are far more numerous than the strong. . . .

How astonishing it is that we do not hate sin more than we do! Sin is the cause of all the pain and disease in the world. God did not create us to be ailing and suffering creatures. It was sin, and nothing but sin, which brought in all the ills that flesh is heir to. It was sin to which we owe every racking pain, and every loathsome illness, and every humbling weakness to which our poor bodies are liable. Let us always bear this in mind. Let us hate sin with a godly hatred.

J. C. RYLE

JUST ONE TOUCH

MATTHEW 9:21 KJV
*For she said within herself, If I may
but touch his garment, I shall be whole.*

Just one touch as He moves along,
Pushed and pressed by the jostling throng,
Just one touch and the weak was strong,
Cured by the Healer divine.

Just one touch as He passes by,
He will list to the faintest cry,
Come and be saved while the Lord is nigh,
Christ is the Healer divine.

Just one touch and He makes me whole,
Speaks sweet peace to my sin sick soul,
At His feet all my burdens roll,
Cured by the Healer divine. . . .

Just one touch! and He turns to me,
Oh, the love in His eyes I see!
I am His, for He hears my plea,
Cured by the Healer divine.

BIRDIE BELL

REACH OUT *and* TOUCH

MARK 5:28 NASB
For she thought, "If I just touch
His garments, I will get well."

Many of us try to have a regular quiet time. As we do so, may each of us touch at least the hem of His garment, and receive wholeness in the matter for which we seek Him.

One knows when this has occurred. It is a day when something happens that is different from just reading our Bible or devotional book, or even just praying and asking for the thing.

We touch Him, and all is changed.

What happens? And who can tell *how* it happens?

We only know that something has passed from Him to us: courage to do the difficult task we feared.

Patience to bear with that one particular trying person. Inner strength to go on when we were sure we could not. A sweet freshness in our spirit, complete inner happiness, deep-flowing peace.

God's way of passing by, of letting His "hem" come near us, is to take some single word in His Book and make it breathe spirit and life to us. Then, relying upon that word—meditating, feeding our soul on it—we find it is suddenly possible to go from strength to strength.

AMY CARMICHAEL

SHE RISKED IT ALL

LUKE 8:46 NIV

But Jesus said, "Someone touched me;
I know that power has gone out from me."

Jesus recognized that someone who was suffering needed Him. How did He react? Was He indignant? Did He ignore the situation by saying, "I've got other business to attend to. I must heal a little girl, who may be dead by now"? No, He stopped and asked the woman to identify herself out of the crowd. . . .

There's great significance to this story for two reasons. First, this woman would have never been out in public. When a Jewish woman bled, she could not be seen in public for fear that she would contaminate others. Second, she would have never touched a rabbi while she was bleeding because that would have contaminated his sacred call—to intercede for the people to seek atonement for their sins. This woman really risked her reputation, her position in the community, her church membership—risked everything—but Jesus understood. He asked her to identify herself, and when she did, He lovingly assured her that He recognized her faith and she had been healed. Her bleeding stopped, and she went home healed and forgiven.

DAVID HAGER

THE COST *of* HEALING

LUKE 8:46 NLT

But Jesus told him, "No, someone deliberately touched me, for I felt healing power go out from me."

This passage tells us something . . . about Jesus. It tells us *the cost of healing*. Every time Jesus healed anyone it took something out of him. Here is a universal rule of life. We will never produce anything great unless we are prepared to put something of ourselves, of our very life, of our very soul into it. No pianist will ever give a really great performance if he glides through a piece of music with faultless technique and nothing more. The performance will not be great unless at the end of it there is the exhaustion which comes of the outpouring of self. . . .

The greatness of Jesus was that he was prepared to pay the price of helping others, and that price was the outgoing of his very life. We follow in his steps only when we are prepared to spend, not our substance, but our souls and strength for others.

WILLIAM BARCLAY

NO LABELS

——

MARK 5:32-33 NRSV

He looked all around to see who had done it.
But the woman, knowing what had happened
to her, came in fear and trembling, fell down
before him, and told him the whole truth.

The lovely thing about this story is that from the moment Jesus was face to face with the woman, there seemed to be nobody there but he and she. It happened in the middle of a crowd; but the crowd was forgotten and Jesus spoke to that woman as if she was the only person in the world. She was a poor, unimportant sufferer, with a trouble that made her unclean, and yet to that one unimportant person Jesus gave all of himself.

We are very apt to attach labels to people and to treat them according to their relative importance. To Jesus a person had none of these man-made labels. He or she was simply a human soul in need. Love never thinks of people in terms of human importances.

WILLIAM BARCLAY

SHE FOUND A FRIEND

LUKE 8:48 NLT
*"Daughter," he said to her, "your faith
has made you well. Go in peace."*

If anybody needed a friend, she did. No one paid her the time of day. Her life was punctuated with loneliness. For twelve years she'd been housebound. A dreaded disease dogged her steps. Doctors could offer no hope for healing her humiliating feminine disorder that left her slowly bleeding continuously. As far as she was concerned, it was a slow death. It left her "unclean"—no friends, no corporate worship, no hope.

But then she found a friend. His name was Jesus. . . .

The faith of a determined (and very sick) woman had been rewarded. The smile that crept across Jesus' face reassured the woman that faith like that would get her a long way. In fact, it still does. When we refuse to accept our plight apart from the Lord and move in His direction, we are rewarded with His friendship—now and eternally.

GREG ASIMAKOUPOULOS

MIRACLES: THE THRILL
OF ORTHODOXY

———

MATTHEW 9:28 NRSV

*When he entered the house, the blind men came
to him; and Jesus said to them, "Do you believe that
I am able to do this?" They said to him, "Yes, Lord."*

People have fallen into a foolish habit of speaking of
orthodoxy as something heavy, humdrum, and safe.
There never was anything so perilous or so exciting as
orthodoxy. It was sanity: and to be sane is more dramatic
than to be mad. . . . It is easy to be a madman: it is easy
to be a heretic. It is always easy to let the age have its head;
the difficult thing is to keep one's own. It is always easy to
be a modernist; as it is easy to be a snob. . . . It is always
simple to fall; there are an infinity of angles at which one
falls, only one at which one stands. To have fallen into any
one of the fads from Gnosticism to Christian Science
would indeed have been obvious and tame. But to have
avoided them all has been one whirling adventure; and in
my vision the heavenly chariot flies thundering through
the ages, the dull heresies sprawling and prostrate, the wild
truth reeling but erect.

G. K. CHESTERTON

BELIEVE YE?

MATTHEW 9:28 KJV

*And when he was come into the house, the blind men
came to him: and Jesus saith unto them, Believe ye that
I am able to do this? They said unto him, Yea, Lord.*

It is thus that the Master speaks to us: "Believe ye" that
I am able to make you happy, though you are cut off
from the light and gladness of the world? "Believe ye" that
I am able to enrich you in poverty, strengthen you in
weakness, and raise you even out of death itself, so that
the barren rod may bear blossom and fruit? "Believe ye"
that I am able to give a knowledge of God which eye hath
not seen nor the heart of man conceived?

It may be with a trembling faith that we answer, "Yea,
Lord." But how blessed is the soul that dares to say "Yea"
to the Master's challenge. Understand that there is no
limit to what he will do for you, if only you will trust
him. The measure of his giving is according to the measure of your faith, and the measure of your faith will be
according to the measure of your abandonment to him.
Spread abroad his fame. Pharisees hate him, but demons
flee.

F. B. MEYER

ADVANCING HIS KINGDOM

MATTHEW 9:28-29 MSG

*When Jesus got home, the blind men went in with him.
Jesus said to them, "Do you really believe I can do
this?" They said, "Why, yes, Master!" He touched
their eyes and said, "Become what you believe."*

When two blind men cried out, "Mercy, Son of
David! Mercy on us!" Jesus kept walking. He
didn't stop and say, "Tell me what it's been like to have
been blind all these years." Instead, when they followed
him home, still crying out for mercy, Jesus said, "Do you
really believe I can do this?" When they answered yes, he
said, "Become what you believe." He touched their eyes,
and they could see (see Matthew 9:27-29).

These blind men saw the light of heaven with the eyes
of their souls. When they confessed their faith, Jesus gave
another sign that the kingdom was indeed present. I see
little of a warm empathic conversation followed by an
even warmer act of healing. I see the Messiah advancing
his kingdom.

LARRY CRABB

FAITH IS OUR LIGHT

MATTHEW 9:29 NIV

*Then he touched their eyes and said, "According
to your faith will it be done to you."*

Everything exists in God. All we can perceive is the
activity of nature, but with faith we can see God at
work. . . .

There is hardly a moment when God does not
approach us disguised as a challenge or responsibility. Our
response to such opportunities includes and obscures his
activity. Because his action is unobservable, we are taken
by surprise and can interpret what happened only in ret-
rospect. If we could lift the curtain and observe what is
really happening, we would see God constantly at work.
We would be rejoicing all the time, "It is the Lord!" (John
21:7 NIV). We would accept every experience that came
our way as a gift from God.

Faith is God's interpreter. Without faith, all we hear is
a noisy babbling. Faith identifies God at work. . . . In this
life, faith is our light. With it we can know what we can't
see, we can touch what we can't feel, we can strip the
world of everything superficial. Faith is the combination
to God's vault.

JEAN-PIERRE DE CAUSSADE

No Reservations

MATTHEW 13:54, 57-58 KJV
*And when he was come into his own country,
he taught them in their synagogue. . . . They
were offended in him. . . . And he did not many
mighty works there because of their unbelief.*

When Jesus was in Nazareth he had the same power to heal, to change the direction of men's lives, to teach, to work miracles, as he had demonstrated in other towns in which he sojourned. But the people in his home town were so charged with indifference, skepticism, unbelief, that he could do no mighty works.

It seems reasonable to suppose that God has the power to answer prayer in our lives as he has answered it in countless other lives. But we have the power to make his power ineffective. Praying with mental reservations is a stone wall between the petitioner and God. To pray for a project we will not support with our money, to pray for people with whom we would not be willing to eat or work—such praying defeats God's mighty works. We would not think of withholding cooperation from the doctor or the lawyer, after paying them to help us, but we hang on to our mental reservations when dealing with Almighty God.

MARGUERITTE HARMON BRO

THE IMPORTANCE *of* FAITH

MATTHEW 13:58 KJV
*And he did not many mighty
works there because of their unbelief.*

We have an illustration of the importance of faith as the condition on which the exercise of Christ's power was based, or the channel through which it flowed, in the incident of a visit He made to Nazareth with its results, or rather its lack of results. . . .

Those people at Nazareth may have prayed our Lord to raise their dead, or open the eyes of the blind, or heal the lepers, but it was all in vain. The absence of faith, however much of performance may be seen, restrains the exercise of God's power, paralyzes the arm of Christ, and turns to death all signs of life. Unbelief is the one thing which seriously hinders Almighty God in doing mighty works. Matthew's record of this visit to Nazareth says, "And he did not many mighty works there because of their unbelief." Lack of faith ties the hands of Almighty God in His working among the children of men. Prayer to Christ must always be based, backed and impregnated with faith.

E. M. BOUNDS

HE CANNOT

MATTHEW 13:58 NASB
*And He did not do many miracles
there because of their unbelief.*

The other side of the coin of this amazing matter of cooperation with God is that there are things even God cannot do. He cannot because He has chosen to assign certain powers to His people. If they will not, His hands are tied (cf. also Mt. 23:37). . . .

Some would argue that although it is proper to say that God will not and does not, it is not proper to say that He cannot. I would reply that given the terms of His relationship to us, the people He loved and called, He *cannot* force us, for He *cannot* deny Himself. To force us would be to deprive us of the freedom He granted when He made us, and thus to deny Himself.

Yet we pray, "Make me to do Thy will!" And so we should, for in that prayer we express our will to cooperate with Him. "Our wills are ours to make them Thine" (Tennyson).

ELISABETH ELLIOT

MOVED *with* THEIR SUFFERING

MATTHEW 14:14 NASB

When He went ashore, He saw a large crowd,
and felt compassion for them, and healed their sick.

When this huge crowd gathered, Jesus looked out and saw broken people with broken lives. They had brought their sick and their lame, people with all manner of problems. And Jesus felt compassion for them. . . .

Jesus was moved with their suffering. And when you bring your needs to Jesus today, you're coming to someone who knows what you are talking about, not only because He is God, and therefore He knows everything, but also because He is man, and He can feel what you feel. That's why Jesus is the only One who can be the mediator between God and us.

But please take note. Jesus can do much more than just sympathize with you. His power can overrule your circumstances. His compassion can deal with your situation. He healed the sick that day (Matthew 14:14), and He fed them too. I don't know what impossible situation you may be facing today, but when you bring Jesus Christ into the equation, you have someone who can surmount the insurmountable.

TONY EVANS

FAITH TAKES HOLD

—

MATTHEW 14:34–36 KJV

And when they were gone over, they came into the land of Gennesaret. And when the men of that place had knowledge of him, they sent out into all that country round about, and brought unto him all that were diseased; and besought him that they might only touch the hem of his garment: and as many as touched were made perfectly whole.

Whithersoever Christ went, he was doing good. They brought unto him all that were diseased. They came humbly beseeching him to help them. The experiences of others may direct and encourage us in seeking for Christ. As many as touched, were made perfectly whole. Those whom Christ heals, he heals perfectly. Were men more acquainted with Christ, and with the diseased state of their souls, they would flock to receive his healing influences. The healing virtue was not in the finger, but in their faith; or rather, it was in Christ, whom their faith took hold upon.

MATTHEW HENRY

THE WAY *of* POWER

MARK 6:56 KJV

And whithersoever he entered, into villages, or cities, or country, they laid the sick in the streets, and besought him that they might touch if it were but the border of his garment: and as many as touched him were made whole.

It wasn't a question of the power inherent in Jesus. It was all there. It was a question of touching Him by an appropriating faith. *All* who touch Him now by an appropriating faith recover—recover from whatever ails them.

But many of us are like the Chinese gentleman in Penang who, sitting in his new Ford car, had coolies push him up and down the street. When asked if there wasn't any power in the machine, he replied, "Yes, but I'm afraid to turn it on." We are afraid to turn on the power—it's here unused. That power is nothing less than the power of the Holy Spirit. The Way is the way of the Holy Spirit. A Holy Spiritless Christianity is different from Christianity. It is a devitalized Christianity; it is less than, and therefore other than, Christianity. It is sub-Christian. The Way is the way of power, power to live the things it teaches.

E. STANLEY JONES

HE JUST HEALED

MATTHEW 15:31 NIV

*The people were amazed when they saw the mute
speaking, the crippled made well, the lame walking and
the blind seeing. And they praised the God of Israel.*

Let your imagination go. Can you see the scene?
Can you see the blind husband seeing his wife for the
first time? His eyes gazing into her tear-filled ones like she
was the queen of the morning?

Envision the man who had never walked, now walking! Don't you know that he didn't want to sit down?
Don't you know that he ran and jumped and did a dance
with the kids?

And what about the mute who could speak? Can you
picture him sitting by the fire late into the night and talking? Saying and singing everything and anything that he
had ever wanted to say and sing.

And the deaf woman who could now hear. What was
it like when she heard her child call her "Mamma" for the
first time?

For three days it went on. Person after person. Mat after
mat. Crutch after crutch. Smile after smile. No record is
given of Jesus preaching or teaching or instructing or
challenging. He just healed.

MAX LUCADO

INVISIBLE

MARK 7:32 NKJV

*Then they brought to Him one who was deaf
and had an impediment in his speech, and
they begged Him to put His hand on him.*

This man was both deaf and dumb. . . . He was living
in a silent world of complete isolation from all those
around him. Thus he represents a very difficult kind of
person to reach. Our Lord leads him aside from the multitude to deal with him privately.

There he did some unusual things: He put his fingers
into the man's ears. Then he spat on his fingers and
touched the man's tongue. Then, looking into the heavens, he sighed—all this before he said the wonderful
word, "Be opened." . . . He puts his fingers into his ears,
to indicate to the man that he intends to heal them. He
wets his fingers and touches the man's tongue to indicate
that he is going to heal the tongue, and that words will
flow freely from it. He looks up into heaven to indicate
that the power for this must come from God. And he
sighs—not so much a sign as a breathing out—to convey
to the man that it is by the invisible agency of the power
of God that he will be made well.

RAY C. STEDMAN

TAKEN ASIDE

MARK 7:33 KJV

And he took him aside from the multitude, and put his fingers into his ears, and he spit, and touched his tongue.

Taken aside by Jesus,
   To feel the touch of His hand;
To rest for a while in the shadow
   Of the Rock in a weary land.

Taken aside by Jesus,
   In the loneliness dark and drear,
Where no other comfort may reach me,
   Than His voice to my heart so dear.

Taken aside by Jesus,
   To be quite alone with Him,
To hear His wonderful tomes of love
   'Mid the silence and shadows dim.

Taken aside by Jesus,
   Shall I shrink from the desert place;
When I hear as I never heard before,
   And see Him face to face?

AUTHOR UNKNOWN

HE SIGHED

MARK 7:34–35 NIV
*He looked up to heaven and with a deep sigh said
to him, "Ephphatha!" (which means, "Be opened!").
At this, the man's ears were opened, his tongue
was loosened and he began to speak plainly.*

When Jesus looked into the eyes of Satan's victim, the only appropriate thing to do was sigh. "It was never intended to be this way," the sigh said. "Your ears weren't made to be deaf, your tongue wasn't made to stumble." The imbalance of it all caused the Master to languish. . . .

And in the agony of Jesus lies our hope. Had he not sighed, had he not felt the burden for what was not intended, we would be in a pitiful condition. Had he simply chalked it all up to the inevitable or washed his hands of the whole stinking mess, what hope would we have?

But he didn't. That holy sigh assures us that God still groans for his people. He groans for the day when all sighs will cease, when what was intended to be will be.

MAX LUCADO

FINDING RELIEF

MARK 7:37 KJV

And were beyond measure astonished, saying,
He hath done all things well: he maketh both
the deaf to hear, and the dumb to speak.

Here is a cure of one that was deaf and dumb. Those who brought this poor man to Christ, besought him to observe the case, and put forth his power. Our Lord used more outward actions in the doing of this cure than usual. These were only signs of Christ's power to cure the man, to encourage his faith, and theirs that brought him. Though we find great variety in the cases and manner of relief of those who applied to Christ, yet all obtained the relief they sought. Thus it still is in the great concerns of our souls.

MATTHEW HENRY

HE ANSWERS

MARK 8:22 KJV

*And he cometh to Bethsaida; and they bring a blind
man unto him, and besought him to touch him.*

O Lord God Almighty, I know that I owe You the
devotion of all my words and thoughts as my main
duty. The greatest reward of speech You have given me is
the opportunity to serve by preaching You and displaying
You as You are to a blind and rebellious world. For You
are our Father and Father of God the Only-begotten Son.
But I am only expressing my own desires. I must also pray
for your help and compassion. Then Your Spirit's breath
will fill the sails of faith and confession which I have
spread out, and a favorable wind will move me forward
on my voyage of instruction. We can trust the promise of
Christ who said, "Ask, and it shall be given you, seek, and
ye shall find, knock, and it shall be opened unto you." In
whatever we lack, we will pray for the things we need.
We will be untiring and energetic as we study Your
prophets and apostles. We will knock to enter every gate
of hidden knowledge. But You are the One who answers
these prayers, who gives us the things we seek, who opens
the door we beat on.

HILARY OF POITIERS

SEEING CLEARLY

MARK 8:23-25 KJV

*He asked him if he saw ought. And he looked up,
and said, I see men as trees, walking. After that he put
his hands again upon his eyes, and made him look up:
and he was restored, and saw every man clearly.*

First, let us see in this gradual restoration to sight a vivid
illustration the manner in which the Spirit frequently
works in the conversion of our souls. Conversion is an
illumination, a change from darkness to light, from blindness to seeing the kingdom of God. Yet few unconverted
people see things clearly at first. The nature and propor-
tion of doctrines, practices and ordinances of the Gospel
are dimly seen by them, and imperfectly understood.
They are like the man before who at first saw people like
trees walking about. Their vision is dazzled and unaccus-
tomed to the new world into which they have been intro-
duced. It is not till the work of the Spirit has become
deeper and their experience has been somewhat matured
that they see everything clearly, and give to each part of
religion its proper place. This is the history of thousands
of God's children. They begin with seeing people like
trees walking around; they end by seeing everything
clearly. Happy are those who have learned this lesson well,
and are humbly distrustful of their own judgment.

J. C. RYLE

AN INVITATION *to* FAITH

MARK 8:25 NCV

*Again Jesus put his hands on the man's eyes. Then
the man opened his eyes wide and they were healed,
and he was able to see everything clearly.*

God, who made the visible heaven and earth, does
not disdain to work visible miracles in heaven or
earth, that He may thereby awaken the soul which is
immersed in things visible to worship Himself the
Invisible. . . .

He restored to the blind those eyes which death was
sure some time to close; He raised Lazarus from the dead,
who was to die again. And whatever He did for the
health of bodies, He did it not to the end that they should
exist for evermore; whereas at the last He will give eternal health even to the body itself. But because those
things which were not seen were not believed, by means
of those temporal things which were seen He built up
faith in those things which were not seen. Let no one
therefore say that our Lord Jesus Christ doeth not those
things now, and on this account prefer the former to the
present ages of the Church. . . . The Lord did those things
to invite us to the faith.

AUGUSTINE

THE WAY IS OPEN

LUKE 17:12–14 NIV

As he was going into a village, ten men who had
leprosy met him. They stood at a distance and called
out in a loud voice, "Jesus, Master, have pity on us!"
When he saw them, he said, "Go, show yourselves to
the priests." And as they went, they were cleansed.

Leprosy is a wasting disease. It destroys the cells of the body, taking away appendages. . . .

But perhaps the most devastating consequence of all to lepers in biblical times was that their contagiousness meant isolation. They lived in caves, huddled together, wrapped in rags, shunned by all society but each other.

No wonder Jesus had pity on the ten leprous men. No wonder he answered their prayer. . . .

In some way, all of us are like the lepers. We all live at times with our feelings numbed by the harsh realities of life; at times we feel the wasting effects of the enemy's warfare, and at other times we feel bitterly isolated from others.

But the Lord showed us in this story that the way to his healing is open when we pray the way the Samaritan leper did: with faith to ask the Lord for what we need. Faith to listen for his instructions and follow them. And faith to return to him with gratitude in our hearts.

CLAIRE CLONINGER

THE SUNSHINE *of* GRATEFULNESS

LUKE 17:15–16 KJV

*And one of them, when he saw that he was healed,
turned back, and with a loud voice glorified God,
and fell down on his face at his feet, giving
him thanks: and he was a Samaritan.*

I have never interpreted the parable of the Ten Lepers to mean that only one was grateful. All the ten, surely, were grateful, but nine of them hurried home first. . . . One of them, however, had a disposition which made him act at once as his feelings bade him; he sought out the person who had helped him, and refreshed his soul with the assurance of his gratitude.

In the same way we ought all to make an effort to act on our first thoughts and let our unspoken gratitude find expression. Then there will be more sunshine in the world, and more power to work for what is good. But as concerns ourselves, we must all of us take care not to adopt as part of a theory of life all people's bitter sayings about the ingratitude of the world. A great deal of water is flowing underground which never comes up as a spring. In that thought we may find comfort. But we ourselves must try to be the water which does find its way up; we must become a spring at which men can quench their thirst for gratitude.

ALBERT SCHWEITZER

RECEIVED BACK

LUKE 17:17-19 NIV

Jesus asked, "Were not all ten cleansed? Where are the other nine? Was no one found to return and give praise to God except this foreigner?" Then he said to him, "Rise and go; your faith has made you well."

In commending the leper who returned while criticizing the others he highlights the point. It was the one with least cause to trust Jesus who returned. In first of all obeying Jesus, and then returning to show his gratitude, the Samaritan overcomes his prejudice and inherited grudge. The purpose of sending the lepers to the priest was in order that they might be received back into the community. The Samaritan is received back, not only into his own home but into the life of Jesus' kingdom as he worships at the "temple" which replaces all human shrines.

Clearly the Samaritan . . . was no longer a leper, but healing was completed when he rendered his loyalty to Jesus. His relationships were renewed and he was freed from the stigma which termed him a "foreigner." Jesus refused to travel around Samaria and his respect for the Samaritan's faith was a living challenge to all who would maintain attitudes of division, hatred and racial superiority.

JUNE OSBORNE & CHRIS SUGDEN

DO YOU BELIEVE?

MATTHEW 20:30 KJV

And, behold, two blind men sitting by the way side,
when they heard that Jesus passed by, cried out, saying,
Have mercy on us, O Lord, thou son of David.

L et us listen to these blind men, who were better than
many that see. For neither having a guide, nor being
able to see Him when come near to them, nevertheless
they strove to come unto Him, and began to cry with a
loud voice, and when rebuked for speaking, they cried
the more. For such is the nature of an enduring soul, by
the very things that hinder, it is borne up. But Christ suffered them to be rebuked, that their earnestness might the
more appear, and that thou mightest learn that worthily
they enjoy the benefits of their cure. Therefore He doth
not so much as ask, "Do ye believe?" as He doth with
many; for their cry, and their coming unto Him, sufficed
to make their faith manifest. Then, when they said what
they wished, He had compassion on them, and touched
them. For this alone is the cause of their cure, for which
also He came into the world.

CHYRSOSTOM

HAVE YOU SEEN HIM?

MARK 10:51 NCV

Jesus asked him, "What do you want me to do for you?" The blind man answered, "Teacher, I want to see."

Few are the people who don't suffer from some form of blindness. Amazing, isn't it? We can live next to something for a lifetime, but unless we take time to focus on it, it doesn't become a part of our life. Unless we somehow have our blindness lifted, our world is but a black cave.

Think about it. Just because one has witnessed a thousand rainbows doesn't mean he's seen the grandeur of one. One can live near a garden and fail to focus on the splendor of the flower. . . .

And a person can be all that goodness calls him to be and still never see the Author of life.

Being honest or moral or even religious doesn't necessarily mean we will see him. No. We may see what others see in him. Or we may hear what some say he said. But until we see him for ourselves, until our own sight is given, we may think we see him, having in reality seen only a hazy form in the gray semidarkness.

Have you seen him?

Have you caught a glimpse of His Majesty?

MAX LUCADO

WHAT DO YOU WANT?

———

LUKE 18:41 NLT

Then Jesus asked the man, "What do you want me to do for you?" "Lord," he pleaded, "I want to see!"

Jesus' question puzzles some people. If He's really the Messiah, then why should He have to *ask* the man what he wanted? Wouldn't it be obvious? It doesn't take a medical doctor to identify a blind beggar who for years has been crawling around, seeking handouts. Why *did* Jesus ask, "What do you want Me to do for you?"

First, we should remember that God often asks us questions, not to gain information but to get us to admit our need. . . .

Second, the Bible makes it clear that while "all things are possible with God" (Mark 10:27, NIV), it reminds us that we can't expect to tap into His miracle-working power without explicit prayer. . . .

So Jesus turns to this sightless man and asks, "What do you want Me to do for you?"

The man doesn't wait to respond. He knows his need. He believes he is speaking with Israel's long-promised Messiah. And so he says simply, "Lord, that I may receive my sight." . . .

May we have the spiritual insight of the man *formerly* known as the blind beggar from Jericho!

GREG LAURIE

THE MOST BEAUTIFUL SIGHT

LUKE 18:42 NIV
Jesus said to him, "Receive your sight;
your faith has healed you."

Perhaps it was one of those incredibly beautiful days. Brilliant sun, bright blue sky, and not too hot. But for Bartimaeus, one of Jericho's familiar beggars, beautiful was not a word he normally used to describe days. You see, Bartimaeus couldn't see. He'd been blind from birth. What others took for granted, Bartimaeus was oblivious to. But on this beautiful day all that would change. A caring man who redefined the meaning of beautiful passed through the town. . . .

When Bartimaeus heard that Jesus was walking by, he called out, "Jesus, Son of David, have mercy on me!" (Luke 18:38 NIV). Struggling to his feet and slowly feeling his way toward the visiting rabbi, Bartimaeus felt warm hands on his weathered face. And the next thing he knew, he was healed. Seeing the eyes of Jesus and the smile that creased His bearded face was not only the first thing Bartimaeus ever saw. It would forever be the most beautiful thing he ever saw.

GREG ASIMAKOUPOULOS

WE SHALL SEE

LUKE 18:42 KJV
*And Jesus said unto him, Receive thy sight:
thy faith hath saved thee.*

When the blind suppliant in the way,
  By friendly hands to Jesus led,
Prayed to behold the light of day,
  "Receive thy sight," the Saviour said.

At once he saw the pleasant rays
  That lit the glorious firmament;
And, with firm step and words of praise,
  He followed where the Master went.

Look down in pity, Lord, we pray,
  On eyes oppressed by moral night,
And touch the darkened lids and say
  The gracious words, "Receive thy sight."

Then, in clear daylight, shall we see
  Where walked the sinless Son of God;
And, aided by new strength from Thee,
  Press onward in the path He trod.

WILLIAM CULLEN BRYANT

ONE HEALER

JOHN 12:37 KJV
But though he had done so many miracles
before them, yet they believed not on him.

It is sadly possible to bear the Name of Christ and yet
live a life totally unworthy of God. And in some cases
those who behave like this do it deliberately. They want
to be known as Christians so as to infiltrate your ranks
and cause as much trouble for you as they can. Like mad
dogs, their bite is sudden and unexpected, but once you
are bitten, healing is a slow and painful matter—and not
all recover.

In fact, there is only one Healer, from this or any other
wound, physical or spiritual. He is the One who had no
beginning, and yet was born on earth; who is God, and
yet is also man; who won true life through dying; who is
the Son of Mary and also the Son of God; who suffered
once, but suffers no more: Jesus Christ, our Lord.

IGNATIUS OF ANTIOCH

THE FINAL ACT

LUKE 22:49–51 NIV

When Jesus' followers saw what was going to happen,
they said, "Lord, should we strike with our swords?"
And one of them struck the servant of the high priest,
cutting off his right ear. But Jesus answered, "No more
of this!" And he touched the man's ear and healed him.

The disciples who possess the "two swords" (22:38) react, thinking that this is the time to use force. (Verse 49 also has no counterpart in Matthew or Mark and is inserted here by Luke to link vv. 35–38 to the act of striking the slave.) One of them (John 18:10 tells us that it was Simon Peter) struck the servant of the high priest (or chief priest), cutting off his right ear. Only Luke notes that it was the right ear and only Luke tells us that Jesus healed the man's wound. (Do we have here a hint of Luke's medical interest?) Here we see Jesus' last act of healing, and it is ironic that the one healed was one of those about to arrest him.

CRAIG A. EVANS

OPPORTUNITIES *to* REPENT

LUKE 22:51 NIV
But Jesus answered, "No more of this!"
And he touched the man's ear and healed him.

When the disciples saw what was happening they assumed Jesus wanted them to fight. He had, after all, told them to carry swords (Luke 22:36) and they had brought two along with them (v. 38). Peter swung his sword and struck a glancing blow against the head of the high priest's servant, slicing his right ear off. Jesus told his disciples not to fight, however, and then he healed the servant's ear.

Then Jesus rebuked those who came to arrest him. The crowd included chief priests, elders, and officers of the temple guard. These were not minor officials; the conspiracy reached all the way to the top. Jesus asked them why they had come out against him with swords and clubs. "Have I been leading a rebellion?" he asked. "You saw me every day in the temple. Why didn't you arrest me then?" . . .

Even in his time of greatest trial, the Savior of the world gave his enemies new opportunities to repent by rebuking them, healing them, and warning them to flee the wrath to come.

R. C. SPROUL

WE CRY *to* THEE

PSALM 147:3 NASB
He heals the brokenhearted and binds up their wounds.

Dear Lord, whose loving eyes can see
Each troubled mind without, within,
We bring our week of life to thee,
All soiled and worn and marred with sin.

We bring our bitterness of heart,
Our hate and want of charity.
Help us to choose the better part,
And learn to love, dear Lord, like thee.

We bring our care for daily bread,
The fear that turns the heart to stone.
We cry to thee; lift up our head
And show us we are not alone. . . .

Lord, make us pure; enrich our life
With heavenly love for evermore.
Give us thy strength to face the strife,
And serve thee better than before.

EDWIN GILBERT

STRANGE GIFT, INDEED

2 CORINTHIANS 12:7 KJV

*And lest I should be exalted above measure through
the abundance of the revelations, there was given to me
a thorn in the flesh, the messenger of Satan to buffet me.*

Strange gift indeed!—a thorn to prick,
   To pierce into the very quick;
To cause perpetual sense of pain;
   Strange gift!—and yet, 'twas given for gain.

Unwelcome, yet it came to stay;
   Nor could it e'en be prayed away.
It came to fill its God-planned place,
   A life-enriching means of grace.

God's grace-thorns—ah, what forms they take;
   What piercing, smarting pain they make!
And yet, each one in love is sent,
   And always just for blessing meant.

And so, whate'er thy thorn may be,
   From God accept it willingly;
But reckon Christ—His life—the power
   To keep, in thy most trying hour. . . .

J. DANSON SMITH

THIS, TOO, IS A MIRACLE

1 PETER 2:24 NRSV
He himself bore our sins in his body on the cross,
so that, free from sins, we might live for righteousness;
by his wounds you have been healed.

This afternoon, I went to a local hospital to visit an elderly parishioner who is suffering from what appears to be terminal cancer. As I sat by her bed, she spoke about her trust in Jesus and told me of an occasion many years ago when she was seriously ill and was prayed for by a former vicar. Unexpectedly, she had made a remarkable recovery. . . .

She asked for prayer again, and I laid hands on her and focused the healing power of the Holy Trinity upon her. I have to say that this time I will be very surprised if she makes a physical recovery, and not at all surprised if she dies in the next few days. But it still seemed right to hold her hand and gently to urge her to "keep looking forward," because one of two things must happen. Against all the odds, there could be a new surge of life in this world—a miracle. Or, if she moves into death, and through death with her trust in Jesus, there will be a new surge of spiritual life for her in eternity. This, too, is a miracle.

ROY LAWRENCE

NO PRAYER IS WASTED

—

JAMES 5:15 NKJV
*And the prayer of faith will save the sick,
and the Lord will raise him up.
And if he has committed sins, he will be forgiven.*

Scripture tells us "the prayer of faith will save the sick" (James 5:15). Yet all of us can doubtless recall times— many times—when we prayed for a healing and it did not occur. . . . Does that mean that God is not listening? that your faith is too weak? or that your prayers have not been fervent enough? I think not, but I also think it is fruitless to try to find an answer to why some people are healed and some are not.

Much of what happens on our earthly journey will remain a mystery until we get to risen life. . . .

I do not think we can ever say prayer is wasted. Although prayer may not change a situation and give us the miracle we want, *prayer changes us.* Through prayer, we become more aware of God's presence. Through prayer, we find inner resources and strength we didn't know we had. Through prayer, we are no longer facing our fears and pain alone: God is beside us, renewing our spirit, restoring our soul, and helping us carry the burden when it becomes too heavy for us to bear alone.

RON DELBENE WITH MARY AND HERB MONTGOMERY

WE HAVE COME

ISAIAH 53:5 NRSV

But he was wounded for our transgressions, crushed for our iniquities; upon him was the punishment that made us whole, and by his bruises we are healed.

O Christ, the healer, we have come
  To pray for health, to plead for friends.
How can we fail to be restored
When reached by love that never ends?

From every ailment flesh endures
Our bodies clamor to be freed;
Yet in our hearts we would confess
That wholeness is our deepest need. . . .

In conflicts that destroy our health
We recognize the world's disease;
Our common life declares our ills.
Is there no cure, O Christ, for these?

Grant that we all, made one in faith,
In your community may find
The wholeness that, enriching us,
Shall reach the whole of humankind.

FRED PRATT GREEN

JESUS' MIRACLES OVER EVIL SPIRITS

---

*"If it is by the finger of God that
I cast out the demons, then the kingdom
of God has come to you."*
LUKE 11:20 NRSV

JESUS' MIRACLES
OVER EVIL SPIRITS

We have been reminded by C. S. Lewis and others that we commit twin errors if we either ignore the reality of evil or become fascinated with it. Somehow our age has managed to combine the errors, glorifying evil for its entertainment value, all the while maintaining that it's nothing more than a troubling figment of our imaginations. But evil is more than movie special effects. While we declare people "basically good," we too often find ourselves appalled at the evil they commit. Our efforts to reduce and rename evil using terms like *mistakes*, *misunderstandings*, and *errors in judgment* end up exposed as frantic efforts at denial. Evil is a stubborn reality.

The possibility of created spiritual beings who have chosen evil is actually no more strange than knowing physical beings who have made the same choice. Jesus spoke to evil spirits. They acknowledged His identity long before many humans realized who He was. In this section, we will reflect on some of those encounters.

HEALING MINDS

MATTHEW 12:22 NIV

Then they brought him a demon-possessed man
who was blind and mute, and Jesus healed him,
so that he could both talk and see.

To those who saw the outward manifestations of an epileptic or some mental disorder which made a man violently destructive, it was not unnatural to think of him as possessing or being possessed by "a devil." Indeed those of us who have ever been in the presence of the violently deranged and looked into their eyes could easily agree that some evil power appears to be possessing the patient. It seems that Jesus was in many cases able to get to the storm-centre of the disturbance and resolve it with authoritative love. We do not know even yet how far the mind affects the body (or the body the mind) or how far either of them is influenced by spiritual power—by intercessory prayer, for example. We know how to "cure" certain diseases with fair accuracy, but what we are really doing is removing the obstacles which are preventing a natural ability to heal itself which both the human body and mind possess. It does not seem to me in the least unreasonable that a man of concentrated spiritual power should be able to remove these obstacles instantaneously.

J. B. PHILLIPS

THE LAST LAUGH

But when the Pharisees heard it, they said,
"This man casts out demons only by
Beelzebul the ruler of the demons."

Obviously Christ had to answer this charge, which
might easily impress the ignorant, but how was He
to do it? Again we find Him using the strategy of laughter. "And if I cast out demons by Beelzebul, by whom do
your sons cast them out?" (Matt. 12:27 ESV). The laugh is
turned on the critics, since everyone who listens will realize that the subtle question has no possible answer. Either
they do *not* cast them out, in which case they look silly,
or, as is more likely, if they claim to be effective in this
effort, they have already, by implication, suggested that
they also are possessed. Christ's question really means, "By
what demonic agency do you perform your miracles?" It
is easy to see that the humorous question is a far more
effective rejoinder than would have been a serious argument about demons. The severest critics of Christ could
not stand ridicule, for seriousness was their central
strength.

ELTON TRUEBLOOD

HE BROUGHT GOD

MATTHEW 12:28 KJV
*But if I cast out devils by the Spirit of God,
then the kingdom of God is come unto you.*

As he came among men he did not try to prove the existence of God—he brought him. He lived in God and men looking upon his face could not find it within themselves to doubt God. He did not argue, as Socrates, the immortality of the soul—he raised the dead. He did not speculate on how God was a Trinity—he said, "If I by the Spirit of God cast out devils, the kingdom of God is come nigh unto you." Here the Trinity—"I," "Spirit of God," "God"—was not something to be speculated about, but was a Working Force for redemption—the casting out of the devils and the bringing in of the Kingdom.

E. STANLEY JONES

HIS KINGDOM COME

LUKE 11:20 KJV

But if I with the finger of God cast out devils,
no doubt the kingdom of God is come upon you.

With the incarnation of Jesus Christ, power over the demonic forces is a keynote of the arrival of the new kingdom and an establishment of a new order. . . . While much of the opposition to this new kingdom of Christ was human—priests, scribes, establishment and tradition—Jesus clearly saw that occult powers were behind this opposition, unmasked openly in the demoniacs, who represented society's fringe failures and the limitations of religious humanism.

Seeing these powers as the hub of his opposition, Jesus said, "If it is by the finger of God that I drive out the devils, then be sure the kingdom of God has already come upon you." Looking towards future generations, Jesus predicted that his followers would, if they believed, perform greater signs than even he had. Paul, anticipating the consummation of the kingdom, describes it as a time when all the occult forces will be disarmed by Christ and the earth will be seen to be God's.

OS GUINNESS

HIS WAY *of* WORKING

LUKE 11:20 NRSV

"But if it is by the finger of God that I cast out the demons, then the kingdom of God has come to you."

Those who object to the way miracles have been handled in the past have at least this to be said for their point of view: the miracles are not something extra, something added to the revelation in order to accredit it. They are part of the revelation. We see the Kingdom of God in the fact that mighty powers are in operation (Lk. 11:20). They are not devices to which God had to resort when He could not do what He wished by normal means, but part of His plan. . . . What we term "miracle" is His way of working. When we have the entry of a Being of a different order into the human sphere of life we must expect to see happenings which cannot be explained by the laws governing human conduct. And those happenings are part of the evidence which indicates that such an entry has, in fact, occurred.

LEON MORRIS

NO ONE *beyond* HIS REACH

LUKE 8:26-27 NIV

They sailed to the region of the Gerasenes, which
is across the lake from Galilee. When Jesus stepped
ashore, he was met by a demon-possessed man from
the town. For a long time this man had not worn
clothes or lived in a house, but had lived in the tombs.

The demoniac was a damned man—forgotten and
alone. Jesus battled a storm on the sea and rowed
seven-and-a-half miles to the region of the damned.

"The other side" was outside of the disciples' comfort
zone. But Jesus engaged this madman on his turf, in an
area where the people did not look, dress, act, talk or
think like Jews. Gerasenes was a cesspool for human
depravity. It was a place of moral and ethical decay. It was
a place where sin was rampant and death was a stench on
people's clothes. But Jesus still went there to meet the
demoniac.

The next time I feel beyond Jesus' reach, or I see people around me as beyond his reach, I will remember the
lengths he went to in order to save a madman from
destruction. If he was willing to do it then, he is willing
to do it now. No matter how far we have fallen, or how
desperate we are, Jesus is ready and willing to meet us.

RICK EZELL

THE DEMONS' UNDOING

MATTHEW 8:28-29 NLT

Two men who were possessed by demons met him. They lived in a cemetery and were so dangerous that no one could go through that area. They began screaming at him, "Why are you bothering us, Son of God? You have no right to torture us before God's appointed time!"

The two demoniacs who accosted Jesus when He landed on the south-eastern shore of the lake lived a solitary life, for, as Matthew alone tells us, they were regarded as so dangerous that no other human beings dared to come near the burial-place which they haunted ([v.] 28). But when they saw Jesus, they knew instinctively that they were confronting no ordinary person, but the *Son of God*—who had the power to destroy them. In consequence, they who struck terror into the hearts of others were now the victims of fear themselves. . . . But if the time for them to be exorcized had in fact arrived, they requested that they might not remain disembodied but be reincarnated in the herd of swine which was grazing some distance away. The favour was granted, but it proved to be the demons' undoing.

TYNDALE NEW TESTAMENT
COMMENTARIES—MATTHEW

JESUS GIVES HOPE

LUKE 8:29 NLT

*This spirit had often taken control of the man.
Even when he was shackled with chains, he simply
broke them and rushed out into the wilderness,
completely under the demon's power.*

This dangerous and frightening individual furnishes a picture of Satan's ultimate goal, his "finished product." What steps led to this state we can only imagine, but here we see "the package deal"—sin, Satan, and death working together. The power of Satan was so intertwined with this man that most observers could not see the hurting soul deep inside. When they looked at him, they saw only a crazed, suicidal maniac roaming the graveyard.

Satan's goal was to destroy this man.

And what did Jesus do for the man? He sought him out in his spooky little graveyard and offered him hope. . . .

Jesus is still in the people-changing business. It thrills me to look at some Christians and know how different they are now from what they once were. . . .

None of us has the power to overcome Satan in our own strength. Neither can we count on society to give us the help we need. But if we cry out to Jesus, He can step in and transform us—no matter what kind or how many "demons" may torment us.

GREG LAURIE

THEIR TIME HAD COME

MATTHEW 8:29, 31 NKJV

*And suddenly they cried out, saying, "What have
we to do with You, Jesus, You Son of God? Have
You come here to torment us before the time?" . . .
So the demons begged Him, saying, "If You cast us
out, permit us to go away into the herd of swine."*

The evil spirits were sensible that Christ was come to
dispossess them, and that their time was now come,
when they must leave the bodies of these two men; for
when Christ comes, who is stronger than the strong man
armed, all must fall before him; they could not stand
against the power of Christ. And here we may observe,
that though the devil is an enemy, yet he is a chained one;
he cannot hurt a poor swine until he has power given him
from above: and we may likewise see the malice of the
devil, that he would hurt a poor swine rather than do no
mischief; and the devil would, if in his power, destroy each
of your souls, but Christ, by his mighty power, prevents
him.

GEORGE WHITEFIELD

THE DEMONS' DESIRE

MATTHEW 8:30-31 KJV

And there was a good way off from them an herd of many swine feeding. So the devils besought him, saying, If thou cast us out, suffer us to go away into the herd of swine.

The demon spirit seems still to tenant the lives of human beings. To what else can we attribute the paroxysms of passion, the awful cruelties and inhumanities of men? There is only one devil, but many demons; only one prince of the power of darkness, but many emissaries. Take heed, lest you open the door of your nature to the spirit of evil and he possess you. Watch and pray, and trust the keeping of your soul to the hands of Christ. He is stronger than the strong man.

Notice that the demon is set upon destruction. If he may not destroy the souls of men, he will destroy swine. This is the mark of evil. It is always destructive; whereas the Spirit of God is constructive and builds up from the ruins of Satan's work a new Heaven and a new earth, both in the soul and in the universe.

All the city besought Jesus to depart, because men count their gains more valuable than his presence. The same spirit rules in the commercial world of today. Let us beware. What shall it profit to gain the world if we lose our souls?

F. B. MEYER

SUBLIME POWER

———

MARK 5:8, 13 NKJV

For He said to him, "Come out of the man,
unclean spirit!" . . . Then the unclean spirits went
out and entered the swine (there were about two
thousand); and the herd ran violently down the
steep place into the sea, and drowned in the sea.

You can see the disciples, still alarmed and frightened, yet unwilling to leave Jesus by himself in the presence of this monster. But they need not have feared for their Master. With the voice of unmistakable authority Jesus says, "Come out of the man!" At once a change comes over the wild man. The taut, tense muscles of his arms relax. The sharp, bloody stones drop from his hands. The wild look fades from his face; and the look of reason, the look of humanity, the look of a man in the image of God takes its place. With a sigh of immense relief and deliverance as the demons depart from him, he sinks down at the feet of Jesus. One of the disciples wipes the blood from his face with a cloth, and another takes a mantle and casts it over his naked body. There he is, at the feet of Jesus. clothed and in his right mind. . . . Mighty, beautiful, sublime example of the power of Jesus to restore and redeem the human soul!

CLARENCE EDWARD MACARTNEY

DRAW ME CLOSE

LUKE 8:35 NIV

The people went out to see what had happened.
When they came to Jesus, they found the man from
whom the demons had gone out, sitting at Jesus' feet,
dressed and in his right mind; and they were afraid.

He hid among the tombstones at night. During the day he dodged visitors by remaining in the shadows. Viewed as dangerous by those who knew of him, this mysterious man was bound by iron chains. But the links couldn't hold him. He tore them off just like he did his clothes. Although he managed to keep the manacles from his feet, he was hardly free. Demons held him hostage. That is, until the day Jesus walked into his cemetery and cemented his future. . . .

So Jesus cast out the demons. . . . The next picture we have of the wild-eyed man is of him sitting quietly, clothed and sane, at the feet of his Savior.

Maybe you relate. Can you recall a time when your heart was far from free even though you boasted of an independent spirit? Can you remember the moment when you saw the emptiness of your life and called out to Jesus to draw you close? Do you need that today? Turn to Him. He promises to cleanse you and clothe you in His righteousness. Let Him draw you close in His loving arms.

GREG ASIMAKOUPOULOS

A PASSION *to* TELL

LUKE 8:38–39 NKJV
*But Jesus sent him away, saying,
"Return to your own house, and tell what
great things God has done for you."*

A despicable man lived in a graveyard and cut his flesh with rocks. Every time people tried to tie him up, he burst his bonds and ran back to the tombs or to the desert, wherever the demons drove him (Luke 8:29).

No wonder he was overcome with gratitude when Jesus set him free from demonic dominion. The healed man fell down and begged his newfound Savior to let him come along. Nothing else mattered to him; Jesus had restored him, and he understood that now his life belonged to Him, in wholeness and completion. He knew the horror of the existence from which Jesus had saved him, so he was thrilled all the more for a chance to start over.

When you recognize the sin and hopelessness from which Jesus has pulled you by His matchless grace, you have the same deep, abiding appreciation. . . . You love your Savior because He loved you first and He gives you a new life that you cannot get for yourself. Do you have a passion to tell others what He has done for you? You cannot be silent when you feel the fullness of His love.

CHARLES STANLEY

TELL YOUR STORY

MARK 5:19 NIV

Jesus did not let him, but said, "Go home to your family and tell them how much the Lord has done for you, and how he has had mercy on you."

The Bible tells us the story of a man who was so thankful for what Jesus had done for Him that he immediately went out and told people about his experience. The man is not named in Scripture, but he could represent any one of us. He was beyond all human help, yet Jesus set him free. The man was so thankful, he begged Jesus to be allowed to join Him. But Jesus sent the man back to his own hometown to share what had happened to him. So the man told everyone about the great things Jesus had done for him, and people were awestruck by his story (Mark 5:1–20).

What is your salvation story? Can you boil it down to three minutes and have it ready to tell at a moment's notice? The apostle Peter advises, "Always be prepared to give an answer to everyone who asks you to give the reason for the hope that you have" (1 Peter 3:15 NIV).

If someone asked you about your faith, what would you say about the hope that you have?

CAROL CHAFFEE FIELDING

NO NEUTRALITY

MATTHEW 9:32–34 NRSV

*A demoniac who was mute was brought to him.
And when the demon had been cast out, the one who
had been mute spoke. . . . But the Pharisees said,
"By the ruler of the demons he casts out the demons."*

There are few passages which show better than this
the impossibility of an attitude of neutrality towards
Jesus. . . .

The crowds looked on Jesus with wonder, because they
were simple people with a crying sense of need; and they
saw that in Jesus their need could be supplied in the most
astonishing way. Jesus will always appear wonderful to the
man with a sense of need; and the deeper the sense of
need the more wonderful Jesus will appear to be.

The Pharisees saw Jesus as one who was in league with
all the powers of evil. They did not deny his wondrous
powers; but they attributed them to his complicity with
the prince of the devils. . . .

The man with a sense of need will always see wonders
in Jesus Christ. The man who is so set in his ways that he
will not change, the man who is so proud in his self-
righteousness that he cannot submit, the man who is so
blinded by his prejudices that he cannot see, will always
resent and hate and seek to eliminate him.

WILLIAM BARCLAY

HANG ON

MATTHEW 15:22 NIV

A Canaanite woman from that vicinity came to him, crying out, "Lord, Son of David, have mercy on me! My daughter is suffering terribly from demon-possession."

At first, Jesus appears to pay no attention to her agony, and ignores her cry for relief. He gives her neither eye, nor ear, nor word. Silence, deep and chilling, greets her impassioned cry. But she is not turned aside, nor disheartened. She holds on. . . .

This last cry won her case; her daughter was healed in the self-same hour. Hopeful, urgent, and unwearied, she stays near the master, insisting and praying until the answer is given. What a study in importunity, in earnestness, in persistence, promoted and propelled under conditions which would have disheartened any but an heroic, a constant soul. . . .

An answer to prayer is conditional upon the amount of faith that goes to the petition. To test this, he delays the answer. The superficial pray-er subsides into silence, when the answer is delayed. But the man of prayer hangs on, and on. The Lord recognizes and honors his faith, and gives him a rich and abundant answer to his faith-evidencing, importunate prayer.

E. M. BOUNDS

SHE BELIEVED; SHE CAME

MATTHEW 15:24 KJV
*But he answered and said, I am not sent but
unto the lost sheep of the house of Israel.*

Our poor friend who was buffeted by our Lord's word was secretly upheld by the sight of his person. What can a word be compared with a person—compared with such a person as that of Jesus, the Sinner's Friend? She believes *him* rather than his way of speaking. He says that he is not sent, but there he is. He says that he is not sent but to the lost sheep of the house of Israel: and yet *here he is.* . . . She seems to say to herself, "Whether he was sent or not, here he is. He has come among Tyrians and Sidonians, and I have come to him, therefore he is not kept from me by his commission. I do not understand his language, but I do understand the look of his face, I do understand his manner. I do understand the winsomeness of his blessed person. I can see that compassion dwells in the Son of David. I am sure that he has all power given to him to heal my daughter; and here he is. I do not know about his commission, but I do know himself, and I shall still plead with him." So she came to Jesus there and *then,* and why should not you?

CHARLES HADDON SPURGEON

HARD, YET GRACIOUS, WORDS

MATTHEW 15:26 KJV

*But he answered and said, It is not meet to take
the children's bread, and to cast it to dogs.*

The Lord was once at a marriage feast, and they had
no wine. They had run out of it, and He made
more. That was gracious; but that is not what I am going
to speak about at present. He did it, but He did not go
there intending to do it; He did not want to do it. It was
at the entreaty of His mother, and to please His mother
that He did it; of course, if it had been wrong He would
not have done it to please His mother or anybody else.
His time was not come—He did not mean to begin it;
but as she wanted it He could afford to do it, and He did
it, and there is the grace of our Lord Jesus Christ.

Yes; and some of His hardest words are full of graciousness. Sometimes, for the sake of others, He inflicted pain
even upon those to whom He spoke; but, oh! how He
yielded afterward: "It is not meet to take the children's
bread, and to cast it to dogs." But we do not see how He
looked when He said it.

GEORGE MACDONALD

TONGUE *in* CHEEK

MATTHEW 15:27-28 NIV

"Yes, Lord," she said, "but even the dogs eat the crumbs that fall from their masters' table." Then Jesus answered, "Woman, you have great faith! Your request is granted."

Could it be that Jesus' tongue is poking his cheek? Could it be that he and the woman are engaging in satirical banter? Is it wry exchange in which God's unlimited grace is being highlighted? Could Jesus be so delighted to have found one who is not bartering with a religious system or proud of a heritage that he can't resist a bit of satire?

He knows he can heal her daughter. He knows he isn't bound by a plan. He knows her heart is good. So he decides to engage in a humorous moment with a faithful woman. In essence, here's what they said:

"Now, you know that God only cares about Jews," he says smiling.

And when she catches on, she volleys back, "But your bread is so precious, I'll be happy to eat the crumbs."

In a spirit of exuberance, he bursts out, "Never have I seen such faith! Your daughter is healed."

This story does not portray a contemptuous God. It portrays a willing One who delights in a sincere seeker.

Aren't you glad he does?

MAX LUCADO

GREAT THOUGHTS *of* CHRIST

MATTHEW 15:27 NKJV
*And she said, "Yes, Lord, yet even the little dogs
eat the crumbs which fall from their masters' table."*

She wanted . . . the devil cast out of her daughter. It was a very great thing to her, but she had such a high esteem of Christ that she said, "It is nothing to Him; it is but a crumb for Christ to give." This is the royal road to comfort. Great thoughts of your sin alone will drive you to despair; but great thoughts of Christ will guide you into the haven of peace. "My sins are many, but oh, it is nothing to Jesus to take them all away. The weight of my guilt presses me down as a giant's foot would crush a worm, but it is no more than a grain of dust to Him, because He has already borne its curse in His own body on the tree. It will be only a small thing for Him to give me full remission, although it will be an infinite blessing for me to receive it." The woman opens her needy soul very wide, expecting great things of Jesus, and He fills it with His love. Dear reader, do the same. *She won the victory by believing in Him.*

CHARLES HADDON SPURGEON

SAVIOR *to* ALL

MARK 7:29–30 NRSV

Then he said to her, "For saying that, you may go—
the demon has left your daughter." So she went home,
found the child lying on the bed, and the demon gone.

She smiled triumphantly, for she believed, beyond reason or evidence, in Jesus' power to overcome evil and
his willingness to bestow God's best gifts upon Gentiles as
well as Jews. . . . He pronounced the words she so greatly
desired to hear. "The evil spirit has left your daughter."

The Greek woman hurried home to find her daughter
lying quietly in bed, her demon departed and her torment ended. Like the Capernaum official's son and the
centurion's servant, this girl was delivered from her affliction by one whom she never saw, one to whom distance
was no barrier to the exercise of his healing power. The
most noteworthy aspect of her cure was that she, a Gentile girl, was healed by a Jew. This healing symbolized, as
had the coming of the wise men to Jesus' cradle, the
extension of Christ's kingdom to all nations. The old
mold in which men tried to contain God's saving power
for Israel alone was broken.

ALICE PARMELEE

DESCENDING *to the* VALLEY

LUKE 9:37-38 NRSV

*On the next day, when they had come down
from the mountain, a great crowd met him. Just then
a man from the crowd shouted, "Teacher, I beg you
to look at my son; he is my only child."*

The healing of the epileptic boy is definitely bound in
with the Transfiguration. Raphael in his great paint-
ing of the Transfiguration has caught this connection by
placing both scenes on one canvas. The scene of glory on
the Mount reveals the wonder and beauty of God's world,
where sin and death have no place. The scene of wretch-
edness below reveals the terribleness of the human plight,
where man is subjected to evils with which he cannot
cope. Had Christ, as Peter suggested (vs. 33), stayed on
the Mount of glory, the scene below would have remained unchanged. He had to leave the height, descend
once more into the valleys of human need, and confront
again the unbelief and stupidity of his own followers (vss.
45-50), the forces of evil which had man in their power,
the rejection of his people, the blindness of the religious
leaders, the mockery of the powers of world empire. All
this was brought to a focus in the Cross.

DONALD G. MILLER

LACKING PRAYER

LUKE 9:40 NASB
*"And I begged Your disciples to cast it out,
and they could not."*

Wherein lay the difficulty with these men? They had been lax in cultivating their faith by prayer and, as a consequence, their trust utterly failed. They trusted not God, nor Christ, nor the authenticity of his mission, or their own. So has it been many a time since, in many a crisis in the church of God. Failure has resulted from a lack of trust, or from a weakness of faith, and this, in turn, from a lack of prayerfulness. Many a failure in revival efforts has been traceable to the same cause. Faith had not been nurtured and made powerful by prayer. Neglect of the inner chamber is the solution of most spiritual failure. And this is as true of our personal struggles with the devil as was the case when we went forth to attempt to cast *out* devils. To be much on our knees in private communion with God is the only surety that we shall have him with us either in our personal struggles, or in our efforts to convert sinners.

E. M. BOUNDS

HARD REALITIES

MATTHEW 17:17 RSV
And Jesus answered, "O faithless and perverse
generation, how long am I to be with you?
How long am I to bear with you?"

In this incident the Apostles fall from the loftiest sum-
mits to the hard realities of daily life. Is it not often so
with us? A man throws himself at Jesus' feet and implores
his help for his son. His disciples have not been able to
cure him! Jesus has a singularly severe word which applies
both to his disciples and to ourselves. He accuses his contemporaries of being a "faithless and perverse generation."
He does not hide the fact that he has difficulty in enduring them. The impotence of the disciples shows how little is their faith! What is faith, for Jesus? It is not a simple
creedal belief; it is the assurance that everything is possible
to God, the assurance that he gives what he promises and
what he ordains. Faith is a power which "moves mountains." To remove mountains is to know that there is no
burden so heavy that God cannot help us to carry it, no
problem so insoluble that he cannot resolve it. If Jesus
accused his first disciples of unbelief, what does he think
of us today? What patience must he have to continue to
tolerate us?

SUZANNE DE DIETRICH

THINGS *as* THEY REALLY ARE

MARK 9:22 NKJV

"And often he has thrown him both into the fire and into the water to destroy him. But if You can do anything, have compassion on us and help us."

After every time of exaltation, we are brought down with a sudden rush into things as they really are, where it is neither beautiful, poetic, nor thrilling. The height of the mountaintop is measured by the dismal drudgery of the valley, but it is in the valley that we have to live for the glory of God. We *see* His glory on the mountain, but we never *live* for His glory there. It is in the place of humiliation that we find our true worth to God—that is where our faithfulness is revealed. . . .

When you were on the mountaintop you could believe anything, but what about when you were faced with the facts of the valley? You may be able to give a testimony regarding your sanctification, but what about the thing that is a humiliation to you right now? The last time you were on the mountain with God, you saw that all the power in heaven and on earth belonged to Jesus—will you be skeptical now, simply because you are in the valley of humiliation?

OSWALD CHAMBERS

BELIEF *and* UNBELIEF

MARK 9:23-24 NIV

"'If you can'?" said Jesus. "Everything is possible for him who believes." Immediately the boy's father exclaimed, "I do believe; help me overcome my unbelief!"

The father of the boy told him the sad story of his son's condition and of the helpless disciples. Then the Lord saw what the real problem was. The man was trying to get help and the disciples were trying to give it, all without faith in the God who could do it. . . .

Jesus asked to see the boy. When they brought him, his father said, "If you can do anything, take pity on us and help us." Now when the father said that, he was doing what many people do when they are in trouble. They know God can do anything but they think He won't, so they are really blaming God for letting things happen. Like them, this man's problem was not with Jesus or with His disciples, but with his own unbelief. He was not sure that Jesus wanted to help him.

Then Jesus told him plainly, "Everything is possible for him who believes." The man knew Jesus was right and he asked Him to help him with his problem of unbelief. Then when the Lord healed his son, he knew that Jesus could and would help those who completely trust in Him.

RALPH N. WALTER

IF YOU CAN

MARK 9:23 NASB

And Jesus said to him, "'If You can!'
All things are possible to him who believes."

Now there was an "if" in the question, but the poor trembling father had put the "if" in the wrong place. Jesus Christ, therefore, without commanding him to retract the "if," kindly puts it in its legitimate position. "Actually," He seemed to say, "there should be no 'if' about My power nor concerning My willingness; the 'if' lies somewhere else. *If you can believe,* 'all things are possible [to him] who believes.'" . . . There is a lesson here that we need to learn. We, like this man, often see that there is an "if" somewhere, but we are continually blundering by putting it in the wrong place. "If Jesus can help me"—"if He can give me grace to overcome temptation"—"if He can grant me pardon"—"if He can make me successful." No; *if* you can believe, He both can and will. You have misplaced your "if." If you can confidently trust, even as all things are possible to Christ, so will all things be possible to you. . . . My soul, can you believe your Lord tonight?

CHARLES HADDON SPURGEON

Faith *and* Doubt

———

Mark 9:24 KJV

And straightway the father of the child cried out, and said with tears, Lord, I believe; help thou mine unbelief.

What that father said showed a condition that is common to the heart of man, with faith and unbelief coexisting there. When we think of the great things of life, of our duty and our destiny and our salvation, both the voice of faith and the voice of doubt will speak. . . . So faith and unbelief grapple with one another in the soul of man. But what was true of this heartbroken father when he said to Jesus, "Lord, I believe; help thou mine unbelief," is true of all of us: we have the power and the will to choose the side of faith as against the side of unbelief. And when we make that choice we can count on the help and the sympathy of God. This father, troubled no doubt and somewhat mystified by what Jesus had said to him, and yet putting his trust in Jesus, resolved to be guided by his belief rather than his unbelief. He confessed his faith, and whatever doubt was left in him he asked Christ to overcome.

Clarence Edward Macartney

ROUTINE DEMANDS

LUKE 9:42 NLT

As the boy came forward, the demon knocked him
to the ground and threw him into a violent convulsion.
But Jesus rebuked the evil spirit and healed the boy.
Then he gave him back to his father.

He was ready to face the Cross and he was ready to
face the common problem just as either came. It is
characteristic of human nature that we can face the great
crisis-moments of life with honour and dignity, but allow
the routine demands of everyday to irritate and annoy us.
We can face the shattering blows of life with a certain
heroism, but allow the petty pinpricks to upset us. Many
a man can face a great disaster or a great loss with calm
serenity and yet loses his temper if a meal is badly cooked
or a train late. The amazing thing about Jesus was that he
could serenely face the Cross, and just as calmly deal with
the day-to-day emergencies of life. The reason was that
he did not keep God only for the crisis as so many of us
do. He walked the daily paths of life with him.

WILLIAM BARCLAY

HIS AUTHORITY

MARK 9:28 NIV
After Jesus had gone indoors, his disciples asked him privately, "Why couldn't we drive it out?"

Each ministry of Jesus—preaching, teaching, counseling, and healing—seems to draw strength from the other. For instance, the healing of the epileptic boy led to a closed seminar with the disciples; Jesus' sermon in the synagogue produced a debate with the scribes; and his counseling with the rich young ruler prompted a parable on the danger of riches. As his balanced style renewed his spirit, his complementary ministries increased his *authority*. Jesus could soar in the realm of ideas and yet drive home the truth with a pragmatic hammer. Because he lived on the raw edge of human need, his proclamation of truth always had a personal touch in which men and women saw themselves. In contrast to the pedantic utterances of the scribes and Pharisees, Jesus gained added vitality and authority from his versatility. No wonder the people marveled, "No man ever spoke like that" (John 7:46).

DAVID L. McKENNA

WHAT IS *between* YOU *and* JESUS?

MARK 9:29 NKJV
So He said to them, "This kind can come
out by nothing but prayer and fasting."

We can remain powerless forever, as the disciples were in this situation, by trying to do God's work without concentrating on His power, and by following instead the ideas that we draw from our own nature. We actually slander and dishonor God by our very eagerness to serve Him without knowing Him.

When you are brought face to face with a difficult situation and nothing happens externally, you can still know that freedom and release will be given because of your continued concentration on Jesus Christ. Your duty in service and ministry is to see that there is nothing between Jesus and yourself. Is there anything between you and Jesus even now? If there is, you must get through it, not by ignoring it as an irritation, or by going up and over it, but by facing it and getting through it into the presence of Jesus Christ. Then that very problem itself, and all that you have been through in connection with it, will glorify Jesus Christ in a way that you will never know until you see Him face to face.

OSWALD CHAMBERS

YOU MUST ASK

MATTHEW 17:21 NKJV

*"However, this kind does not go out
except by prayer and fasting."*

This divine teacher of prayer lays himself out to make it clear and strong that God answers prayer, assuredly, certainly, inevitably; that it is the duty of the child to ask, and to press, and that the Father is obliged to answer, and to give for the asking. In Christ's teaching, prayer is no sterile, vain performance, not a mere rite, a form, but a request for an answer, a plea to gain, the seeking of a great good from God. It is a lesson of getting that for which we ask, of finding that for which we seek, and of entering the door at which we knock.

A notable occasion we have as Jesus comes down from the Mount of Transfiguration. He finds his disciples defeated, humiliated, and confused in the presence of their enemies. . . .

Their faith had not been cultured by prayer. They failed in prayer before they failed in ability to do their work. They failed in faith because they had failed in prayer. That one thing which was necessary to do God's work was prayer. The work which God sends us to do cannot be done without prayer.

E. M. BOUNDS

Love *in* Action

Mark 16:9 NKJV
*Now when He rose early on the first day of
the week, He appeared first to Mary Magdalene,
out of whom He had cast seven demons.*

Mary Magdalene has been mentioned earlier in this Gospel as one of the women at the cross and at the tomb (15:40, 47; 16:1). Mark reminded his readers of the reason for her devotion to Jesus: He had cast seven demons from her (see also Luke 8:2). The specifics of that particular healing are not recorded in any of the Gospels, although several accounts of Jesus casting out demons show the extreme horror of demon possession. It was to this devoted and sorrowful woman that Jesus made his first appearance after the Resurrection.

We don't know why Mary was chosen as the first, but that fact should be very encouraging. She was a sinner, a woman with a severely troubled past. Yet her simple faith, courage, and love mark her as praiseworthy, not just for her quiet faith, but for her love in action.

Life Application Bible Commentary—Mark

A MIRACLE *of* GRACE

MARK 16:9 NASB
*He first appeared to Mary Magdalene,
from whom He had cast out seven demons.*

Mary of Magdala was *the victim of a fearful evil*. She was possessed not just by one demon, but by seven. These dreadful inmates caused much pain and pollution to the poor frame in which they had found a lodging. Hers was a hopeless, horrible case. She could not help herself, and no human power could set her free. But Jesus passed that way, and without being asked and probably while being resisted by the poor demoniac, He uttered the word of power, and Mary of Magdala became *a trophy of the healing power of Jesus*. All seven demons left her, left her never to return, forcibly ejected by the Lord of all. What a blessed deliverance! What a happy change! From delirium to delight, from despair to peace, from hell to heaven! . . . Grace found her useless and made her useful, cast out her demons and gave her to behold angels, delivered her from Satan and united her forever to the Lord Jesus. May we also be such miracles of grace!

CHARLES HADDON SPURGEON

JESUS' MIRACLES
OVER DEATH

———

Jesus said to her,
"I am the resurrection and the life."
JOHN 11:25 NIV

JESUS' MIRACLES OVER DEATH

Compared to His other miracles, Jesus raised few people from the dead. Only three are described at any length: two young people and Lazarus. This little group represents hundreds of people each day who have not lived full lives yet die. It was not Jesus' purpose to reverse the effects of the Fall. People still die. Those three just mentioned eventually died again. But their temporary resurrections demonstrated that death isn't final. Through them, Jesus showed us that death can be—and will be—defeated.

These death-defying miracles also had other objectives. They provided startling lessons in how far Jesus was willing to go to glorify His Father. For example, He risked deeply offending His dear friends Mary, Martha, and Lazarus by disappointing them in order to give them an even greater gift of delight! And through it all, God received glory. By faith, your own death will give Jesus yet another opportunity to glorify God! Keep that possibility in mind as you reflect on these instances of Jesus' power over death.

PREPARE *for* ETERNITY

ROMANS 8:38-39 KJV
For I am persuaded, that neither death, nor life, nor angels, nor principalities, nor powers, nor things present, nor things to come, Nor height, nor depth, nor any other creature, shall be able to separate us from the love of God, which is in Christ Jesus our Lord.

To whatever world death introduce you, the best conceivable preparation for it is to labour for the highest good of the world in which you live. Be the change which death brings what it may, he who has spent his life in trying to make this world better can never be unprepared for another. . . .

Live in this, find your dearest work here, let love to God and man be the animating principle of your being; and then, let death come when it may, and carry you where it will, you will not be unprepared for it. The rending of the veil which hides the secrets of the unseen world, the summons that calls you into regions unknown, need awaken in your breast no perturbation or dismay; for you cannot in God's universe go where love and truth and self-devotion are things of naught, or where a soul, filled with undying faith in the progress and identifying its own happiness with the final triumph of goodness, shall find itself forsaken.

JOHN CAIRD

GIVEN ANOTHER LIFE

LUKE 7:12 NRSV

*As he approached the gate of the town, a man
who had died was being carried out. He was his
mother's only son, and she was a widow; and with
her was a large crowd from the town.*

The world has for Him no chamber of terror. He
walks to the door of the sepulcher, the sealed cellar
of His Father's house, and calls forth its four-days dead.
He rebukes the mourners, He stays the funeral, and gives
back the departed children to their parents' arms. The
roughest of its servants do not make Him wince; none of
them are so arrogant as to disobey His word; He falls
asleep in the midst of the storm that threatens to swallow
His boat. Hear how, on that same occasion, He rebukes
his disciples! The children to tremble at a gust of wind in
the house! God's little ones afraid of the storm! Hear Him
tell the watery floor to be still. . . .

GEORGE MACDONALD

DON'T CRY

LUKE 7:13 NIV
*When the Lord saw her, his heart went
out to her and he said, "Don't cry."*

Do you remember the widow of Nain who had only one son, and when he died she went out to bury him (Luke 7:11—17)? Jesus met the funeral procession and touched the bier where the dead man was lying. This was absolutely incredible to the Jews who were there. Surely Jesus had defiled Himself by touching a dead body. But His touch resurrected the young man. When Jesus first met the widow, she was mourning. (This was, after all, her only son and she might now become destitute.) Jesus simply said to her, "Don't cry." What does this comment tell us about Jesus' heart? He cared for women. He cared for this widow, and He cared for her dead son. He touched the dead and they arose. He was life; He was resurrection.

JILL BRISCOE

HE UNDERSTANDS

———

LUKE 7:14 NIV
Then he went up and touched the coffin,
and those carrying it stood still. He said,
"Young man, I say to you, get up!"

Compassion is another important lesson Jesus taught us. He often broke with tradition and had little regard for the status quo. One of the greatest examples of this can be found in Luke 7:11-15, when Jesus stopped a funeral procession and spoke to the woman who had just lost her only son. For a Jewish widow to lose a son was devastating because now she had lost her total support. Her husband and son were both gone. But Jesus had such compassion for this grieving woman that He stopped the funeral procession and touched the dead boy. This was unheard of in Jewish custom, because Jews feared contamination from a corpse. But Jesus told the dead boy to rise, and the boy sat up, spoke, and was returned to his mother. Jesus understands your grief. Maybe you've lost a child, maybe you've had a miscarriage, maybe you have infertility, maybe you have an illness and you've been told you don't have long to live. Whatever the problem, Jesus understands your grief. His arms are open wide, and He wants to touch you with His compassion, His mercy, and His grace.

DAVID HAGER

HE SAW HER

LUKE 7:15 NLT

Then the dead boy sat up and began to talk to those around him! And Jesus gave him back to his mother.

The one thing that stands out so visibly to me in this encounter Jesus had with the widow is that he "saw her" (Luke 7:13 NLT). This woman never called for help, did not exercise faith and sought no miracle. Yet Jesus saw her sadness, her grief and her hurt. He did not look beyond her, like we have a tendency to do. He really saw her.

Jesus not only saw the widow of Nain, "his heart went out to her" (Luke 7:13 NIV). He didn't just acknowledge that she was in pain, he suffered with her. A woman with sorrows met the man of sorrows. . . .

God sees you and he feels for you. When you hurt, he hurts. When you are in pain, he is in pain. His love for us moves him to great compassion.

That day in Nain, Jesus crossed the path of a funeral procession. In so doing, he raised a mother's only son to life. But the miracle wasn't for the boy; it was for the mother. Jesus raised a dead man to life, not to bring attention to himself, but to show compassion toward this woman.

RICK EZELL

THE LAST RESORT?

MATTHEW 9:18 NRSV

*While he was saying these things to them, suddenly
a leader of the synagogue came in and knelt before him,
saying, "My daughter has just died; but come and
lay your hand on her, and she will live."*

It is clear that such a man would come to Jesus only as
a last resort. He would be one of those strictly ortho-
dox Jews who regarded Jesus as a dangerous heretic; and
it was only when everything else had failed that he turned
in desperation to Jesus. Jesus might well have said to him,
"When things were going well with you, you wanted to
kill me; now that things are going ill, you are appealing for
my help." And Jesus might well have refused help to a
man who came like that. But he bore no grudge; here was
a man who needed him, and Jesus' one desire was to help.
Injured pride and the unforgiving spirit had no part in the
mind of Jesus. . . .

Jesus that day in Capernaum rescued a Jewish maid
from the grasp of death.

WILLIAM BARCLAY

CALM SERENITY

MARK 5:40 NRSV

*They laughed at him. Then he put them all outside,
and took the child's father and mother and those who
were with him, and went in where the child was.*

There is the contrast between *the unrestrained distress* of
the mourners and *the calm serenity* of Jesus. They
were wailing and weeping and tearing their hair and
rending their garments in a paroxysm of distress; he was
calm and quiet and serene and in control.

Why this difference? It was due to Jesus' perfect confidence and trust in God. The worst human disaster can be
met with courage and gallantry when we meet it with
God. They laughed him to scorn because they thought
his hope was groundless and his calm mistaken. But the
great fact of the Christian life is that what looks completely impossible with men is possible with God. What
on merely human grounds is far too good to be true,
becomes blessedly true when God is there. They laughed
him to scorn, but their laughter must have turned to
amazed wonder when they realized what God can do.
There is nothing beyond facing, and there is nothing
beyond conquest—not even death—when it is faced and
conquered in the love of God which is in Christ Jesus our
Lord.

WILLIAM BARCLAY

BELIEVE ONLY

LUKE 8:50 KJV
But when Jesus heard it, he answered him,
saying, Fear not: believe only.

Only believe what? *She* was dead; it was all over! Only believe that the Almighty One is still beside you, Jairus; only believe what your heart sensed when you first saw in His eyes that He would go with you; only believe in the dark what He told you in the light a few moments ago; only believe that He does all things well, that nothing is too hard for Him! And believing to what must have seemed the bitter end, Jairus found that the delight of assurance that had been dimmed by delay and dismay into desperation and utter disillusionment came to be the dawning and culmination of desire, when his daughter was restored whole, and hungry, to him. . . .

He tests us that we may trust Him, He waits that we may know His grace, He tarries that we may learn with Jairus and Mary and Martha, that if we believe we shall see the glory of God—not only in heaven, but right here and now!

He arises and goes with us.

V. RAYMOND EDMAN

WAKE UP!

MARK 5:41 KJV
*And he took the damsel by the hand,
and said unto her,* Talitha cumi; *which is,
being interpreted, Damsel, I say unto thee, arise.*

Talitha cumi" was an expression of the Aramaic that the little girl would have understood. It was her native tongue and I think it could be translated "Little lamb, wake up!" That's what He said to her and that is a sweet, lovely thing. We find that our Lord raised a little girl, He raised a man in the vigor of young manhood (the widow's son at Nain), and then probably a mature man or even a senior citizen, Lazarus. He raised them all the same way. He spoke to them!

I think this little girl represents the little folks, those little ones before they reach the age of accountability. And He said to her in this lovely way, "Little lamb, wake up." I know right now I'm speaking to a lot of folk who have lost little ones. When we lost our first little one, what a sad thing it was for us. It's wonderful for me to know that although she has been in His presence for many years, one of these days He's going to speak those words again, "Little lamb, wake up!"

J. VERNON MCGEE

An Open Door

MARK 5:41–42 NKJV

*Then He took the child by the hand, and said
to her, "Talitha, cumi," which is translated, "Little girl,
I say to you, arise." Immediately the girl arose and
walked, for she was twelve years of age. And they
were overcome with great amazement.*

In Aramaic *talitha cumi* means "little girl, get up." . . .
The occasion took place at the man's house. There was
plenty of the kind of sorrow you expect when anybody
that young dies. And that's one of the great uses of funer-
als surely, to be cited when people protest that they're bar-
baric holdovers from the past, that you should celebrate
the life rather than mourn the death, and so on. Celebrate
the life by all means but face up to the death of that
life. . . .

The child was dead, but Jesus, when he got there, said
she was only asleep. He said the same thing when his
friend Lazarus died. Death is not any more permanent
than sleep is permanent is what he meant apparently. That
isn't to say he took death lightly. When he heard about
Lazarus, he wept, and it's hard to imagine him doing any
differently here. But if death is the closing of one door, he
seems to say, it is the opening of another one. *Talitha cumi.*

FREDERICK BUECHNER

HIS ULTIMATE OFFER

Now a certain man was ill, Lazarus of Bethany, the village of Mary and her sister Martha. . . . So the sisters sent a message to Jesus, "Lord, he whom you love is ill." But when Jesus heard it, he said, "This illness does not lead to death; rather it is for God's glory, so that the Son of God may be glorified through it."

The miracles are pictures of what Jesus offers to do in the human heart. His opening the eyes of a blind beggar, Bartimaeus, is a picture of the new vision He offers to us all. His healing of paralyzed people is a picture of the new power He makes available to those who put their lives in His hand. His turning of water into wine shows how He can change the ordinary drudgery of life into high-octane living. His feeding of the multitude shows how He longs to be the bread that satisfies the believer's heart. His raising of Lazarus from the grave points to His ultimate offer: to give new and eternal life to all who trust themselves to Him. That is one of the main reasons why Jesus worked miracles. He wanted to make concrete before the imaginations of His contemporaries (and their successors) the spiritual revolution He was longing to bring about in their lives.

MICHAEL GREEN

HIS SILENCE

JOHN 11:6 NKJV
*So, when He heard that he was sick, He stayed
two more days in the place where He was.*

Has God trusted you with His silence—a silence that has great meaning? God's silences are actually His answers. Just think of those days of absolute silence in the home at Bethany! Is there anything comparable to those days in your life? Can God trust you like that, or are you still asking Him for a visible answer? God will give you the very blessings you ask if you refuse to go any further without them, but His silence is the sign that He is bringing you into an even more wonderful understanding of Himself. Are you mourning before God because you have not had an audible response? When you cannot hear God, you will find that He has trusted you in the most intimate way possible—with absolute silence, not a silence of despair, but one of pleasure, because He saw that you could withstand an even bigger revelation. If God has given you a silence, then praise Him—He is bringing you into the mainstream of His purposes.

OSWALD CHAMBERS

THE GRANDER ANSWER

JOHN 11:6 KJV

When he had heard therefore that he was sick,
he abode two days still in the same place where he was.

And so the silence of God was itself an answer. It is not merely said that there was no audible response to the cry from Bethany; it is distinctly stated that the absence of an audible response was itself the answer to the cry—it was *when* the Lord heard that Lazarus was sick that *therefore* He abode two days still in the same place where He was. I have often heard the outward silence. A hundred times have I sent up aspirations whose only answer has seemed to be the echo of my own voice, and I have cried out in the night of my despair, *"Why art Thou so far from helping me?"* But I never thought that the seeming farness was itself the nearness of God—that the very silence was an answer.

It was a very grand answer to the household of Bethany. They had asked *not too much,* but *too little.* They had asked only the life of Lazarus. They were to get the life of Lazarus and a revelation of eternal life as well.

GEORGE MATHESON

A TRULY DIVINE WORK

JOHN 11:14–15 KJV

Then said Jesus unto them plainly, Lazarus is dead. And I am glad for your sakes that I was not there, to the intent ye may believe; nevertheless let us go unto him.

His power would have been less illustriously displayed if he had instantly given assistance to Lazarus. For the more nearly the works of God approach to the ordinary course of nature, the less highly are they valued, and the less illustriously is their glory displayed. This is what we experience daily; for if God immediately stretches out his hand, we do not perceive his assistance. That the resurrection of Lazarus, therefore, might be acknowledged by the disciples to be truly a divine work, it must be delayed, that it might be very widely removed from a human remedy. . . .

The fatherly kindness of God towards us is here represented in the person of Christ. When God permits us to be overwhelmed with distresses, and to languish long under them, let us know that, in this manner, he promotes our salvation. At such a time, no doubt, we groan and are perplexed and sorrowful, but the Lord rejoices on account of our benefit, and gives a twofold display of his kindness to us in this respect.

JOHN CALVIN

WAIT *for* HIM

JOHN 11:14–15 NKJV

Then Jesus said to them plainly, "Lazarus is dead.
And I am glad for your sakes that I was not there,
that you may believe. Nevertheless let us go to him."

The case of Lazarus was an instance of where there was delay, where the faith of two good women was sorely tried: Lazarus was critically ill, and his sisters sent for Jesus. But, without any known reason, our Lord delayed his going to the relief of his sick friend. The plea was urgent and touching—"Lord, behold, he whom thou lovest is sick"—but the master is not moved by it, and the women's earnest request seemed to fall on deaf ears. What a trial to faith! Furthermore: our Lord's tardiness appeared to bring about hopeless disaster. While Jesus tarried, Lazarus died.

But the delay of Jesus was exercised in the interests of a greater good. Finally, he makes his way to the home in Bethany.

Fear not, O tempted and tried believer, Jesus *will* come, if patience is exercised, and faith holds fast. His delay will serve to make his coming the more richly blessed. Pray on. Wait on. You cannot fail. If Christ delay, wait for him. In his own good time, he *will* come, and will not tarry.

E. M. BOUNDS

THE BETTER ANSWER

JOHN 11:25 NIV
Jesus said to her,
"I am the resurrection and the life."

Standing at their brother's tomb, Mary and Martha grieved their loss. Martha questioned Jesus' timing. "If you had been here," Martha said, "my brother would not have died!"

But Jesus is never late. Gently he reminded Martha of his awesome power and limitless love. "I am the resurrection and the life," he said. Then he called to Lazarus, the dead man, and commanded that he come forth. And Lazarus did, still wrapped in his burial clothes.

What loss threatens to unravel your life? As you stand among the gravestones, what questions or demands do you have for the Lord? Remember, Jesus is never late. In his infinite understanding, perfect timing, and deep concern, he will hear your cry, answer your prayer, and bring life. In the meantime, keep resting in his sovereignty and trusting in his love.

DAVE VEERMAN

HE IS NEVER LATE

JOHN 11:25-26 NIV

Jesus said to her, "I am the resurrection and the life.
He who believes in me will live, even though he dies;
and whoever lives and believes in me will never die.
Do you believe this?"

Some prayers are followed by silence because they are
wrong, others because they are bigger than we can
understand. Jesus stayed where He was—a positive staying, because He loved Martha and Mary. Did they get
Lazarus back? They got infinitely more; they got to know
the greatest truth mortal beings ever knew—that Jesus
Christ is the Resurrection and the Life. It will be a wonderful moment for some of us when we stand before God
and find that the prayers we clamored for in early days
and imagined were never answered, have been answered
in the most amazing way, and that God's silence has been
the sign of the answer.

OSWALD CHAMBERS

DO YOU BELIEVE?

JOHN 11:26 NKJV
"Do you believe this?"

Martha believed in the power available to Jesus Christ; she believed that if He had been there He could have healed her brother; she also believed that Jesus had a special intimacy with God, and that whatever He asked of God, God would do. But—she needed a closer personal intimacy with Jesus. . . .

Is the Lord dealing with you in the same way? Is Jesus teaching you to have a personal intimacy with Himself? Allow Him to drive His question home to you—"Do you believe this?" Are you facing an area of doubt in your life? Have you come, like Martha, to a crossroads of overwhelming circumstances where your theology is about to become a very personal belief? This happens only when a personal problem brings the awareness of our personal need. . . .

Then, when I stand face to face with Jesus Christ and He says to me, "Do you believe this?" I find that faith is as natural as breathing. And I am staggered when I think how foolish I have been in not trusting Him earlier.

OSWALD CHAMBERS

IN HIS IMAGE

JOHN 11:26 KJV
Believest thou this?

He is asking Martha and all of us whether we really believe that He is able to give a sure and certain expectation to each of us, that we may know in our thinking and in our emotions, in our "bones," so to speak, that His death and Resurrection will give us future changed bodies over which death can have no power. The victory which Christ died to give us has a future aspect that we know will one day take place and then be history. *That* victory is the one that will destroy death. Bodies, those same bodies, are to be raised from the dead in exact likeness to Christ's body after His Resurrection. He, who made us in His image, came in a body like ours—which died for us and rose for us. That resurrected form shows us what *we* are to be like through all eternity, in the image of the resurrected Christ.

EDITH SCHAEFFER

HE WEEPS

JOHN 11:35 KJV
Jesus wept.

Over the centuries, Christians have cherished this amazing passage, which demonstrates Jesus' power over life and death. But by focusing on the dramatic miracle of Lazarus's resurrection, have we overlooked the importance of Jesus' tears? . . .

For more than thirty years, he walked this earth, tasting the joys and tragedies of ordinary life. In time his deep love would lead him to pay the ultimate price—sacrificing his own life on the cross in order to save us from our sin.

Jesus' tears show that he feels as we do.

As with our own tears, his came only after he could no longer contain the swelling waves of sorrow. The droplets that spilled down his face reveal that he can understand our broken dreams, our dashed hopes, and the many pains that come from dealing with life and loss.

Jesus understands, and the Savior who raised Lazarus will someday raise us.

STEVE AND LOIS RABEY

Come Out!

John 11:39 NCV

Jesus said, "Move the stone away." Martha, the sister of the dead man, said, "But, Lord, it has been four days since he died. There will be a bad smell."

What Jesus did with Lazarus, he is willing to do with us. Which is good to know, for what Martha said about Lazarus can be said about us, "But, Lord, it has been four days since he died. There will be a bad smell" (John 11:39). Martha was speaking for us all. The human race is dead, and there is a bad smell. We have been dead and buried a long time. We don't need someone to fix us up; we need someone to raise us up. In the muck and mire of what we call life, there is death, and we have been in it so long we've grown accustomed to the stink. But Christ hasn't.

And Christ can't stand the thought of his kids rotting in the cemetery. So he comes in and calls us out. We are the corpse, and he is the corpse-caller. We are the dead, and he is the dead-raiser. Our task is not to get up but to admit we are dead. The only ones who remain in the grave are the ones who don't think they are there.

Max Lucado

TRUE *to* HIS PROMISE

JOHN 11:40 NIV
*Then Jesus said, "Did I not tell you that if you
believed, you would see the glory of God?"*

And even though Mary and Martha spent time with
Jesus on a regular basis, it was hard for them to
believe when He said their brother Lazarus's "sickness will
not end in death." Really, who could blame Mary and
Martha? When Lazarus died, the situation looked impos-
sibly bleak. How would Jesus stay true to His word that
the sickness wouldn't end in death when Lazarus had
already died?

Well, it's likely you know the rest of the story. Jesus
raised Lazarus from the dead and, like always, Jesus remained true to His promise. . . .

Yes, God continues to perform miracles today by freeing people from the bondage they experience. Bodies are
healed, lives are healed, homes are healed. Perhaps you
have experienced some kind of physical or emotional
healing, or you know someone who has. Whatever we
may have experienced in the way of modern miracles,
no miracle compares to the miracle of salvation that Jesus
performs every day when people are forgiven and healed
of the spiritual disease of sin.

DEREK WEBB

THAT YOU MAY BELIEVE

JOHN 11:41–42 NIV

So they took away the stone. Then Jesus looked up
and said, "Father, I thank you that you have heard me.
I knew that you always hear me, but I said this for
the benefit of the people standing here, that they
may believe that you sent me."

Nowhere else had Jesus prayed with an over-the-shoulder audience in mind, like a Shakespearean actor who turns to the crowd to deliver an aside. At this moment Jesus seemed self-consciously aware of his dual identity, simultaneously the One who came down from heaven and the Son of Man born on earth.

The public prayer, the loud voice, the gestures—these have all the marks of a spiritual battle under way. Jesus was making a point, working out a "sign" in full public view, and here as nowhere else he acknowledged the in-between state of God's creation. Jesus knew, of course, that Lazarus was now whole and content, in every way better for having shuffled off this mortal coil. . . .

At that very moment Jesus himself hung between two worlds. . . . That his own death would also end in resurrection did not reduce the fear or the pain. He was human: he had to pass through Golgotha to reach the other side.

PHILIP YANCEY

I THANK THEE

JOHN 11:41-42 KJV

Then they took away the stone from the place where
the dead was laid. And Jesus lifted up his eyes, and
said, Father, I thank thee that thou hast heard me.
And I knew that thou hearest me always: but because
of the people which stand by I said it, that they
may believe that thou hast sent me.

There are these things remarkable in Christ's raising
Lazarus from the dead (John 11:41): that he called
upon God before he did it, to do it for him, and thanked
him that he had heard him and told him that he knew
that he heard him always. When he spoke to him he
called him Father and told him that he spoke to him for
this end: that others that stood by, when they should see
that what he asked of him was granted in such an extraordinary thing, might believe that he sent him. Now can it
be imagined that God would thus hear an impostor? Or
so order or suffer it that so extraordinary a thing should
be done immediately, in consequence of the request and
act of an impostor, who was so impudent when he asked
it as to call him Father, told him that he always heard him,
and told him that he spoke thus that others might see that
he did indeed give a testimony to his mission and authority, by doing it at his request, in such a manner?

JONATHAN EDWARDS

I LIVE

JOHN 11:43 KJV
*And when he thus had spoken, he cried
with a loud voice, Lazarus, come forth.*

After one moment when I bowed my head
And the whole world turned over and came
upright,
And I came out where the old road shone white,
I walked the ways and heard what all men said,
Forests of tongues, like autumn leaves unshed
Being not unlovable but strange and light;
Old riddles and new creeds, not in despite
But softly, as men smile about the dead.

The sages have a hundred maps to give
That trace their crawling cosmos like a tree,
They rattle reason out through many a sieve
That stores the sand and lets the gold go free:
And all these things are less than dust to me
Because my name is Lazarus and I live.

G. K. CHESTERTON

WHERE WERT THOU?

———

JOHN 11:44 KJV

*And he that was dead came forth, bound hand and foot
with graveclothes: and his face was bound about with a
napkin. Jesus saith unto them, Loose him, and let him go.*

When Lazarus left his charnel-cave,
    And home to Mary's house returned,
    Was this demanded—if he yearned
To hear her weeping by his grave?

"Where wert thou, brother, these four days?"
    There lives no record of reply,
    Which telling what it is to die
Had surely added praise to praise.

From every house the neighbours met,
    The streets were filled with joyful sound
    A solemn gladness even crowned
The purple brows of Olivet.

Behold a man raised up by Christ!
    The rest remaineth unrevealed;
    He told it not; or something sealed
The lips of that Evangelist.

ALFRED, LORD TENNYSON

BREAKING *the* POWER *of* DEATH

MATTHEW 27:52-53 NIV

The tombs broke open and the bodies of many holy
people who had died were raised to life. They came
out of the tombs, and after Jesus' resurrection they
went into the holy city and appeared to many people.

In Scripture, earthquakes symbolized God's mighty acts
(see Judges 5:4; 1 Kings 19:11; Psalm 114:7-8; Isaiah
29:6; Joel 3:16; Nahum 1:5-6; Matthew 28:2; Acts 16:26;
Revelation 6:12; 8:5). The opening of the tombs and
people coming back to life revealed that by Jesus' death,
the power of death was broken. Whether this event happened at Jesus' death or at his resurrection (for the people
did not go into the city until after Jesus' resurrection), the
resurrection of Jesus and of these holy people inaugurated
the new age of salvation, the beginning of the "Last
Days." (See also Ezekiel 37:1-14 and Daniel 12:2 for the
Jewish expectation of a bodily resurrection.)

LIFE APPLICATION BIBLE COMMENTARY—MATTHEW

DON'T FORGET

JOHN 14:11 NIV
*"At least believe on the evidence
of the miracles themselves."*

How could the disciples forget, or if they hadn't for-gotten, *how could they so easily dismiss the miracles* they had seen firsthand? . . .

He had changed water into wine.

He had restored mobility to a man who had been paralyzed for thirty-eight years.

He had healed the royal official's son without ever even going to see him.

He had fed five thousand people until they were full using only five loaves and two fish.

He had walked on the surface of the Sea of Galilee.

He had created sight in a man born blind.

He had raised Lazarus from the dead.

And those were only the miracles that John could quickly tick off in his mind! There were so many others. . . . The disciples must have lost count of them all. The list could go on and on. How could they have rationalized that the miracles were anything other than *proof* that Jesus *was God* in their midst? And if Jesus was God in their midst, He could most certainly be taken at His Word.

ANNE GRAHAM LOTZ

JESUS' MIRACULOUS RESURRECTION

—

"Because I live, you will live also."
JOHN 14:19 NKJV

JESUS' MIRACULOUS RESURRECTION

As with all of Christ's miracles, the resurrection was not an end but a means. Jesus didn't rise from the grave to prove that He could; He rose from the grave to highlight every other promise He made. He rose from the grave to defeat death and Satan. He died on the cross to obtain our pardon, but He left the tomb to personally guarantee our forgiveness. He rose from the grave to give us a prelude for eternal life.

The resurrection of Jesus places Christianity in a category of its own. Without the bodily resurrection of Jesus, His followers are just another large group of believers in a more-or-less religious system. Without the resurrection, Christianity is a major religion. With a risen Lord, however, Christianity is a supernatural relationship between the Son of God and those who trust Him. Those who reject the resurrection of Jesus are left with little but the despair of their own efforts to merit eternal benefits. The infinitely better choice involves the hope-filled realization that because Jesus lives, so can we.

THE GREATEST MIRACLE

———

1 CORINTHIANS 15:20 NRSV
*But in fact Christ has been raised from the dead, the
first fruits of those who have died.*

We are talking about the *resurrection* of Jesus. We are
not talking about his 'survival' of death in some
vague way. We are not talking about appearances of his
"ghost." We are certainly not talking simply about his
continued influence in the world. We are talking about
the resurrection of his dead body, about his personal victory over death, about a tomb that was empty, not because
the body had dissolved but because he was gloriously
alive again. We are using the term "resurrection" in its
normal dictionary meaning, "restoration to life." . . .

The Lord Jesus performed many miracles himself. The
gospels record in detail quite a number of them. Many of
them deal with diseases of various kinds, or with cases of
demon possession. In such phenomena death casts its
shadow before it, and Christ's touch of life banished some
part of that shadow. But in his resurrection, Christ was
both the subject and the object of the greatest miracle,
and he dealt with no symptom of man's subjection to
death, but with death itself.

GEOFFREY W. GROGAN

GATEWAY *to* LIFE

1 CORINTHIANS 15:20 NKJV
*But now Christ is risen from the dead, and has
become the firstfruits of those who have fallen asleep.*

Why is it so important to believe in the Resurrection? . . . The picture Paul gives us is of the firstfruits of a harvest, the promise of what is to come. He is the firstfruits of God's harvest of souls—and we are the rest of the harvest.

Paul says the hope of the Resurrection is the reason he is willing to go through intense suffering for Christ. What would be the point he asks, if Christ were not truly alive? By far the biggest problem in life is death. We spend billions of dollars trying to put off the evil day that none of us can escape. But for the Christian the stone has been rolled away from the tomb of death. It's empty! Death for the Christian is the gateway into life. Christ has gone before to tell us there is a new world ahead of us and we can face the grave with utmost confidence in that promise.

JILL BRISCOE

FIRSTFRUITS

—

1 CORINTHIANS 15:23 KJV

*But every man in his own order: Christ the firstfruits;
afterward they that are Christ's at his coming.*

It is, indeed, in accordance with the nature of the invisible God that He should be thus known through His works; and those who doubt the Lord's resurrection because they do not now behold Him with their eyes, might as well deny the very laws of nature. They have ground for disbelief when works are lacking; but when the works cry out and prove the fact so clearly, why do they deliberately deny the risen life so manifestly shown? Even if their mental faculties are defective, surely their eyes can give them irrefragable proof of the power and Godhead of Christ. A blind man cannot see the sun, but he knows that it is above the earth from the warmth which it affords; similarly, let those who are still in the blindness of unbelief recognize the Godhead of Christ and the resurrection which He has brought about through His manifested power in others. . . .

He it is Who has destroyed death and freely graced us all with incorruption through the promise of the resurrection, having raised His own body as its first-fruits, and displayed it by the sign of the cross as the monument to His victory over death and its corruption.

ATHANASIUS

HOW CAN WE KNOW?

MARK 10:34 NCV

"They will beat him with whips and crucify him. But on the third day, he will rise to life again."

How do we *know* Jesus rose from the dead? . . . Before any of the events had occurred, Jesus made no less than ten specific predictions about His death and resurrection, all of which came true. . . .

Even critics agree Jesus was crucified and died at Roman hands and that the location of His tomb was public knowledge. Nor can anyone logically deny that a one- to two-ton stone was rolled over the face of the grave. A highly trained Roman military guard was set at the grave to prevent anyone from stealing the body. But almost everyone agrees, critics included, that the tomb was found empty on Sunday morning. . . .

There were numerous resurrection appearances of Christ after His death. He appeared to many different people—to disciples who did not believe it at first, to a crowd of 500, and to selected individuals. He appeared to them in many different ways, locations, and circumstances. These appearances eventually compelled belief, despite skepticism, as the accounts reveal.

JOHN ANKERBERG & JOHN WELDON

COME ON *and* CELEBRATE!

MATTHEW 28:6 NIV
He is not here; he has risen, just as he said.
Come and see the place where he lay.

The most exciting three words in the English language are "He is risen." The angel beside Jesus' open tomb spoke these words to the women who had come to anoint Jesus' dead body. The angel asked them why they were looking in a grave for someone who was alive. Jesus was no longer there! He is alive! He is risen! He lives forevermore.

Surely those three days while Jesus lay in the tomb were filled with darkness. Jesus had died, and along with Him seemed to go the dreams and hopes of so many. The women who came to anoint His body surely believed that the story was over. Perhaps a few of Jesus' followers remembered His words, "Three days later [I] will rise" (Mark 10:34 NIV). But most seem to have missed it somehow.

When Jesus arrived among His followers after His resurrection, they were filled with joy! Can you picture it? We serve a Savior who died and rose again. Because He lives, we, too, will live forever. Join in! Come on and celebrate the resurrection of our Lord!

DEBBIE CARSTEN

LOVE IS *the* LESSON

———

LUKE 24:6 KJV
He is not here, but is risen.

Most glorious Lord of life that on this day
    Didst make Thy triumph over death and sin,
And having harrowed hell didst bring away
    Captivity thence captive us to win;
    This joyous day, dear Lord, with joy begin
And grant that we, for whom Thou didest die
    Being with Thy dear blood clean washed from sin,
May live forever in felicity.
And that Thy love we weighing worthily,
    May likewise love Thee for the same again;
And for Thy sake that all like dear didst buy,
    With love may one another entertain.
So let us love, dear love, like as we ought,
Love is the lesson which the Lord us taught.

EDMUND SPENSER

HE LIVES

MARK 16:6 NLT

The angel said, "Do not be so surprised. You are
looking for Jesus, the Nazarene, who was crucified.
He isn't here! He has been raised from the dead!
Look, this is where they laid his body."

Downcast and despairing, a young woman made her way in the early morning darkness to a fresh grave. Her heart was breaking and her body was aching. And for good reason. Her best friend had been executed the day before and she had not slept all night. . . . Sorrow, horror, fear. In her mind's eye she could see Jesus looking at her with love. She also could see Him convulsing on the cross, bleeding and struggling for breath. She saw His limp body lowered to the ground. But her momentary replay of what she had witnessed was interrupted by a voice. "The one you are looking for is not here. He is risen!" As she looked up, she not only saw the glowing messenger who spoke these words, she saw that the once-sealed tomb was now wide open. It was a miracle! It was more than she could have imagined! As she ran back to tell her friends what she had seen and heard, she heard herself speaking three words over and over again. "My Redeemer lives!"

GREG ASIMAKOUPOULOS

WITH JOY

SMATTHEW 28:8 NIV
So the women hurried away from the tomb, afraid yet filled with joy, and ran to tell his disciples.

W*hat on earth has happened* to make us celebrate with such irrepressible joy, whether in Washington, San Francisco, Seoul, or Sydney? For a start, Christ came. He visited planet Earth—like a meteor from outer space that struck with such an impact that the world has never been the same since. But that was only the beginning. When the worst our world could muster—death—was brought down on him, he rose from the dead. Yes, he blasted it open, brushed it aside and now the entire universe itself will never be the same. Where once it was a claustrophobic death-locked cell, a gaping hole for freedom has been torn by the resurrection. Those two events, the crucifixion and the resurrection of Jesus, have changed everything.

REBECCA MANLEY PIPPERT

NOT VERY GOOD *at* BELIEVING

JOHN 20:6, 8–10 NRSV

*Simon Peter came, following him, and went
into the tomb. . . . Then the other disciple, who
reached the tomb first, also went in, and he saw and
believed; for as yet they did not understand the
scripture, that he must rise from the dead. Then the
disciples returned to their homes.*

We don't know exactly what happened when Jesus
left the tomb in which he had been buried. We
do know that he was never recognized by sight, but only
by voice, or in the breaking of bread, or the eating of fish.
When the women told the men that an angel had told
them that Jesus was risen, no one believed them. When
Peter and John saw the empty tomb for themselves they
just went away and didn't shout aloud to the rest of the
disciples and their friends what had happened. We are not
very good believers most of the time, we human beings.

MADELEINE L'ENGLE

FELLOWSHIP *with* US

JOHN 20:16 NRSV

Jesus said to her, "Mary!" She turned and said to him in Hebrew, "Rabbouni!" (which means Teacher).

The resurrection means that the limitations of space and time are abolished. We do not need to be born again as first-century Palestinians to encounter Christ, in that the risen Christ finds us and calls us, whatever our situation. Christ breaks down historical and cultural barriers—and ultimately the barrier of death itself—precisely because he is risen and alive. For man, death means a severing of relationships, in that he is cut off from those whom he knew and loved. In the case of Jesus, we find that his death had exactly the opposite effect on account of the resurrection—it restored him to fellowship with those whom he loved (Mary Magdalene being a good example) and opened up the possibility of fellowship with those whom (so to speak) he had never known—like us.

ALISTER MCGRATH

THE PROOF

"In the past God overlooked such ignorance, but now he commands all people everywhere to repent. For he has set a day when he will judge the world with justice by the man he has appointed. He has given proof of this to all men by raising him from the dead."

In light of this, we might wish to consider the well noted "wager" of Blaise Pascal the eminent mathematician (the computer language Pascal is named after him), physicist, and genius, which is basically an argument of logical self-preservation. God either exists or not, and we must of necessity lay odds for or against Him. If I wager for Him and He does not exist, there is no loss. If I wager for Him and He exists, there is infinite gain. If I wager against Him and He does not exist, there is neither loss nor gain. But if I wager against Him and He exists, there is infinite loss. There is a single hypothesis where I am exposed to the loss of everything. Wisdom, therefore, instructs me to make the wager which ensures my winning all or, at worst, losing nothing.

JOHN ANKERBERG & JOHN WELDON

THE REASON WE HOPE

ROMANS 5:10–11 NIV

For if, when we were God's enemies, we were reconciled to him through the death of his Son, how much more, having been reconciled, shall we be saved through his life! Not only is this so, but we also rejoice in God through our Lord Jesus Christ, through whom we have now received reconciliation.

The disposition of hope is rooted in the fundamental biblical truth that all possibilities for life and its future are under the care and goodness of God. Reconciliation is a possibility for us because it begins with, and remains rooted in, God's love for us. The good news of Christian faith is that God's love is constant and undefeatable. This is most clearly evident in Jesus' being raised from the dead. The resurrection of Jesus (the best of all possible futures) is our ultimate warrant for hope. We cannot engage in or experience it, if we do not believe in God's love for us as a constant, undefeatable love—that is to say, unless we believe in "amazing grace." To accept God's unconditional love for us is fundamental to the process of reconciliation in life and in sacrament.

RICHARD M. GULA

THE END *of* DEATH

ROMANS 6:9 MSG
When Jesus was raised from the dead it was
a signal of the end of death-as-the-end.

For three days Jesus' body decayed. It did not rest, mind you. It decayed. The cheeks sank and the skin paled. But after three days the process was reversed. There was a stirring, a stirring deep within the grave . . . and the living Christ stepped forth.

And the moment he stepped forth, everything changed. . . .

The resurrection is an exploding flare announcing to all sincere seekers that it is safe to believe. Safe to believe in ultimate justice. Safe to believe in eternal bodies. Safe to believe in heaven as our estate and the earth as its porch. Safe to believe in a time when questions won't keep us awake and pain won't keep us down. Safe to believe in open graves and endless days and genuine praise.

Because we can accept the resurrection story, it is safe to accept the rest of the story.

Because of the resurrection, everything changes.

MAX LUCADO

THE KEY

I CORINTHIANS 6:14 KJV
*And God hath both raised up the Lord, and
will also raise up us by his own power.*

The entire plan for the future has its key in the resurrection. Unless Christ was raised from the dead,
there can be no kingdom and no returning King. When
the disciples stood at the place where Jesus left this earth,
which is called the place of ascension, they were given
assurance by angels that the Christ of resurrection would
be the Christ of returning glory: "Men of Galilee, . . . why
do you stand here looking into the sky? This same Jesus,
who has been taken from you into heaven, will come back
in the same way you have seen him go into heaven"
(Acts 1:11 NIV).

The resurrection is an event which prepares us and
confirms for us that future event when He will return
again.

Yes, Jesus Christ is alive.

Obviously Christ's physical resurrection is an essential
part of God's plan to save us. Have you given yourself to
this living Christ?

BILLY GRAHAM

294   HIS MIRACLES

A LIVING SAVIOR

---

1 CORINTHIANS 15:3-4 NLT

*I passed on to you what was most important and
what had also been passed on to me—that Christ
died for our sins, just as the Scriptures said.
He was buried, and he was raised from the dead
on the third day, as the Scriptures said.*

During the course of human history, this world has witnessed some wonderful and significant events, but the most glorious day this world has known was the day Jesus of Nazareth rose from the dead. . . .

The crux of the gospel is not only that Christ died for our sins, but that he rose again the third day according to the Scriptures (1 Cor. 15:3–4). He was delivered for our offenses and raised again for our justification. Had Christ remained in the tomb, it would have been the grave of all hope. But the Resurrection is true, and it proves many things. It proves that Jesus was the Son of God. It proves that his atonement for sin was complete, sufficient, and acceptable. It proves that Jesus' words are true and we can rely upon them. It proves that there is resurrection in store for us, as well. Today we worship a living Savior. It takes such a Savior to save us when we are lost, to comfort us when we grieve, to strengthen us when we are weak, and to take us to heaven when we die.

PHILIP W. COMFORT & WENDELL C. HAWLEY

JESUS DEFEATED DEATH

1 CORINTHIANS 15:55 KJV
O death, where is thy sting?
O grave, where is thy victory?

What could have produced that Church? A dead Christ? It would have been an effect all out of harmony with the cause. After the battle of Waterloo the news was signaled: "Wellington defeated . . ." A mist came over at that point. England plunged into sadness. Then the mists arose, and the full message came: "Wellington defeated Napoleon." Sadness turned to joy. The news was signaled from a hill called Calvary, "Jesus defeated . . ." and the mists came over for three days—the saddest days of human history. Then on Easter morning the mists cleared, and the world got the full message, "Jesus defeated death." And the world has never been the same since. Nor has death been the same since. "O death, where is thy sting? O grave, where is thy victory?" Earth's blackest day and earth's brightest day are only three days apart. But those three days divide the ages. On one side, doubt and despair; on the other, hope and happiness.

E. STANLEY JONES

JESUS' MIRACLES AFTER HIS RESURRECTION

*Jesus told him, "Because you have seen me,
you have believed; blessed are those who
have not seen and yet have believed."*

JOHN 20:28–29 NIV

JESUS' MIRACLES AFTER HIS RESURRECTION

The days following Jesus' resurrection revealed a new relationship between the Creator and His creation. The effects were almost immediate. Jesus left the tomb, appeared to several people, then joined two disciples on the road to Emmaus, patiently interacting with them until even they were convinced that the risen Lord was their companion. Later, He appeared to the disciples in a room with locked doors. Jesus exercised a wider freedom within His creation than He had previously displayed. His earlier miracles demonstrated His mastery within Creation; His post-resurrection miracles demonstrated His mastery over Creation.

Jesus did not transform the post-resurrection world into a place where miracles are passé; He simply highlighted the miraculous possibilities related to God's sovereignty. To those who insist on a predictable existence Jesus still says, "What is impossible from a human perspective is possible with God" (Luke 18:27 NLT). The following thoughts will help us appreciate the power Jesus made available to those who trust Him.

HURTING HEARTS

LUKE 24:15-16 NCV

While they were talking and discussing, Jesus
himself came near and began walking with them,
but they were kept from recognizing him.

There is a line, a fine line, which once crossed can be fatal. It's the line between disappointment and anger. Between hurt and hate, between bitterness and blame. If you are nearing that line, let me urge you, don't cross it. Step back and ask this question: How long am I going to pay for my disappointment? How long am I going to go on nursing my hurt?

At some point you have to move on. At some point you have to heal. At some point you have to let Jesus do for you what he did for these men.

Know what he did? First of all, he came to them. . . . He didn't sit back and cross his arms and say, "Why can't those two get with the program?" He didn't complain to the angel and say, "Why won't they believe the empty tomb? Why are they so hard to please?"

What did he do? He met them at their point of pain. Though death has been destroyed and sin annulled, he has not retired. The resurrected Lord has once again wrapped himself in flesh, put on human clothes, and searched out hurting hearts.

MAX LUCADO

THE LONELY ROAD

LUKE 24:15 KJV
*And it came to pass, that, while they
communed together and reasoned, Jesus himself
drew near, and went with them.*

A night in Spring . . . and two men walking the
Emmaus road—saddened by their master's death—
bowed down beneath their load, when suddenly *Another*
overtakes them as they walk. A *Stranger* falls in step with
them, and earnestly they talk—of what is in their hearts—
moved by a warm soul-stirring glow—and when they
reach Emmaus they are loth to let Him go; and so they
bid Him stay awhile and share their simple board. And as
He breaks the bread . . . *they know.* They know it is the
Lord.

Oh, may He *overtake* us as the Path of Life we tread!
Along our way of sorrow may His radiant Light be shed
. . . Oh, may He come to warm the heart and ease the
heavy load—and walk with us as long ago He walked the
Emmaus Road.

Take the road . . . the lonely road—courageous, unafraid;
ready for the journey when the twilight shadows fade . . .
God whose Love is Omnipresent—will He fail us then?—
or forget the covenant that He has made with men?

PATIENCE STRONG

THE WRONG CONCLUSION

LUKE 24:21 NKJV
*"But we were hoping that it was He who was
going to redeem Israel. Indeed, besides all this, today
is the third day since these things happened."*

Every fact that the disciples stated was right, but the
conclusions they drew from those facts were wrong.
Anything that has even a hint of dejection spiritually is
always wrong. . . . What have I been hoping or trusting
God would do? Is today "the third day" and He has still
not done what I expected? Am I therefore justified in
being dejected and in blaming God? Whenever we insist
that God should give us an answer to prayer we are off
track. The purpose of prayer is that we get ahold of God,
not of the answer. . . .

We look for visions from heaven and for earth-shaking
events to see God's power. Even the fact that we are
dejected is proof that we do this. Yet we never realize that
all the time God is at work in our everyday events and in
the people around us. If we will only obey, and do the
task that He has placed closest to us, we will see Him.
One of the most amazing revelations of God comes to us
when we learn that it is in the everyday things of life that
we realize the magnificent deity of Jesus Christ.

OSWALD CHAMBERS

WE HAD HOPED . . .

LUKE 24:21 NIV
*"We had hoped that he was the one
who was going to redeem Israel."*

"We had hoped," say the travellers to the Lord. "We had hoped that things would go like this. . . ." We had our plans, but now. . . .

Easter is utterly disconcerting, because it is the power and mystery of God taking hold of our frail mortality, our limited hopes. "Don't you see," their unrecognized fellow-pilgrim asks them. Don't you see that it had to be like that? Was it not written? Isn't it what all the Scriptures are about, from end to end? Don't you understand that the Christ had to suffer and so enter into his glory? Don't you understand that it can't be otherwise for you? You have to jettison your small plans, because the Father's plans for you are unthinkably greater and more wonderful. You have to leap into [God's] hands, say an unconditional "Yes" and be born anew. [God's] love exceeds all that you deserve or even desire.

MARIA BOULDING

WHEN WILL YOU BELIEVE?

LUKE 24:25 NIV

He said to them, "How foolish you are, and how slow of heart to believe all that the prophets have spoken!"

How did Jesus Christ deal with the foolishness of the two disciples on the road to Emmaus? This is the stupidity on another line: a stupidity of simple souls, honest and true, who had become blinded by their own grief and their own point of view.

Jesus said to them: "O fools, and slow of heart to believe all that the prophets have spoken!" (Luke 24:25 KJV) Here the word *fools* might be translated, "My little children, when will you believe what the prophets have written?" This is stupidity of a totally different order—a stupidity that Jesus deals with very pointedly, but very patiently. It is a stupidity that obliterates one's understanding of the Word of God because of personal grief, sorrow, or perplexity.

Is Jesus Christ saying to you, "My child, when will you believe what I say?" Is there a particular problem in your life that has made you become slow of heart to believe? Do not let the stupidity grow. Seek what the Word of God has to say about it.

Oh, there is such a need for people who will search the Bible and learn what God is saying to them!

OSWALD CHAMBERS

HIS DEATH WAS A MUST

LUKE 24:26 NIV

*"Did not the Christ have to suffer these
things and then enter his glory?"*

The Bible teaches that in the death of Christ is found
his triumph over Satan. It also teaches that his death
was *necessary*. It was to win something that could be won
in no other way. This repels the idea that the Lord was
helpless before the Jewish authorities who plotted against
him. His enemies were fitting in with his plan. His death
was a *must*. . . .

Jesus had to die. He was compelled not by circumstances but because there was no other way to do what he
came to do. Any voice that sought to deflect him from
his course was to Jesus the voice of Satan himself.

When we ask what made that death so necessary, the
Bible does not mince words. He died to *redeem people* and
to *forgive sin*. And since, as we have already seen, his death
was a must, we conclude that there was no other way in
which he could redeem and forgive.

JOHN WHITE

DECLARE WHAT GOD HAS DONE

LUKE 24:31, 33 NASB

*Then their eyes were opened and they recognized Him;
and He vanished from their sight. . . . And they got
up that very hour and returned to Jerusalem.*

When the two disciples had reached Emmaus and were refreshing themselves at the evening meal, the mysterious stranger who had so enchanted them on the road took bread and broke it, made Himself known to them, and then vanished out of their sight. They had constrained Him to stay with them because the day was far spent; but now, although it was much later, their love was a lamp to their feet, indeed wings also. They forgot the darkness, their weariness was all gone, and immediately they headed back the seven miles to tell the wonderful news of a risen Lord who had appeared to them on the road. They reached the Christians in Jerusalem and were received by a burst of joyful news before they could tell their own tale. These early Christians were all on fire to speak of Christ's resurrection and to proclaim what they knew of the Lord; they happily shared their experiences. . . . We also must bear our witness concerning Jesus. . . . Let us rise and march to the place of duty, and there declare what great things God has shown to our soul.

CHARLES HADDON SPURGEON

BEHIND CLOSED DOORS

JOHN 20:19 NLT

That evening, on the first day of the week, the disciples were meeting behind locked doors because they were afraid of the Jewish leaders. Suddenly, Jesus was standing there among them! "Peace be with you," he said.

Mary's announcement (John 20:18) must have stunned the disciples. Later the news that the Lord was alive came from two travelers who had unknowingly spent the day walking to Emmaus with Jesus (Luke 24:15-16). Confused, elated, doubtful, and fearful, the disciples stayed close together, hoping to endure the waiting in one place. They were huddled behind locked doors when Jesus appeared to all of them.

There is no real safe place in the world without Jesus, but his presence makes the most dangerous places bearable. When Jesus appeared to his disciples on this occasion he left them five gifts: (1) his own presence; (2) his peace; (3) a mission: "I am sending you"; (4) a companion—the Holy Spirit; and (5) a message of forgiveness. . . .

Whatever God has asked you to do, remember: (1) Your authority comes from God, and (2) Jesus has demonstrated by words and actions how to accomplish the job he has given you. As the Father sent his Son, Jesus sends his followers . . . and you.

LIFE APPLICATION BIBLE COMMENTARY—JOHN

HIS MIRACLES

THE FIRST *and* FINEST MISSIONARY

JOHN 20:21 NKJV
"As the Father has sent Me, I also send you."

God had one Son and He sent Him to be a mission-ary. . . . Jesus' mission was to go on a cross-cultural journey to tell the people He found about God. He left His home and family, traveled a long way, and identified with the people. He learned their language, ate their food, wore their clothes, and endured their sicknesses. He lived among the poorest folk in the obscurest village, and understood the deepest needs of the community. . . .

In the world's eyes, He failed in His missionary endeavors, and was crucified for His trouble. But in God's sight, His mission was gloriously accomplished and He returned home to a marvelous welcome and a grand reward. He paid the ultimate price a missionary is ever asked to pay—laying down His life for His God on the foreign mission field. But like other humble servants that followed after Him, He lives forever in heaven, surrounded by His converts. Jesus was the first and finest missionary!

JILL BRISCOE

MEANINGFUL FAITH

JOHN 20:27 NIV

Then he said to Thomas, "Put your finger here;
see my hands. Reach out your hand and put it
into my side. Stop doubting and believe."

Jesus appears again and turns *immediately* to Thomas. Rather than to condemn, the appearance was designed to deal directly with his doubt. To paraphrase Jesus' words, "Put your finger in, touch my hand, put your hand in my side. And when you are done, put aside any doubt as to who and what is spiritually real for your life. I want you to see that what I told you is true. I am who I said: the way and the truth and the life."

And Thomas believed. . . .

But Jesus said something intriguing to Thomas: "Because you have seen me, you have believed; blessed are those who have not seen and yet have believed" (John 20:29 NIV). This verse leads many people to view Thomas' doubt in a negative light, yet it is less a word to Thomas, perhaps, than to the nature of meaningful faith. God could inspire the most rationally conclusive argument for his existence; he could appear in all of his glory and stun the world into spontaneous worship. But God seeks relationships with free people who choose to bow before him in uncoerced love and devotion.

JAMES EMERY WHITE

HOPE IS NOT *in* VAIN

JOHN 20:27 NKJV

"Do not be unbelieving, but believing."

There may come a time when little makes sense, and evil and chaos seem to be winning the day. These might be times when we feel hopelessness and confusion, when we do not see even a flicker of light. And the lesson of Jesus' scars is to hold on, to be patient and to trust God, even when we cannot see any reason to do so. He will help us. He may not take away the suffering, but he will walk with us through it. And that alone has the power to transform us. How can we be sure? Because the joy of the resurrection was preceded by the agony of Good Friday. . . . There is a loving God who can sustain us, enable us to endure, and mold us into someone better than we were before. The cross prepares us for the difficult times. The resurrection proves that God is greater than evil, and it gives us confidence and hope during the dark times. Because the risen Christ's wounds show us that our hope is not in vain.

REBECCA MANLEY PIPPERT

THE DOUBTER

"My Lord and my God!"

Thomas, too, was a doubter who needed faith. Even after his best friends returned from the empty tomb and described what they had seen, Thomas refused to believe. It was only when Jesus appeared to the disciples a week later and invited Thomas to touch his wounds and satisfy his doubts that Thomas found the faith he required.

"Put your finger here; see my hands. Reach out your hand and put it into my side," the Master said. "Stop doubting and believe." And Thomas exclaimed, "My Lord and my God!" (John 20:24-28)

The Bible invites any of us who lack faith to pray in the words of the father who doubted: "I do believe; help me overcome my unbelief."

This is a prayer that God delights to answer. Faith is a gift that he delights to give. God knows what we lack and what we need. He made each of us as we are, and in our character is the raw material he will use to make us who we can become.

CLAIRE CLONINGER

SEEING IS NOT BELIEVING

JOHN 20:28-29 NIV

Thomas said to him, "My Lord and my God!"
Then Jesus told him, "Because you have seen me,
you have believed; blessed are those who have
not seen and yet have believed."

Seeing is never believing: we interpret what we see in the light of what we believe. Faith is confidence in God before you see God emerging, therefore the nature of faith is that it must be tried. To say, "Oh, yes, I believe God will triumph," may be so much credence smeared over with religious phraseology; but when you are up against things it is quite another matter to say, "I believe God will win through." The trial of our faith gives us a good banking account in the heavenly places, and when the next trial comes our wealth there will tide us over. If we have confidence in God beyond the actual earthly horizons, we shall see the lie at the heart of the fear, and our faith will win through in every detail. Jesus said that men ought always to pray and not "cave in"—"Don't look at the immediate horizon and don't take the facts you see and say they are the reality; they are actuality; the reality lies behind with God."

OSWALD CHAMBERS

GONE FISHIN'

JOHN 21:3 NRSV
Simon Peter said to them, "I am going
fishing." They said to him, "We will go with you."

Some interpreters find it difficult to imagine that the disciples, after two memorable encounters with Jesus in Judea and having heard his command to go into the world, would then waste time fishing in Galilee. I am not so sure! It takes time for the pieces to fit together in a person's life, especially if the way of discipleship has freedom in it. Peter has experienced the victory of Christ and he is glad of that true event. But he had fallen hard in his denial of Jesus. It takes time for a person to resolve the feelings of depression that result from a moral defeat like denial. What can Peter do? In his own eyes, before himself, he is discredited. . . .

It makes sense to me that Peter is doing what you and I would tend to do with feelings of loose ends. He returns to what he knows best and feels good about. He may not be a great man of faith, but a fisherman he is. It is my view that a depressed Peter decides to go fishing, and just as the disciples had stayed with Thomas through his battle for faith, so now they stay with a struggling Peter through his lonely battle.

EARL F. PALMER

THE SAME MIRACLE

JOHN 21:6 NLT

Then he said, "Throw out your net on the right-hand side of the boat, and you'll get plenty of fish!" So they did, and they couldn't draw in the net because there were so many fish in it.

The disciples, tired as they were, responded to the obvious authority in the voice, and cast their nets to starboard—and a miracle occurred! This recalls Luke 5:1-11, another occasion where Peter and the other disciples were fishing on the sea, catching nothing. Jesus gave a command to go out into the deep water. Peter, though doubtful, followed Jesus' orders. When they obeyed, a miracle occurred! When Peter saw the first miracle, "he fell down at Jesus' knees, saying, 'Go away from me, Lord, for I am a sinful man!'" (Luke 5:8 NRSV). He recognized beyond Jesus' power a holiness that was not part of his own life.

On this occasion, Peter is again a central character. Jesus identified himself by his unexpected and seemingly useless request. The fishermen's actions involved them in another miracle. If the request did not give them a clue, the results unmistakably pointed to the power of their Lord. Both John and Peter recognized that Jesus was behind the overwhelming catch of fish.

LIFE APPLICATION BIBLE COMMENTARY—JOHN

IT IS *the* LORD!

JOHN 21:7 NKJV

*Therefore that disciple whom Jesus
loved said to Peter, "It is the Lord!"*

The last time the disciples had eaten with Jesus was at the Last Supper, right before his death. But now they were seaside with the risen Lord, as he prepared the first meal of their new life together. . . .

In the entire Gospel of John, the author records his own words only twice. The first time is when Jesus said one of the disciples would betray him. John said, "Is it I?" He knew, as I know about myself, that he was fully capable of betraying the Lord on any given day. And the second time he recorded his own words? It was this occasion. When they realized the man on the shore was none other than the risen Lord, it was John who stated the obvious "It is the Lord!"

The moral of the story: Keep your eyes and ears and heart open to the truth. Who knows when you, in a time of defeat and uncertainty, might hear a stranger call to you from across the open water and say, "Cast your nets on the other side"? And what once was a day of fruitless struggle becomes a day of laughter and tears of joy.

PAUL S. WILLIAMS

WHAT WILL IT TAKE?

MATTHEW 28:16–17 KJV

Then the eleven disciples went away into Galilee, into a mountain where Jesus had appointed them. And when they saw him, they worshipped him: but some doubted.

I told them to meet me at this particular mountain. After they had been there awhile, I appeared to them. Some of the disciples by then were getting accustomed to my new power and reacted ecstatically when I appeared. But others still doubted that it was really I. They still thought I was a ghost. The critics who paint my men as easily-duped fools are far from the truth. My disciples came fighting the whole way.

As we were eating supper, I confronted them about their own belief. I talked about their stubborn refusal to believe me, the Scriptures, and the women who had seen the angels. They were just like modern men and women who can't believe in miracles. I asked them what it would take for them to believe me. The prophets had told them what would happen, I had told them myself, and it had occurred exactly as we all predicted. Now I was sitting with them. They could touch me, again, just as we all had predicted. I wanted to know what it would take for them to trust me.

I let them think about that.

ANDREW G. HODGES

HIS HOLY SPIRIT

ACTS 1:2-3 NASB

He had by the Holy Spirit given orders to the apostles
whom He had chosen. To these He also presented Him-
self alive, after His suffering, by many convincing proofs,
appearing to them over a period of forty days and speak-
ing of the things concerning the kingdom of God.

From the earliest days of His ministry, it was evident
that the Holy Spirit would have a major role in what
Jesus would say and do. . . .

All that Christ did, He accomplished by the power and
energy of the Spirit (cf. Acts 1:1-2). For example, Jesus'
many miracles and the people's reaction to them demonstrated that His ministry was supernaturally empowered
(see Matt. 8:23-27 and how the disciples reacted to His
calming the storm). His opposition (most notably the
Pharisees), on the other hand, did not acknowledge the
Spirit's role in Jesus' ministry. In fact, the Pharisees
astoundingly came to the conclusion that Jesus was
empowered by Satan. Their blasphemous accusation
prompted Jesus to issue a strong public statement defend-
ing His actions and declaring the Spirit His real source of
power (cf. Matt. 12:22-33).

JOHN MACARTHUR

DRIVEN *to* BELIEVE

ACTS 1:3 RSV
To them he presented himself alive after his passion by many proofs, appearing to them during forty days, and speaking of the kingdom of God.

But the heart of the matter is beyond doubt: "To them he presented himself alive after his passion [suffering and death] by many proofs" (1:3). These experiences, however mysterious, were not the products of the disciples' fevered imagination. These men were not self-deluded. All the evidence points to the fact that they had never imagined such a thing would happen. They were extremely reluctant to believe one another or their own senses when it did happen. The great fact of the Resurrection, which we find them proclaiming throughout the rest of Acts, was not their invention. They had been driven to believe it against all logic and common sense and all the experience of the human race. Only the real appearance of the Risen Lord can account for their faith.

ALBERT C. WINN

FRESH FIRE

*"But you will receive power when
the Holy Spirit comes on you."*

The disciples had been on a roller coaster of emotions. They had seen Jesus heal the sick, raise the dead, die on a cross, rise from the dead, and ascend to heaven—only to leave them to carry on His work. Now they were expected to go into all the world, preaching the gospel. How were they to accomplish this task? How could God have left such a responsibility in their inexperienced hands? He could do it because He knew, when the Holy Spirit came down upon them, they could change the world. So God sent the Spirit down—and the world has never been the same.

Do you feel weak? Incapable of running the race set before you? You already have the Holy Spirit, but sometimes you need to be ignited with fresh fire; sometimes you need to be refreshed with power sent down like rain into your soul. Ask God to send it on down! At your request, He will pour down His power and refreshment to help you do whatever He has called you to do, no matter how weak you feel.

CAROL CHAFFEE FIELDING

HE WILL BE BACK

ACTS 1:9-10 NIV

After he said this, he was taken up before their very eyes, and a cloud hid him from their sight. They were looking intently up into the sky as he was going, when suddenly two men dressed in white stood beside them.

Why did the disciples stand and look intently into the sky? . . . They may have been saddened by his sudden disappearance and were looking anxiously for him to descend. Or perhaps they were confused and didn't know what else to do.

Whatever their thoughts or motives, however, two angels ("white-robed men") gave them the word. They could stop looking *up* and start looking *around* at the world and its needy people. They could stop waiting and start working to fulfill Christ's commission. They could stop wondering and start living with the assurance that Jesus would come again, just as he had promised.

Although nearly two thousand years have passed since this dramatic event, the angels' message still stands—Jesus will surely return. That truth should continue to motivate believers. In fact, each day that passes provides another day to work for Christ and his kingdom.

Keep hoping, working, loving, sharing the Good News, and living for the Savior. He will come back.

DAVE VEERMAN

The Crowning *of* Jesus

LUKE 24:50–52 NIV
*When he had led them out to the vicinity of Bethany,
he lifted up his hands and blessed them. While he
was blessing them, he left them and was taken
up into heaven. Then they worshiped him and
returned to Jerusalem with great joy.*

We might expect the disciples to be sad at Jesus' departure, but we read that they "worshiped him and returned to Jerusalem with great joy" (v. 52). Were they happy to see him go? Yes, because they now knew why he had to leave. It meant he was going to heaven to sit at the right hand of God the Father. It meant he would soon send the Holy Spirit, as his first act of rule, to empower them to take the good news everywhere. They knew these things because Jesus had "opened their minds so they could understand the Scriptures" (v. 45). . . .

Though the ascension was the glorious climax of Jesus' first coming, there is a more glorious event yet to come. Luke tells us at the beginning of the second part of his two-volume work that "this same Jesus, who has been taken from you into heaven, will come back in the same way you have seen him go into heaven" (Acts 1:11 NIV).

On that day his kingship will become fully visible to all men, even to those who denied it.

R. C. SPROUL

LORD *of* ALL LORDS

LUKE 24:51 NKJV

Now it came to pass, while He blessed them, that He
was parted from them and carried up into heaven.

The transfiguration was completed on the Mount of Ascension. If Jesus had gone to heaven directly from the Mount of Transfiguration, He would have gone alone. He would have been nothing more to us than a glorious Figure. But He turned His back on the glory, and came down from the mountain to identify Himself with fallen humanity.

The ascension is the complete fulfillment of the transfiguration. Our Lord returned to His original glory, but not simply as the Son of God—He returned to His father as the *Son of Man* as well. There is now freedom of access for anyone straight to the very throne of God because of the ascension of the Son of Man. As the Son of Man, Jesus Christ deliberately limited His omnipotence, omnipresence, and omniscience. But now they are His in absolute, full power. As the Son of Man, Jesus Christ now has all the power at the throne of God. From His ascension forward He is the King of kings and Lord of lords.

OSWALD CHAMBERS

BETTER *to* LEAVE

MARK 16:19 NRSV

So then the Lord Jesus, after he had
spoken to them, was taken up into heaven and
sat down at the right hand of God.

It seems to have been a lot easier for Jesus' friends to believe in the Ascension than it had been to believe in the Resurrection. Maybe their acceptance of the marvel of Jesus' resurrection expanded their capacity for belief. Maybe it did look to them as though Jesus were wafted up into heaven. . . .

However the Ascension happened, what we do know is that Jesus did not want his friends to hold on to him. They were thrilled with the Resurrection body, once they recognized it to be the Lord and they wanted to keep him with them forever. But he told them, in no uncertain terms, that it was better for them for him to leave them. He would send them the Holy Spirit; that was the promise. He would go, and then the Comforter would come. . . .

He reiterated that it was better for him to go, that only then would he send them the Comforter, the Holy Spirit, the Third Person of the Trinity, the Person who is hardest for most of us to understand.

MADELEINE L'ENGLE

JESUS'
FOLLOWERS
PERFORM
MIRACLES *in*
HIS NAME

The Lord proved their message was
true by giving them power to do
miraculous signs and wonders.

ACTS 14:3 NLT

JESUS' FOLLOWERS PERFORM MIRACLES *in* HIS NAME

In much the same way that they saw the use of miracles demonstrated by Jesus, His followers displayed a remarkable reticence to resort to miraculous signs as a way to authenticate their message. Many of the wonders that accompanied the apostles seem to have been initiated by God rather than the messengers. In fact, some miracles amazed the apostles as much as they astounded other observers. The disciples were amazed that "even the demons submit to us" (Luke 10:17 NIV). When the Holy Spirit fell on the small group of Jesus' loyal followers, they were empowered to boldly fulfill the commission He had given them. And when they set out, they turned the world upside down (Acts 17:6).

In the power of Jesus' name, the apostles were able to lay the foundation for the early church. The miracles authenticated a message not yet written in the form we have today—the Bible. As you read about the miracles done by Jesus' followers, consider the power of Jesus' name in your life.

LEARNING *by* DOING

MARK 6:6-7 NLT

Then Jesus went out from village to village, teaching.
And he called his twelve disciples together and sent them
out two by two, with authority to cast out evil spirits.

In the training of the twelve disciples, there came a time when Jesus decided it was time to send them out on a mission. At that juncture, the disciples were clearly not polished preachers or teachers. In fact, they didn't even have a firm grasp of their subject—as evidenced by their total surprise when Jesus was crucified, and even greater amazement when he rose from the dead, despite the fact that he had been telling them throughout their training that this would happen! And they certainly were not always proficient when they were called upon to confront evil spirits, or even capable of handling the squabbles that arose in their own fellowship. But Jesus sent them out anyway! . . .

So with a sense of mission, urgency, dependency, apprehension, and expectation they went forth. Uncertain in their own minds, unprepared in their own strength, they went in obedience to Jesus and in dependence on Jesus. They were a blessing—and they were blessed. Ministering as they went, they learned as they worked. God's teaching methods have not changed.

STUART BRISCOE

FREELY GIVE

MATTHEW 10:5, 8 KJV

These twelve Jesus sent forth, and commanded them, saying . . . Heal the sick, cleanse the lepers, raise the dead, cast out devils: freely ye have received, freely give.

Wherever they went they must proclaim, The kingdom of heaven is at hand. They preached, to establish the faith; the kingdom, to animate the hope; of heaven, to inspire the love of heavenly things, and the contempt of earthly; which is at hand, that men may prepare for it without delay. Christ gave power to work miracles for the confirming of their doctrine. This is not necessary now that the kingdom of God is come. It showed that the intent of the doctrine they preached, was to heal sick souls, and to raise those that were dead in sin. In proclaiming the gospel of free grace for the healing and saving of men's souls, we must above all avoid the appearance of the spirit of an hireling.

MATTHEW HENRY

AUTHORITY GIVEN

MARK 6:13 NKJV

And they cast out many demons, and anointed with oil many who were sick, and healed them.

Jesus gave his disciples authority to cast out demons (Mark 3:15), as well as the power to heal the sick. Casting out demons extended Jesus' personal ministry, which was to confront Satan's power and destroy it. As the disciples went throughout Galilee, they would be announcing the arrival of the kingdom of God through their preaching and healing. If they had only preached, people might have thought the kingdom was only spiritual. On the other hand, if the disciples had only been given the power to cast out demons and heal the sick, without preaching, people might not have realized the spiritual importance of their mission. Most of their listeners expected the arrival of God's kingdom and the Messiah to bring wealth and power to their nation; they preferred material benefits to spiritual discernment. But the truth about Jesus is that he is both God and man, both spiritual and physical; and the salvation that he offers is both for the soul and the body.

LIFE APPLICATION BIBLE COMMENTARY—MARK

IN HIS NAME

LUKE 10:17–19 NRSV

The seventy returned with joy, saying, "Lord,
in your name even the demons submit to us!" He said
to them, "I watched Satan fall from heaven like a flash
of lightning. See, I have given you authority to tread
on snakes and scorpions, and over all the power of
the enemy; and nothing will hurt you."

The return of the seventy to Jesus is the occasion for one of the most exalted experiences in his entire career. In his name, demons had been conquered (vs. 17). In this, Jesus saw a promise of the whole ministry of his Church, through which the proclamation of his coming victory over Satan would be carried to the ends of the earth. With an authority given by Jesus, the Church would have power which its enemies could not finally destroy (vss. 18-19). Serpents and scorpions are symbols of spiritual enemies, and are not to be taken literally. Although the Church may rightly rejoice in her achievements through the power of Christ, there is something greater over which to joy—the mercy of God through whom men find salvation.

DONALD G. MILLER

RIGHT REJOICING

LUKE 10:20 NKJV
"Nevertheless do not rejoice in this, that the spirits are subject to you, but rather rejoice because your names are written in heaven."

Jesus Christ is saying here, "Don't rejoice in your successful service for Me, but rejoice because of your right relationship with Me." The trap you may fall into in Christian work is to rejoice in successful service—rejoicing in the fact that God has used you. Yet you will never be able to measure fully what God will do through you if you have a right-standing relationship with Jesus Christ. If you keep your relationship right with Him, then regardless of your circumstances or whoever you encounter each day, He will continue to pour "rivers of living water" through you (John 7:38 NKJV). And it is actually by His mercy that He does not let you know it. Once you have the right relationship with God through salvation and sanctification, remember that whatever your circumstances may be, you have been placed in them by God. And God uses the reaction of your life to your circumstances to fulfill His purpose, as long as you continue to "walk in the light as He is in the light" (1 John 1:7 NKJV).

OSWALD CHAMBERS

THE UPPER ROOM

ACTS 1:13 NKJV

*And when they had entered, they went up into
the upper room where they were staying.*

We make a great deal of "the upper room" now, but in the days of Jesus it was just one room in a home where some of the disciples were staying. Just think of it! God's most precious promise—the promise of the Father (Acts 1:4)—was fulfilled in one of the most ordinary places on earth—a home. This puts Christianity into a different mold from other world religions with their emphasis on places, rites, ceremonies, etc. . . .

The most freeing thing that ever happened in religious history was when God, in the power of His Holy Spirit, came upon His waiting disciples in a home. In this age, God can be found anywhere in the world, providing He is found in Christ. He comes to all, wherever they may be, when they lift up a surrendered and trusting heart to Him.

SELWYN HUGHES

FROM HEAVEN

ACTS 2:2 NRSV

*And suddenly from heaven there came a sound
like the rush of a violent wind, and it filled the
entire house where they were sitting.*

Exactly the same types of events continue in New Testament times. Of course, incarnation in the person of Jesus is the most complete case of "God with us," or "Immanuel." The apostle John, who as a youth was the closest of companions with Jesus, marvels in his old age that he and others had with their physical senses—their ears, eyes, and hands—known the very source of life, which was from the beginning of everything (1 John 1:1).

Thus the sight of Jesus interacting with the enveloping kingdom day after day; his transfiguration and his resurrection presence; his ascension; the coming of the spirit with a sound "from heaven"—that is, out of the atmosphere—where he recently had gone, which then filled the room where his disciples were waiting, resting visibly on them as flames of fire . . . all of these gave the early church the strongest possible impression of the reality and immediate presence of the kingdom of Christ.

DALLAS WILLARD

THE CHURCH IS BORN

ACTS 2:2 NIV

Suddenly a sound like the blowing
of a violent wind came from heaven and filled
the whole house where they were sitting.

It may have been the same upper room where Jesus and
His disciples had shared one last supper. Twelve had fit
a whole lot more comfortably than one hundred and
twenty, but no complaining could be heard. Instead, the
gathered believers were engaged in passionate prayer. . . .

And then it came. The mysterious sound of a gale force
wind. The flames, "tongues of fire," spontaneously ignit-
ing on their heads. Then the Spirit's presence showed
itself in foreign languages "declaring the wonders of
God" (Acts 2:11 NIV). Those who stood on the streets
below, who had journeyed to Jerusalem for the Feast of
Pentecost, had come from a variety of nations. The words
they heard were in their own languages. As the Holy
Spirit descended on the disciples, the glory of God fell.
That day the Church was born!

God is still in the business of working miracles and
growing His church. Like these early believers, pray that
God's glory would fall, making His people strong in His
might. Pray that He would make you ready to make a difference in your world for Him!

GREG ASIMAKOUPOULOS

A NEW ERA

ACTS 2:3 NIV
*They saw what seemed to be tongues of fire that
separated and came to rest on each of them.*

If you draw a line through the pages of the New Testament . . . that line runs straight through an Upper Room. . . . That filling was the dividing line in the moral and spiritual development of humanity. It marked a new era—the era of the Holy Spirit.

On the other side of that dividing line, prior to Pentecost, the disciples were spasmodic in their allegiance and achievements. Sometimes they could rejoice that evil spirits were subject to them, and sometimes they had to ask, "Why could we not cast it out?" Sometimes they appeared ready to go to death with Jesus, and sometimes they quarreled over who should have first place in His Kingdom. Simon Peter could whip out a sword and cut off the ear of the High Priest's servant, and then quail before the gaze of a serving maid. Then came Pentecost. A divine reinforcement took place. They were new men doing new work; no longer spasmodic, but stable. On which side of that dividing line are you? Are you a pre-Pentecost Christian, spasmodic and intermittent, or a post-Pentecost Christian—dynamic and different?

SELWYN HUGHES

MIRACULOUS WORDS

ACTS 2:4 KJV
*And they were all filled with the Holy Ghost,
and began to speak with other tongues,
as the Spirit gave them utterance.*

God invented a way for it to break out when he divided and clove the tongues of the Apostles, so that they might spread among all people what had been delivered to them.

Thus emerges the manifold goodness of God, because a plague and punishment of man's pride was turned into matter of blessing. For whence came the diversity of languages, except so that God could bring the wicked and ungodly counsels of humans to nothing. But God furnishes the Apostles with the diversity of tongues now, that he may bring and call home, into a blessed unity people who wander here and there. I said that this was done for our sake, not only because the fruit of it came to us, but because we know that the Gospel became ours not by chance, but by the appointment of God, who for this very purpose gave the Apostles tongues of fire, lest any nation should lack that doctrine which was committed unto them.

JOHN CALVIN

WORDS *of* PRAISE

ACTS 2:7-8 NASB

They were amazed and astonished, saying,
"Why, are not all these who are speaking Galileans?
And how is it that we each hear them in our
own language to which we were born?"

It was a mind-boggling experience for those who responded to the supernatural sound. First there was surprise at the unusual noise, then there was absolute amazement and perplexity at hearing and understanding what some foreigners (the disciples from Galilee) were saying (Acts 2:7-8). But the disciples were not speaking in other people's languages pridefully or as a way just to attract attention to themselves. Instead, the Acts narrative says the crowd was impressed because "we hear them in our own tongues speaking of the mighty deeds of God" (v. 11). . . .

Everything that happened in Jerusalem on that most important of Pentecosts was orchestrated by the Father to make it clear that the Spirit's coming perfectly fit the divine timetable. . . . No matter how incredible the events surrounding Pentecost may seem to our finite minds, and no matter how hard some would strive to give them a human explanation, there is no escaping the fact that all the credit belongs to God.

JOHN MACARTHUR

SUCH JOY

ACTS 2:23 NRSV
*"This man, handed over to you . . .
you crucified and killed."*

Within a few days after His death, the disciples were charging the leaders of Jerusalem with His death and doing it publicly. Why couldn't these leaders walk straight to the tomb and point out the body of Jesus? It would have settled everything, for them. They didn't. Why? If the weak answer is reiterated that the disciples stole the body while the soldiers slept, then the answer is simple. . . . There were those who proved faithless; wouldn't they divulge the awful secret of the theft and justify their relapse? No whisper has ever come down through the ages of such divulging. Besides, do these disciples look like men who hold a guilty secret, who proclaim a vast hoax, who live on a lie? Do they look like body snatchers? Their hangdog faces would have shown it; the guilty secret would have eaten out their message. . . . But these men, on the contrary, are radiant and irresistible. They laugh their way through persecution, sing their way through prisons, and smile their way through death. For what? A hoax? Well, hoaxes don't produce hallelujahs, nor does body snatching produce transformed lives. Like produces like.

E. STANLEY JONES

HIS FOLLOWERS' WORKS

ACTS 2:43 KJV

*And fear came upon every soul: and many
wonders and signs were done by the apostles.*

It is great and very precious in the Lord's sight, beloved, when all of Christ's people work together at the same duties and every rank and degree of both sexes cooperates with the same intent. How wonderful it is when one purpose motivates everyone to stay away from evil and do good. How excellent it is when God is glorified in His followers' work and the Author of godliness is blessed by heartfelt gratitude. The hungry are nourished, the naked are clothed, the sick are visited. People don't seek their own interests but "that which is another's," as long as they make the most of their own means to relieve others' misery. . . . In such a community there isn't disorder or diversity for the members of the whole body agree on their one purpose—godliness. . . . For the excellence of every person's portion is the glory of the whole body. When we are all led by God's Spirit, we rejoice not only over the things we do on our own but also the things others do.

LEO I

SHARE IT!

———

ACTS 3:6 KJV

*Then Peter said, Silver and gold have I none;
but such as I have give I thee: In the name of Jesus
Christ of Nazareth rise up and walk.*

Dr. Luke begins his historical record of the apostolic church with these words, "Jesus began both to do and teach . . ." He *began* them but He intends that the church, if it be His Church, *continue* what He began in the power of the same Spirit who enabled Him in His ministry. If you had been with Peter and John on your way to pray in the Temple that day, what would you have done? Would you have reached in your pocket, pulled out a few coins and flipped them to the beggar, then walked in pious grandeur to pray in the Temple? Or would you have dared to say, "Silver and gold have I none, but such as I have give I unto you; In the name of Jesus Christ stand up and walk again"? These are thrilling days in which to be alive and know Jesus Christ and His gospel. To have it and share it! If you do not have it, receive it now, and if you have it, in God's name share it.

RICHARD C. HALVERSON

AWESOME NAME

ACTS 3:6 NLT

But Peter said, "I don't have any money for you.
But I'll give you what I have. In the name of
Jesus Christ of Nazareth, get up and walk!"

Some words have the ability to scare us. They are singular words that pack a powerful punch. Words like cancer, Parkinson's, Alzheimer's, divorce. These words can take our breath away. They can make us give up all hope. They are fearful words, sad words, painful words that, when uttered, cause all of life to come crashing in around us. . . .

One day Peter and John came across a lame beggar near the temple in Jerusalem. The man, deprived of his mobility, was hopeful for a couple of coins. But what he got was far beyond what he could have ever imagined. The two disciples confessed that they didn't have any money to give him, but expressed their desire to give him what they had. Reaching down they pulled the man up "in the name of Jesus Christ." Instantaneously, the man was healed.

How awesome is His name.

GREG ASIMAKOUPOULOS

A GREATER POWER

ACTS 8:6-7 NIV

*When the crowds heard Philip and saw the miraculous
signs he did, they all paid close attention to what
he said. With shrieks, evil spirits came out of many,
and many paralytics and cripples were healed.*

The "shrieks" of these spirits revealed their rage at
encountering a power greater than their own.
Demons are never pleased to be told to leave their human
dwellings, but they have no choice but to submit to the
higher authority (see Mark 9:25-26). . . .

Demons, or evil spirits, are ruled by Satan. Most scholars believe that they are fallen angels who joined Satan in
his rebellion against God and who, in some cases, may
cause a person to be mute, deaf, blind, or insane. Demons
also tempt people to sin. Although demons can be powerful, they are not omnipotent or omniscient and cannot
be everywhere at once. Demons are real and active, but
Jesus has authority over them, and he gave this same
authority to his followers. Although Satan is allowed to
work in the world, God is in complete control. God can
drive demons out and end their destructive work in people's lives. Eventually, Satan and his demons will be
thrown into the lake of fire, forever ending their evil work
in the world (Revelation 20:10).

LIFE APPLICATION BIBLE COMMENTARY—ACTS

HIS MIRACLES

THE TRUE TEST

ACTS 9:17 NKJV

*And Ananias went his way and entered the house; and
laying his hands on him he said, "Brother Saul, the
Lord Jesus, who appeared to you on the road as
you came, has sent me that you may receive your
sight and be filled with the Holy Spirit."*

When Paul received his sight, he also received spiritual insight into the Person of Jesus Christ. His entire life and preaching from that point on were totally consumed with nothing but Jesus Christ. . . . Paul never again allowed anything to attract and hold the attention of his mind and soul except the face of Jesus Christ.

We must learn to maintain a strong degree of character in our lives, even to the level that has been revealed in our vision of Jesus Christ.

The lasting characteristic of a spiritual man is the ability to understand correctly the meaning of the Lord Jesus Christ in his life, and the ability to explain the purposes of God to others. The overruling passion of his life is Jesus Christ. . . .

Never allow anything to divert you from your insight into Jesus Christ. It is the true test of whether you are spiritual or not. To be unspiritual means that other things have a growing fascination for you.

OSWALD CHAMBERS

JESUS CHRIST HEALS YOU

ACTS 9:32-34 NIV

As Peter traveled about the country, he went to visit the saints in Lydda. There he found a man named Aeneas, a paralytic who had been bedridden for eight years. "Aeneas," Peter said to him, "Jesus Christ heals you. Get up and take care of your mat." Immediately Aeneas got up.

The apostles would certainly never have attempted to perform miracles unless they had first been certain it was God's will, for the effect was dependent on his will. The Spirit did not give them the power to heal whichever people they wanted to. Christ applied a limit to his miracles and wanted his disciples to perform only those he knew would be useful. Peter did not say these words rashly, for he would have been laying himself open to ridicule if he had not already known that it was God's will. Maybe he prayed privately. The Spirit, who is the author of all miracles and worked through Peter, was directing his tongue at that moment and was moving his heart within him. By these words Peter showed plainly that he was only the minister of the miracle and that it came from Christ's power; thus he ascribed all the praise to Christ.

"Take care of your mat." It increases the glory of the miracle that the man not only had the strength to get up but also could take care of his own mat.

JOHN CALVIN

A GREATER INSTRUMENT

ACTS 9:40 NIV

Peter sent them all out of the room; then he got down on his knees and prayed. Turning toward the dead woman, he said, "Tabitha, get up." She opened her eyes, and seeing Peter she sat up.

Certain fanatics dream that the human soul is just a breath that vanishes until the day of resurrection, and they seize on this passage to prove it. What was the point (they ask) of recalling Tabitha's soul to the prison of her body, to suffer more miseries, if it had been received into blessed rest? As though God had no right to think about his glory in death as well as in life! The true happiness of believers is to live and die to him; and when we dedicate ourselves to him, Christ is a blessing to us as much in life as in death (Philippians 1:20-21). Therefore, there is nothing wrong with the Lord's thinking more of his own glory than of Tabitha herself, although, as the interest of believers is always connected with God's glory, it was to her own advantage to be brought back to life, so that she might be a greater instrument of God's goodness and power.

JOHN CALVIN

AUTHORITY *from* CHRIST

ACTS 13:9, 11 KJV

*Then Saul, (who also is called Paul,) filled with
the Holy Ghost, set his eyes on him. . . . And now,
behold, the hand of the Lord is upon thee, and thou
shalt be blind, not seeing the sun for a season. And
immediately there fell on him a mist and a darkness.*

I call your attention to the fact that Paul had the sign gifts
of an apostle. When he went over there to Paphos, he
couldn't ask them to turn to the New Testament. There
was no New Testament for him to preach from or for
them to turn to. . . . So how will they recognize his
authority? It is by the sign gifts. Today, the New Testament
is written. We are now given a different way to recognize
authority. "If there come any unto you, and bring not this
doctrine, receive him not into your house, neither bid
him God speed" (2 John 10 KJV). This doctrine is in the
Word of God, in the New Testament. . . .

Paul has his authority from the Lord Jesus Christ. He
absolutely dominates the sorcerer by his message of the
gospel of the Lord Jesus Christ. Sergius Paulus comes
to the light. He has been in spiritual darkness but now
believes and is astonished at the doctrine of the Lord.

J. VERNON MCGEE

THE TRUE PURPOSE *of* MIRACLES

ACTS 14:1, 3 NIV

*At Iconium . . . Paul and Barnabas spent
considerable time there, speaking boldly for the Lord,
who confirmed the message of his grace by enabling
them to do miraculous signs and wonders.*

This shows the true purpose of miracles. They are primarily to show us God's power and grace, but because we interpret them wrongly and perversely, God never lets them be separated from his Word, in case they get abused and corrupted. If at any time miracles were performed apart from his Word, it was very seldom, and little fruit came from it. Most of the time God has performed miracles so that the world may know him not just in himself or his majesty but in his Word. In this verse Luke says that the Gospel was confirmed by miracles, so that through Paul's teaching people might be brought to the pure worship of God.

Luke says that the Lord allowed miracles to be done by his servants. Thus he teaches that it was only those who obeyed God who were his ministers, and that God was the one who worked the miracles, using them as agents. . . . He works through people in such a way that his glory is not obscured by their ministry.

JOHN CALVIN

AUTHENTICATED AUTHORITY

ACTS 14:3 NLT
*The apostles stayed there a long time,
preaching boldly about the grace of the Lord.
The Lord proved their message was true by giving
them power to do miraculous signs and wonders.*

In Acts, signs and wonders are key to revealing the work of salvation in Christ and to proclaiming the gospel. They authenticated the apostles' authority and the authority of those associated with them . . . A "sign" *(semeion)* is a miracle whereby God shows himself to be almighty. A "wonder" *(teras)* is an amazing miracle that causes astonishment. In the Old Testament, the word "wonder" referred to God's redemptive activity when Moses led the Hebrews from Egypt (Deuteronomy 26:5-11). In the early church, these great miracles, empowered by the Spirit, showed God's new redemptive work in Christ. . . .

We may wish we could perform a miraculous act that would convince everyone once and for all that Jesus is the Lord. . . . God gave Paul and Barnabas power to do great wonders to confirm that their message was true, but people were still divided. Don't spend your time and energy wishing for miracles. Sow your seeds of Good News on the best ground you can find in the best way you can, and leave the convincing to the Holy Spirit.

LIFE APPLICATION BIBLE COMMENTARY—ACTS

　HIS MIRACLES

LOOKING *for* HANDS *to* USE

ACTS 19:11–12 NKJV

*Now God worked unusual miracles by the hands
of Paul, so that even handkerchiefs or aprons were
brought from his body to the sick, and the diseases
left them and the evil spirits went out of them.*

Throughout this time wonderful deeds were being done. The sweat-band [handkerchief] was what a workman wore round his head to absorb the sweat as he worked. The apron was the girdle with which a workman or servant girded himself. It is very significant that the narrative does not say that Paul did these extraordinary deeds; it says that God did them through Paul's hands. God, said someone, is everywhere looking for hands to use. We may not be able to work miracles with our hands but without doubt we can give them to God so that he may work through them.

WILLIAM BARCLAY

THEY WERE COMFORTED

ACTS 20:9-10 KJV

Eutychus . . . fell down from the third loft,
and was taken up dead. And Paul went down,
and fell on him, and embracing him said,
Trouble not yourselves; for his life is in him.

Paul raised this boy from the dead. You will remember also that Simon Peter raised Dorcas from the dead. This was a gift that belonged to the apostles. After the canon of Scripture was established, the sign gifts were not manifested—they disappeared from the church. When Dr. Luke writes that they "were not a little comforted," he means they were really thrilled that this precious young man had been raised from the dead and was back in their midst. And now Paul continues to preach through the night even until daybreak. What a rebuke that is to us! In some churches there is a chorus of complaint if a pastor preaches ten or even five minutes longer than usual. These early believers sat up all night listening to Paul. I know someone is going to say, "If I could listen to Paul, I'd listen all night, too." Paul probably was nothing more than a humble preacher of the gospel. We do know that Apollos was an eloquent man, but that is not said of Paul. These believers simply wanted to hear the Word of God. How wonderful that is!

J. VERNON MCGEE

SHAKE IT OFF!

ACTS 28:3, 5 AMP.
*Now Paul had gathered a bundle of sticks, and he
was laying them on the fire when a viper crawled out
because of the heat and fastened itself on his hand. . . .
Then [Paul simply] shook off the small creature
into the fire and suffered no evil effects.*

When Paul and his traveling companions were ship-
wrecked on the island of Malta, he was gathering
sticks to make a fire and dry out when he was bitten by
a snake that had been driven out of the flames. The Bible
says that he simply shook it off into the fire. You and I
should do the same—we too should be bold inwardly and
shake it off!

Whatever may be troubling you from the past, *shake it
off!* God has a great future planned for you. The dreams
of the future have no room for the snake bites of the past!

I am trying to build a fire in you that will never go out.
Stir yourself up and refuse to take on a spirit of coldness
and deadness. Fight those negative thoughts that are holding you in bondage. Jesus wants to make you whole. He
doesn't want to fix part of you, He wants to fix all of you:
body, emotions, mouth, mind, attitude, will and spirit.

JOYCE MEYER

CHANNELS *of* BLESSING

ACTS 28:8 NKJV
Publius lay sick of a fever and dysentery.
Paul went in to him and prayed, and he laid
his hands on him and healed him.

It seems that in Malta the Chief of the island was a title; and Publius may well have been the chief Roman representative for that part of the island. His father was ill and Paul was able to exercise his healing gift and bring him relief. But in verse 9 there is a very interesting possibility. That verse says that the rest of the people who had ailments came and *were healed.* The word used is the word for *receiving medical attention;* and there are scholars who think that this can well mean, not only that they came to Paul, but that they came to Luke who gave them of his medical skill. If that be so, this passage gives us the earliest picture we possess of the work of a *medical missionary.* There is a poignant thing here. Paul could exercise the gift of healing; and yet he himself had always to bear about with him the thorn in the flesh. Many a man has brought to others a gift which was denied to him. . . . It is one of the wonders of grace that such men did not grow bitter but were content to be the channels of blessings which they themselves could never enjoy.

WILLIAM BARCLAY

JESUS'
MIRACLES
in YOU

Therefore, if anyone is in Christ,
he is a new creation; the old has gone,
the new has come!

2 CORINTHIANS 5:17 NIV

JESUS' MIRACLES *in* YOU

A s Jesus made clear in His remarks leading up to healing the paralyzed man in Mark 2, the greatest miracles are unseen. He healed the man in an obvious way to underscore the truth of His even greater miracle of giving that man forgiveness. You will not "see" the greatest miracle God can do for you, at least until eternity.

God remains no less able or unwilling to do miracles today than He was in Jesus' day. But unfortunately, many people's approach to miracles bears a chilling resemblance to the taunts Jesus heard—"Show us a miracle, then we'll believe." Demanding that God prove Himself reveals a profound misunderstanding about who's in charge and about humanity's desperate condition before God.

The promise of God's forgiveness, highlighted by the power of Jesus' resurrection, remains the greatest yet most humbling miracle of all. Every day we who believe should be grateful for the miracle of salvation and the miraculous promise of our own eternal life. Beyond that, every other miracle is an unexpected added delight that brings glory to God!

THOU HAST TOUCHED ME

PSALM 34:8 NRSV
O taste and see that the LORD is good;
happy are those who take refuge in him.

Late have I loved thee, beauty so ancient and so new!
Late have I loved thee!
Thou wast within me, and I stood without.
I sought thee here, hurling my ugly self on the beauty
of thy creatures.
Thou wast with me, but I was not with thee.
Thou hast called me, thy cry has vanquished my
deafness.
Thou hast shone, and thy light has vanquished my
blindness.
Thou hast broadcast thy perfume, and I have breathed it:
now I sigh for thee.
I have tasted thee, and now I hunger for thee.
Thou hast touched me, and now I burn with desire for
thy peace.

AUGUSTINE

SHINE *through* US

MATTHEW 5:14 NKJV
*"You are the light of the world.
A city that is set on a hill cannot be hidden."*

Dear Jesus,
Help us to spread your fragrance everywhere
we go.
Flood our souls with your spirit and life.
Penetrate and possess our whole being so utterly
that our lives may only be a radiance of yours.
Shine through us
and be so in us
that every soul we come in contact with
may feel your presence in our soul.
Let them look up and see no longer us
but only Jesus.
Stay with us
and then we shall begin to shine as you shine,
so to shine as to be light to others.
The light, O Jesus, will be all from you.
None of it will be ours.
It will be you shining on others through us.
Let us thus praise you in the way you love best
by shining on those around us. . . . Amen.

MOTHER TERESA

THE FLOWING MIRACLE

JOHN 4:10 NLT
*Jesus replied, "If you only knew the gift God
has for you and who I am, you would ask me,
and I would give you living water."*

In our amazement over Jesus' specific miracles, we often miss the greater miracles in the lives he transformed. He responded to many needs, but he repeatedly offered the deeper miracle of eternal life. He even used a miracle like the healing of the paralytic in Mark 2 to authenticate his more significant claim to be able to forgive sins.

Jesus engaged an apparently healthy woman at the well in a conversation that revealed the yawning depths of her need for spiritual healing. He promised and delivered living water in her soul that immediately flowed into her neighbor's lives. She was transformed from shamed to saved, eager to tell everyone about what Christ had done for her.

Jesus' miracle of living water continues to erupt in unsuspecting lives today as much as ever. If the springs welling up to eternal life do not flow from your inner being, Jesus is still willing to bring that same miracle into your life. He invites you to trust him just as that woman did beside the well so long ago. Go ahead; ask him for living water. He delivers.

NEIL WILSON

DAY 336

THE INDWELLING SOURCE *of* LIFE

JOHN 7:38–39 NKJV
*"He who believes in Me, as the Scripture has said,
out of his heart will flow rivers of living water."
But this He spoke concerning the Spirit, whom
those believing in Him would receive.*

The greatest danger to any ancient city during a time
of siege was not the enemy without; it was the lack
of resources within. More often than not, when an army
like the Assyrians attacked a walled city like Jerusalem,
they would simply surround the city and wait for it to run
out of food and water. Then, when the people were weak
and desperate, the city could be taken almost without a
fight. But Hezekiah made sure that would not happen to
Jerusalem. He rerouted a spring of water outside the city
walls so it flowed inside the walls of the city.

Interestingly, Jesus referred often to the Holy Spirit as
the living water given by God to the believer which con-
stitutes a secret, powerful resource in times of trouble.
When you have the Holy Spirit living inside of you, you
possess a resource that can give you abundant life through
the longest siege of the enemy. The enemy can camp at
your doorstep for an indefinite period of time and it
won't matter to you. The Holy Spirit is your indwelling
source of life.

DAVID JEREMIAH

CALLED *to* BE SAINTS

JOHN 14:12 NKJV

*"Most assuredly, I say to you, he who believes in Me,
the works that I do he will do also; and greater works
than these he will do, because I go to My Father."*

We are called to be saints, who in our humanness
are always saints without halos. . . .

We are asked to be what we are not. We who follow
Christ are called to offer to others what is still unrealized
in us. Lessons of love and life are to be taught by us who
are still learning them. Self-understanding in others is to
be encouraged by us who do not yet understand ourselves. We are to witness, nurture, and admonish others in
their spiritual pilgrimage while still struggling with our
own. We who are sick are asked to heal others. We who
are fractious and cause conflict are called by Christ to be
peacemakers. We who have dark corners in our soul still
unredeemed are sent out to baptize. We who need the
Word ourselves are commissioned to proclaim and to
preach. We who are possessed by irrational urges and
baser motives are sent out to cast out demons. We are
called by Jesus to do what we need, to offer what we ourselves need.

DONALD J. SHELBY

VISITED

JOHN 14:17 NKJV

"The Spirit of truth, whom the world cannot receive, because it neither sees Him nor knows Him; but you know Him, for He dwells with you and will be in you."

We have been visited. Let those words sink into your soul, for no matter what you face, the Visitor is there, bringing a power that can flow to you now because of the visit He made long ago. For you see, He has, in that one grand visit, already accomplished whatever today's or tomorrow's need may demand! And now, God's Holy Spirit has come to interpret for and ignite in us all that is available to us. Because of Christ's condescendence—His coming to visit us—we can not only survive the stress and personal failure of trials, but we can be restored to His highest purposes for us.

Speak it aloud.

Declare it now: "I have been visited! Praise You, Lord! I marvel at Your loving purpose for me—that, in order to assure its fulfillment, You have paid me a visit."

And while you're praising Him for that, further thank Him that He has also promised to abide with you forever.

Never leaving.

Never forsaking.

JACK HAYFORD

TRUE PEACE

JOHN 14:27 NIV

"Peace I leave with you; my peace I give you.
I do not give to you as the world gives. Do not let
your hearts be troubled and do not be afraid."

Everyone wants peace, but very few care for the things that produce it. God's peace is with the humble and the gentle, and especially with the patient. If you will listen to God, and act accordingly, you will enjoy much peace. . . .

Don't think that you have found true peace just because you feel no pain or have no enemies. Never think that life is perfect when you receive everything you want. Never consider yourself God's favorite child because you enjoy a great devotional life. That is not the way to true peace and spiritual growth.

Peace can be found in offering your whole heart to God. Forget your own will in great things and small things, thanking God equally for the pleasant and the unpleasant. Weigh everything in the same balance.

If you are strong enough to willingly suffer more and more without praising yourself, but always praising God's name, then you will be on the road to true peace.

THOMAS À KEMPIS

SHARED MINISTRY

MARK 16:15 NIV
*He said to them, "Go into all the world and
preach the good news to all creation."*

Every Christian has a vocation. We are called to share in
the ministry of Jesus Christ *in* and *through* the
world. . . . Sharing in the ministry of Jesus Christ involves
living in the world as an expression of the holiness we
see in him—a holiness expressed through his compassion,
his concern for justice (righteousness), and through his
healing and reconciling presence in the world. The relationship he offers to us—when entered into with seriousness—results in those qualities we see in him being
expressed through us, sometimes even despite ourselves.

JAMES C. FENHAGEN

The Holy Spirit Came

John 14:16 NKJV
"And I will pray the Father, and He will give you another Helper, that He may abide with you forever."

Is [the Holy Spirit's] presence recognized as it ought to be? We cannot control His working; He is sovereign in all His operations, but are we sufficiently anxious to obtain His help or sufficiently watchful lest we grieve Him and He withdraws His help? Without Him we can do nothing, but by His almighty energy the most extraordinary results can be produced: Everything depends upon His revealing or concealing His power. Do we always look up to Him for our inner life and our outward service with the respectful dependence that is appropriate? Do we not too often run before His call and act independently of His aid? Let us humble ourselves this evening for past neglect, and now entreat the heavenly dew to rest upon us, the sacred oil to anoint us, the celestial flame to burn within us. The Holy Spirit is not a temporary gift—He remains with the church. When we seek Him as we should, we will find Him. He is jealous, but He is full of pity; if He leaves in anger, He returns in mercy. Condescending and tender, He does not grow tired of us but constantly displays His grace.

Charles Haddon Spurgeon

YOU WILL LIVE ALSO

JOHN 14:19 NKJV
"Because I live, you will live also."

It is now all-important for us to cling to this truth that *he,* Jesus Christ, in *his* life, is our present. Not our past is our present. Not the great darkness casting its shadows out of yesterday into today. Not what we rightly or wrongly hold against ourselves and probably against others as well. Not the world with its accusations and we with our counter-accusations. Not even the well-deserved divine wrath against us, let alone our grumbling against God, or our secret thought that there might be no God after all. Therefore, not we ourselves, as we are today or think we are, make up our present. He, Jesus Christ, his life is our present: his divine life poured out for us, and his human life, our life, lifted up in him. This is what counts. This is what is true and valid. From this point on we may continue our journey into the future. And this is the future which grows out of this present: *You will live also.*

KARL BARTH

SET FREE *by* GRACE

ROMANS 6:14 NLT

*Sin is no longer your master, for you are no
longer subject to the law, which enslaves you
to sin. Instead, you are free by God's grace.*

Miracles," wrote Willa Gather, "seem to me to rest
not so much upon faces or voices or healing
power coming suddenly near to us from afar off, but upon
our perceptions being made finer, so that for a moment
our eyes can see and our ears can hear what is there about
us always."

There's real grace for you—God opening our ears
enough to hear the music of life buzzing around us and
widening our eyes to the ever-present, extravagant light
of His love. And this isn't showtime, this is His everyday
fare. A God that even heaven couldn't hold doesn't need
a televised miracle service in order to show up. His grace
happens everywhere—even in the middle of a traffic jam
that has you left with nothing to do but read every
bumper that surrounds you. Remember to look for Him
while you're there.

ROBERTA CROTEAU

He Will Give Life

—

ROMANS 8:11 NASB
But if the Spirit of Him who raised Jesus from
the dead dwells in you, He who raised Christ Jesus
from the dead will also give life to your mortal
bodies through His Spirit who dwells in you.

In the end, the risen Christ will raise us up with him. "If the Spirit of Him who raised Jesus from the dead dwells in you, He who raised Christ Jesus from the dead will also give life to your mortal bodies through His Spirit who dwells in you" (Romans 8:11). "If we have become united with Him in the likeness of His death, certainly we shall also be in the likeness of His resurrection" (Romans 6:5 NASB). Just as Jesus took back his own life from the fangs of death, so he will raise from the dead those who are his. He makes this promise for all who believe: "I Myself will raise him up on the last day" (John 6:40). Thus his resurrection guarantees theirs. . . .

The glory of Christ in the power of his resurrection into invincible life and omnipotent authority will be reflected back to him in the joyful worship of his risen and perfected saints. Who shall enjoy this eternal gift of life? Jesus answers: "I am the resurrection and the life; he who believes in Me . . . will never die" (John 11:25-26).

JOHN PIPER

HELP *in the* HARD TIMES

———

ROMANS 8:26 KJV
The Spirit itself maketh intercession for us
with groanings which cannot be uttered.

Oh, the burdens that we love to bear and cannot understand! Oh, the inarticulate out-reachings of our hearts for things we cannot comprehend! And yet we know they are an echo from the throne and a whisper from the heart of God. It is often a groan rather than a song, a burden rather than a buoyant wing. But it is a blessed burden, and it is a groan whose undertone is praise and unutterable joy. It is a groaning "which cannot be uttered." We could not ourselves express it always, and sometimes we do not understand any more than that God is praying in us, for something that needs His touch and that He understands.

And so we can just pour out the fullness of our heart, the burden of our spirit, the sorrow that crushes us, and know that He hears, He loves, He understands, He receives; and He separates from our prayer all that is imperfect, ignorant and wrong, and presents the rest, with the incense of the great High Priest, before the throne on high; and our prayer is heard, accepted and answered in His name.

A. B. SIMPSON

NEW POWER

2 CORINTHIANS 5:17 NIV
*Therefore, if anyone is in Christ, he is a
new creation; the old has gone, the new has come!*

When people exhibit *new* power to overcome an *old* weakness, I contend that this *is evidence* that the living God lives within them. These changes become powerful proof to all those who witness them that what people could not do on their own *is possible* with God's power—His Holy Spirit—within them! Instead of being under the influence of drugs, alcohol, money, or power, people who ask God to come into and change their lives will experience the supernatural power of the Holy Spirit of God released in them! . . .

If the Holy Spirit's function is to give glory to God, a transformed life is a visual sign or confirmation that Someone powerful—yet unseen—has become a real, indwelling part of us!

BECKY TIRABASSI

A NEW CREATION

2 CORINTHIANS 5:17 NRSV
*So if anyone is in Christ, there is a new
creation: everything old has passed away;
see, everything has become new!*

The philosophy of Christian healing is always forward-looking. The difference Jesus makes begins here and now, and then goes on and on into the infinite mystery of heaven. Meditate now on how Charles Wesley expressed the eternal aspect of healing prayer in one of the greatest of all his hymns:

Finish then thy new creation;
Pure and spotless let us be;
Let us see thy great salvation,
Perfectly restored in thee;
Changed from glory into glory,
Till in heaven we take our place,
Till we cast our crowns before thee,
Lost in wonder, love and praise. Amen.

ROY LAWRENCE

STRENGTH *from* WITHIN

2 CORINTHIANS 12:10 AMP.
So for the sake of Christ, I am well pleased and
take pleasure in infirmities, insults, hardships,
persecutions, perplexities and distresses; for when
I am weak [in human strength], then am I [truly]
strong (able, powerful in divine strength).

The apostle Paul found the strength of God so wonderful that in 2 Corinthians 12:9-10 he actually said he would glory in his weaknesses, knowing that when he was weak, the strength of God would rest upon him and fill up his weaknesses. To put it in our language today, Paul was saying that he was glad when he was weak because then he got to experience the strength of God. . . .

Have you been trying to push through difficulties on your own? If so, make a change right now. Start getting strength from deep within you where the Holy Spirit dwells. If that divine strength does not yet dwell in you, all you need to do to receive it is admit your sins, repent of them, and ask Jesus to be your Savior and Lord. Surrender your life, all that you are and all that you are not, to Him. Ask Him to baptize you in the Holy Spirit and to fill you through and through with the power of the Holy Spirit.

JOYCE MEYER

THE FRUIT *of* CONVERSION

GALATIANS 2:20 NKJV

*I have been crucified with Christ; it is no longer
I who live, but Christ lives in me; and the life which
I now live in the flesh I live by faith in the Son of
God, who loved me and gave Himself for me.*

The Christian life involves more than growth and development. It involves conversion and transformation, a radical turning of the Self toward the God who made us and who continues to sustain us. Christian faith is about an inner transformation of consciousness resulting from our encounter with the living Christ. "I have been crucified with Christ," proclaimed the Apostle Paul, "it is no longer I who live, but Christ lives in me" (Gal. 2:20). "When anyone is united to Christ, there is a new world: the old order has gone, and a new order has already begun" (2 Cor. 5:17). The Christian revelation promises a radical vision of what it means to be a human being. The life of Christ does not change the way we look, nor does it eliminate our peculiarities or the results of our own brokenness and estrangement. What it does do is open us to the Spirit of God in ways that increase in us the capacity for love. The fruit of conversion is a life that can be used by God for the healing of the world.

JAMES C. FENHAGEN

SET FREE

GALATIANS 5:1 NRSV
For freedom Christ has set us free.

This "freedom" is established in heaven's charter—the *Bible*. . . . Come in faith; you are welcome to all the *covenant blessings*. There is not a promise in the Word that will be withheld. In the deepest tribulations let this freedom comfort you; overwhelmed by waves of distress let it cheer you; when sorrows surround you let it be your solace. This is your Father's love-token; you are free in it at all times. You are also given *free access to the throne* of *grace*. It is the believer's privilege to have access at all times to his heavenly Father. Whatever our desires, our difficulties, our wants, we are at liberty to spread them all before Him. It does not matter how much we may have sinned, we can ask and expect pardon. . . . Exercise your right, believer, and enjoy this privilege. You are set free to all that is treasured up *in* Christ—wisdom, righteousness, sanctification, and redemption. It does not matter what your need is, for there is abundant supply in Christ, and it is there *for you*. What a "freedom" is yours!

CHARLES HADDON SPURGEON

His Love *in* Us

GALATIANS 5:22 NLT
*The Holy Spirit . . . will produce this
kind of fruit in us: love . . .*

In his humanity Jesus is the Savior whose unsettling, unnerving, and unpredictable love blows like a tornado through the lives of sinful men and women. His love is beyond description, even by our best words, by the most powerful sermons we have heard and the most profound books we have ever read. The same love in the heart of Jesus as he lay dying on the cross dwells within us this moment through his transforming Spirit. When we are in conscious communion with Jesus, we are aware of the sacredness of others. Beyond society's labels, the indwelling Presence in a brother or sister makes our differences irrelevant. We meet them without needing their affirmation because we rest secure in the unrestricted love of Jesus Christ.

BRENNAN MANNING

THE SAME POWER

EPHESIANS 1:19 JB
*How infinitely great is the power
that he has exercised for us believers.*

Our tragic mistake today is to minimize "how infinitely great is the power that he has exercised for us believers" (Ephesians 1:19)—*the same power* he used in raising Christ from the dead! To settle for mediocrity, to surrender to our addictions, to capitulate to the world, and to resign ourselves to a humdrum life of hoeing cabbage and drinking beer is to nullify the power of the crucified, resurrected Jesus and the total sufficiency of his redeeming work.

The Christ in us is not only our hope for future glory but a transforming presence within who promises, "Whoever believes in me will perform the same works as I do myself, he will perform even greater works" (John 14:12).

BRENNAN MANNING

IN *the* HEAVENLY PLACES

EPHESIANS 2:5-6 KJV

*Even when we were dead in sins, hath quickened
us together with Christ, (by grace ye are saved;)
and hath raised us up together, and made us sit
together in heavenly places in Christ Jesus.*

This is our rightful place, to be seated "in heavenly
places in Christ Jesus," and to "sit still" there. But
how few there are who make it their actual experience!
How few, indeed think even that it is possible for them to
"sit still" in these "heavenly places" in the everyday life of
a world so full of turmoil as this. . . .

A quiet spirit is of inestimable value in carrying on outward activities; and nothing so hinders the working of the
hidden spiritual forces, upon which, after all, our success in
everything really depends, as a spirit of unrest and anxiety.

There is immense power in stillness. . . . A knowledge
of this fact would immensely change our ways of working. Instead of restless struggles, we would "sit down"
inwardly before the Lord, and would let the Divine forces
of His Spirit work out in silence the ends to which we
aspire. You may not see or feel the operations of this silent
force, but be assured it is always working mightily, and will
work for you, if you only get your spirit still enough to
be carried along by the currents of its power.

HANNAH WHITHALL SMITH

TO BE *with* HIM

PHILIPPIANS 2:5 NIV
Your attitude should be the
same as that of Christ Jesus.

To be transformed into the image of Christ I must begin to do the will of the Father in the same place where He began: He emptied Himself. There is for any serious disciple, quite simply, no other starting place. It is a matter of beginning today to say no to yourself—specifically, about something you've been insisting you must have, specifically about something you have been refusing. This is step one. You travel the road "toward Jerusalem" from there, gladly taking up the cross (which is step two: saying yes to God) and following, knowing where the road led Jesus. It did not—and don't forget *this!—end* with a cross.

The third day He rose again from the dead. He ascended into heaven. His prayer for us is, "Father, I desire that these men who are thy gift to me, may be with me where I am" (Jn 17:24 NEB).

ELISABETH ELLIOT

TO KNOW HIM

PHILIPPIANS 3:10 NKJV
*That I may know Him and the
power of His resurrection . . .*

The doctrine of a risen Savior is exceedingly precious. The resurrection is the cornerstone of the entire building of Christianity. . . . Though you cannot, like the disciples, see Him visibly, yet I urge you to aspire to see Christ Jesus by the eye of faith; and though, like Mary Magdalene, you may not touch Him, yet you may be privileged to converse with Him and to know that He is risen, you yourselves being risen in Him to newness of life. To know a crucified Savior as having crucified all my sins is a high degree of knowledge; but to know a risen Savior as having justified me and to realize that He has bestowed upon me new life, having made me a new creature through His own newness of life—this is a noble style of experience. Short of it, none should rest satisfied. May you both "know him and the power of his resurrection." Why should souls who are made alive with Jesus wear the grave-clothes of worldliness and unbelief? Rise, for the Lord is risen.

CHARLES HADDON SPURGEON

DOING GOOD

COLOSSIANS 3:12 NIV

*Therefore, as God's chosen people, holy and
dearly loved, clothe yourselves with compassion,
kindness, humility, gentleness and patience.*

We have great opportunity to show compassion on all around us. How much there is of temporal want! There are the poor and the sick, widows and orphans, distressed and despondent souls, who need nothing so much as the refreshment a compassionate heart can bring. They live in the midst of Christians, and sometimes complain that it seems as if there are children of the world who have more sympathy than those who are only concerned about their own salvation. . . . O brethren, pray earnestly for a compassionate heart, always on the lookout for an opportunity of doing some work of love, always ready to be an instrument of the divine compassion. It was the compassionate sympathy of Jesus that attracted so many to Him on earth. That same compassionate tenderness will still, more than anything, draw souls to you and to your Lord.

ANDREW MURRAY

UNHOOKED *and* SET FREE

1 TIMOTHY 2:5-6 NKJV
*For there is one God and one Mediator between God
and men, the Man Christ Jesus, who gave Himself
a ransom for all, to be testified in due time.*

Simply put, Jesus was the ransom paid for man's
redemption: His blood was the price paid to recover
mankind, the property seized from God's hand. Jesus
came into the marketplace of mankind, found slaves on
the block, and freed them at the expense of Himself. And
He is still coming today to people who are enslaved,
hooked in a thousand different ways: Hooked by pride to
a never-ending treadmill in pursuit of social acceptance,
success, and material possessions; hooked by lust into pursuing the latest trends or easiest relationship, hoping to
satisfy the sensuous cravings of debased tastes; hooked by
intimidating fears, haunting lies from the past, crushing
depression, unceasing pain, or unquenchable hate.

This is the marketplace to which Jesus comes, and it is
there that He offers His blood as the ransom payment.
And as our "mediator," the one making the transaction,
He brings us promise and hope: you can, I can, mankind
can . . . we *all* can be unhooked; set free by the payment
of Christ's blood.

JACK HAYFORD

BROUGHT *to* GLORY

HEBREWS 2:10 NIV

*In bringing many sons to glory, it was fitting that God, for
whom and through whom everything exists, should make
the author of their salvation perfect through suffering.*

Our Lord's cross is the gateway into His life: His resurrection means that He has power now to convey
His life to me. When I am born again from above, I
receive from the risen Lord His very life.

Our Lord's resurrection destiny is to bring "many sons
unto glory" (Heb. 2:10 KJV). The fulfilling of His destiny
gives Him the right to make us sons and daughters of
God. We are never in the relationship to God that the Son
of God is in; but we are brought by the Son into the rela-
tion of sonship. When our Lord rose from the dead, He
rose to an absolutely new life, to a life He did not live
before He was incarnate. He rose to a life that had never
been before; and His resurrection means for us that we are
raised to His risen life, not to our old life. One day we
shall have a body like unto His glorious body, but we can
know now the efficacy of His resurrection and walk in
newness of life. "I would know Him *in the power of His
resurrection*" (see Phil. 3:10).

OSWALD CHAMBERS

ULTIMATE HEALING

JAMES 5:15 NIV
*And the prayer offered in faith will make the
sick person well; the Lord will raise him up.
If he has sinned, he will be forgiven.*

I see no reason why this should not be taken literally.
Many churches exercise this biblical practice with great
profit to their members. God is concerned for all our
needs, physical needs included. Indeed, Christ died for
all our sickness and our sins (Isaiah 53:4-5; Matthew
8:16-17). However, the fact that our ultimate healing is in
the atonement (Revelation 21:4) is no more a guarantee
that we can claim healing for every sickness now than it
is that we can avoid old age and death (Romans 5:12;
8:20-23). Our resurrection is in the atonement too, but
we cannot claim it today. In fact, the ultimate "healing"
of the body will not come until the resurrection, when
we will receive the "redemption of our bodies" (Romans
8:23 NIV). Meanwhile, God graciously heals from time to
time in accordance with His will and in response to "the
prayer offered in faith" (James 5:15).

NORMAN GEISLER

OUR STRENGTHENER

1 PETER 5:10 AMP.
*The God of all grace [Who imparts all blessing
and favor], Who has called you to His [own] eternal
glory in Christ Jesus, will Himself complete and make
you what you ought to be, establish and ground
you securely, and strengthen, and settle you.*

The Holy Spirit also offers His help as our Strength-ener. Just imagine having a well of strength inside you, a source you can draw on anytime you feel the need. When you feel weak or tired or discouraged to the point of giving up, just stop for a few minutes. Close your eyes, if possible, and ask the Holy Spirit to strengthen you. As you wait in His presence, you can often actually feel the strength of God coming to you. . . .

There is so much available to us in the Holy Spirit that we have missed because we have not been properly taught about His wonderful present-day ministry. We always talk about what Jesus did when He was here, but what about what He is doing now through the power of the Holy Spirit? Let us not live in the past, but rather let us fully enter into all that the present holds for us.

JOYCE MEYER

CLEANSED *from* SIN

———

I JOHN 1:7 NASB
The blood of Jesus His Son cleanses us from all sin.

"Cleanses," says the text—not "*shall* cleanse." There are multitudes who think that as a dying hope they may look forward to pardon. Oh, how infinitely better to have cleansing now than to depend on the bare possibility of forgiveness when I come to die. Some imagine that a sense of pardon is an attainment only obtainable after many years of Christian experience. But forgiveness of sin is a *present* reality—a privilege for this day, a joy for this very hour. The moment a sinner trusts Jesus he is fully forgiven. The text, being written in the present tense, also indicates *continuance;* it was "cleanses" yesterday, it is "cleanses" today, it will be "cleanses" tomorrow. This is the way it will always be with you, Christian, until you cross the river; every hour you may come to this fountain, for it cleanses still. . . . Our iniquity is gone, all gone at once, and all gone forever. Blessed completeness! What a sweet theme to dwell upon as one gives himself to sleep.

CHARLES HADDON SPURGEON

GOD'S GREAT MERCY

1 JOHN 1:9 NIV
*If we confess our sins, he is faithful and
just and will forgive us our sins and purify
us from all unrighteousness.*

There are none so wicked that they cannot have a
remedy.

What is that? Enter into your own heart and search its
secrets. Consider your own life. How have you spent your
days? If you find some ugliness in yourself, what will you
do? Ask God to forgive you. You will surely be heard.
Your sins will be forgiven. God will be true to his promise. He sent his only Son into this world to save sinners
like you.

Consider the great love of God the Father. Amend
your life. Avoid temptation. If you will do this, you may
be sure that though you have done all the sins in the book
they will neither hurt nor condemn you. The mercy of
God is greater than all the sins in the world.

HUGH LATIMER

BLAMELESS

JUDE 24 NASB

*Now to Him who is able to keep you from stumbling,
and to make you stand in the presence of His
glory blameless with great joy . . .*

Let your mind revolve around that wonderful word *"blameless"*! We are far from it now; but since our Lord never stops short of perfection in His work of love, we will reach it one day. . . . But how will Jesus make us blameless? He will wash us from our sins in His own blood until we are as white and fair as God's purest angel; and we will be clothed in His righteousness, that righteousness that makes the saint who wears it positively blameless—yes, perfect in the sight of God. . . . Oh, the intense delight of that hour when the everlasting doors will be lifted up, and we, being made fit for the inheritance, will dwell with the saints in light. Sin gone, Satan shut out, temptation past forever, and ourselves "blameless" before God—this will be heaven indeed! Let us be joyful now as we rehearse the song of eternal praise that will soon sound forth in full chorus from all the blood-washed host; let us copy David's exultings before the ark as a prelude to our ecstasies before the throne.

CHARLES HADDON SPURGEON

MADE WHOLE

REVELATION 7:12 KJV

Saying, Amen: Blessing, and glory, and wisdom,
and thanksgiving, and honour, and power, and might,
be unto our God for ever and ever. Amen.

When I utter the name of Jesus, I not only set before my mind a Man who is meek and humble in heart (Matthew 11:29), kind, prudent, chaste, merciful (Titus 1:8), and conspicuous in every honorable and saintly quality, but I also set before me the man who is Almighty God. He it is who heals me, and restores me to spiritual health by His character, and He is the One who helps me so powerfully. All of this is communicated to me, whenever His name is uttered, the name of Jesus. Because He is Man, I can strive to imitate Him. Because He is Almighty God, I can lean upon Him. The examples of His earthly life, I gather like medicinal herbs, and because of His divinity I can blend them. Then the result is a potion no pharmacist can ever prescribe. . . .

For now, you have a remedy for heart and hand. For you have in the name of Jesus the power to correct wrong actions, to perfect those that are imperfect, and the guard to protect your affections from corruption. In this name you will be made whole again.

BERNARD OF CLAIRVAUX

THE FINAL MIRACLE

REVELATION 21:3-4 NRSV
"See, the home of God is among mortals. . . . Death will be no more; mourning and crying and pain will be no more, for the first things have passed away."

It is only the final miracle that really matters. It is not my day-to-day healing that matters, but the final miracle of my resurrection with Christ.

Will I participate in that final miracle that God has prepared for those who know Him and love Him and have come to trust Him? All our experiences of pain and suffering and fear and confusion and discontent, all of those experiences from which we would love to be freed, prepare us to accept Christ's ultimate solution. Should He relieve those circumstances in advance, it is likely that we would never give ourselves wholly to Him—the singular act which assures us of participation in that final miracle.

Still, understand that He has not really withheld anything from us at all. In giving us that final miracle, He gives us all the other miracles. Once that final miracle is ours, all other miracles are ours as well. . . . It is not the individual miracles we are concerned about; we can sacrifice those to receive the final miracle—the everlasting life promised those who place their trust in the Miracle Worker.

PAUL SMITH

CONCLUSION

How much of a difference did Jesus' miracles make in the daily lives of those He touched and healed? How much of a difference have Jesus' miracles made in your life?

We are so prone to rejoice over God's power one moment and forget His presence the next. We can take God's involvement in our lives for granted to such a degree that it loses its sustaining and hopeful effect. We suddenly find ourselves in peril or pain and call out to God as if He has never before shown Himself faithful or caring. Yet, we know this is not God's plan for our lives. How can we live out the confidence that Almighty God is with us and that nothing can separate us from His love?

Jeremiah pointed out that God's faithfulness is "new every morning" (Lamentations 3:23 NIV). Ask God to remind you each day to consider the inexhaustible truth of His faithfulness. You will find yourself much more aware of God's miraculous presence in your life. Indeed, *you* are one of His miracles.